Exchange Rate Alignments

Exchange Rate Alignments

John Mills
Economist, John Mills Ltd

First published 2012 by
PALGRAVE MACMILLAN

Palgrave Macmillan in the UK is an imprint of Macmillan Publishers Limited,
registered in England, company number 785998, of Houndmills, Basingstoke,
Hampshire RG21 6XS.

Palgrave Macmillan in the US is a division of St Martin's Press LLC,
175 Fifth Avenue, New York, NY 10010.

Palgrave Macmillan is the global academic imprint of the above companies
and has companies and representatives throughout the world.

Palgrave® and Macmillan® are registered trademarks in the United States,
the United Kingdom, Europe and other countries

ISBN: 978–1–137–02296–7

This book is printed on paper suitable for recycling and made from fully
managed and sustained forest sources. Logging, pulping and manufacturing
processes are expected to conform to the environmental regulations of the
country of origin.

A catalogue record for this book is available from the British Library.

A catalog record for this book is available from the Library of Congress.

10 9 8 7 6 5 4 3 2 1
21 20 19 18 17 16 15 14 13 12

Printed and bound in Great Britain by
CPI Antony Rowe, Chippenham and Eastbourne

Contents

Illustrations

Tables

Figure

Preface

This book is not about doom and gloom. Its tone, very specifically, is quite the opposite. Its message is that the austerity, unemployment, cuts in public expenditure, slow growth and decline vis-à-vis most of the rest of the world which nearly everyone in Britain assumes are in store for us – indeed, for many other Western countries, too – are unnecessary and avoidable. None of these poor outcomes is inevitable. On the contrary, the dismal economic prospects we currently face are largely, if not entirely, the result of bad policies which could easily have been different and which it would not be particularly difficult to change quite quickly for the better. The object of this book is to explain what these mistaken policies are and what needs to be done to put them right.

To show what has gone wrong and what needs to change, the text which follows is essentially in three parts. The first five chapters explain what causes and hinders economic growth, explore the crucial role of exchange rates, review what we should and should not do about inflation, determine what can be done to bring back full employment and consider all these issues in the light of the need for sustainability. None of this is particularly complicated, and there is no reason why it should be. I agree with Professor J. K. Galbraith when he says that he had 'long felt that there is no economic proposition that can't be stated in clear accessible language.'[1]

The next five chapters are about economic history. Their role is first to provide a test bed to see whether the previous chapters' explanations of how economies work can explain adequately and convincingly why economic history has unfolded in the way it has and second to do so by addressing some important questions to which there are no very obvious answers. Why have some economies grown much faster than others? Why has the UK – dropped from having the highest living standards in the world to now appearing way down the league table? Why is it that so high a proportion of the world's manufactured goods are made in China? Why is unemployment an intractable problem in most of the West, whereas for most of the 1950s and 1960s only a tiny fraction – about 2 per cent – of the potential labour force, at least in Europe, was then out of work? Why did inflation suddenly become a major problem in the 1970s, and were sensible policies adopted to get it down? Once inflation had fallen from the 1990s onwards to the point where it was little more than 2 per cent per annum in almost all developed countries, was it really sensible to make keeping inflation this low the principal economic priority? How can the Chinese economy go on growing at about 10 per cent per annum – with many other countries on the Pacific Rim doing nearly as well – while we seem to consider ourselves lucky nowadays to be able to achieve any economic growth at all? Why has the distribution of wealth and income become so much more uneven in the West in recent years? Are there factors which link the answers to all these questions? The test is whether the analysis in this book's early chapters can show what the linkages are and explain convincingly how they operate and why they have led to our present condition.

The last part of this book turns to remedies. What can we do to reverse all the trends which have impacted us so adversely? How do we get back to economic growth and full employment, combined with relatively low inflation and a reasonable prospect of a sustainable future? The key here is to understand what went wrong and why we are therefore not in this position already. Once this has been explained, seeing what we need to do to vastly improve our prospects becomes relatively easy. Major obstacles to moving in the right direction, to finding solutions to our economic predicament, are then likely to be, not insuperable technical or operational difficulties, but entrenched attitudes. The UK's biggest problem is that generations of politicians, civil servants, commentators and academics have all become inured to pursuing and supporting the wrong policy objectives. Getting them to look at things in a different way and to change their minds is not going to be easy or trouble-free.

Getting people to change their minds however may now be much easier than it has been at any time previously, largely because our current economic condition is unsustainable. We cannot go on borrowing huge sums, as we are now, when we have an economy which is not growing. It will not be forever before the markets realise that the maths do not add up. Sooner or later – perhaps before very long – we are, like Greece, going to run out of people prepared to lend us more money. Perhaps the key message in this book is that we need to get a grip on the situation and change our ways while we still have time to do so in an orderly fashion. If we don't, there will be a major financial crisis from which, no doubt, we will recover but only after having wasted years in futile attempts to avoid policy changes we ought to have engineered long ago. We need to change strategy now to stop this disaster materialising.

Acknowledgements

There are many people to whom thanks are due for their help in getting this book published. The ideas and recommendations it contains are not those usually found in books about economics, and I am therefore particularly grateful to Palgrave Macmillan, especially Taiba Batool, their Senior Economics Commissioning Editor, for being willing to publish it against a background of a fair bit of scepticism from established academic economists. I do not think this project would have gone ahead without the support of Professor John Black, Geoffrey Gardiner, Jeremy Hardie and Ruth Lea, all of whom acted as referees. I owe a big debt of gratitude to all of them.

There is also a wider circle of people who have contributed in different ways to the book. Bryan Gould and Austin Mitchell have always shared the views which are set out in the pages which follow. So did Shaun Stewart, who sadly died in 1997, from whom I learnt a huge amount, not least because of his almost unbelievable mastery of trade statistics and awe-inspiring rigour of analysis. He left me his library of statistical material, which I have mined ever since. Peter Moyes, who shared Professor Black with me as Economics Tutor when we were at Oxford together, produced a large volume of helpful comments. Damon de Laszlo at the Economic Research Council and David Green at Civitas have been kind enough to give me a platform at their think tanks, which has sparked a lot of very helpful correspondence. Too many others to mention individually have made contributions, and I thank them all.

1
Economic Growth

The economic history of the developing world since the start of industrialisation has been remarkably uneven. Britain experienced an unprecedented period of rapid growth in the first half of the nineteenth century, but then slowed down between 1850 and 1900. The USA grew rapidly during the whole of the nineteenth century and, more intermittently, through to 1945, but then slowed relative to new challengers. Germany and the Netherlands did much better during the second half of the nineteenth century than the first, and better still during the early years of the twentieth century, leading up to World War I. The 1930s were a particularly interesting and important period, with the USA and France languishing, Britain doing far better than previously and Germany surging ahead at an astonishing pace. There have been decades when most of the most prosperous economies of the time were expanding very quickly, as they did in the 1950s and 1960s, although the USA's did not grow as fast as others' during these decades. In the 1970s, after the post-war boom, increases in output slowed in the developed countries. The world's growth rate of 4.9 per cent per annum cumulatively between 1950 to 1973 slowed to 3.0 per cent from 1973 to 1992[1] and then rose a little, to 3.4 per cent, between 1992 and 2009.[2] Crucially, however, lower growth rates in the later periods were far more marked in those economies where relatively high standards of living already prevailed, notably in western Europe and Japan, where they averaged 2.2 per cent over the years 1992–2009.[3] It was the already industrialised countries' poor performance which pulled down the world average, since China, India and other countries on the Pacific Rim, particular the so-called tiger economies – South Korea, Taiwan, Hong Kong and Singapore – surged ahead.

Why did these changes in relative performance occur? Why was growth so much faster in some periods than others? What can policymakers do to create the conditions where growth takes place? How can they avoid it slowing down? If it is possible to identify the reasons why some economies have grown fast and others slowly and why some have succeeded in employing their resources of labour and other factors of production more fully than others, it may then become possible to see more clearly not only what has happened in the past but also what might be done to alter the course of future events.

The starting point is to understand the circumstances which allow and encourage economic expansion to take place. Growth is achieved by creating conditions where the output of goods and services rises. Essentially, two approaches are required. The first is to increase inputs – to employ more labour, to educate and train it better and to use more capital equipment, land and buildings. The second is to achieve more output in relation to inputs than was attained before – increasing total factor productivity. This is done by investment in more highly productive machinery, by improved management, by better design, by development of new materials and more attractive products and by enhanced production efficiency generally. Any convincing explanation of the way output can be increased needs to take account of both these components of the growth process.

High growth rates are achieved by keeping all the factors of production, particularly labour and capital, in use as intensively as possible. The economic expansion thus achieved will be reflected in increased output per head, which is how productivity is raised. At the level of the individual enterprise, this is accomplished in three principal ways: first by an investment in machinery and equipment which makes it possible for the existing labour force to achieve increased production; second by better management and training of the workforce and enhancement of its skills and experience; and third by increasing sales, so that all the available resources of labour and capital are used to maximum capacity.

The potential for improved production as a result of capital investment is a familiar concept. The power, efficiency and speed that machinery can produce made the Industrial Revolution possible. During the past two centuries, the development of a huge range of machines has been accompanied by many other output-increasing inventions and technological developments – from internal combustion engines to electronics, from steamships to airliners, from new building techniques to plastics. All these developments have made it possible to produce goods and services of increased value per labour hour. There is, however, a huge variation in the return on different types of investment. Some are very much more productive and therefore more conducive to expanding output than others. One of the ways of increasing economic growth, thus making it much easier to achieve, is to create conditions in which the economy is biased towards the most highly productive uses of investment. It is also the case that productivity increases are much easier to secure in some types of economic activity than others. This, too, is a factor of major policy significance.

The quality of management is extremely important. Many improvements in working practices which lead to more production or to changes in output designed to make it more attractive to consumers involve little capital outlay but a great deal of human skill. Some of the latter comes from good education and training. An even more important factor than having skilled labour is ensuring that the best available managerial talent is concentrated in those areas where it can be used most effectively to improve economic achievement. Where talent is actually employed depends critically on economic rewards and on the social status accompanying them. Another element in improving economic achievement involves shifting both rewards and social status towards those involved in running the parts of the economy where good management has the best chance of improving performance.

A third vital component involves creating enough demand pressure on the economy to ensure that all the available resources of capital and labour are, in so far as possible, fully utilised. To achieve the most from capital equipment, it needs to be used as intensively as possible. To get the best out of the labour force, it needs to be fully employed. When there is a shortage of jobs, it may make sense to increase output by using relatively low productivity machinery and more employees. As supplies of labour run short, this tactic ceases to be a viable option. There is then no alternative to labour-saving equipment. At the level of the enterprise, a full order book at profitable prices is needed, with highly efficient machinery that is used to capacity to produce goods the market is hungry to buy, operated by a well trained and motivated labour force, led by able managers. It is because these conditions still widely prevail in Korea and Taiwan and, even more so, in the fast-developing parts of China and India that these economies are expanding rapidly. They were also replicated in Germany, France and Italy – indeed, over most of western Europe – in the 1950s and 1960s, when all these countries were growing much faster than they are now.

There is nothing mysterious about the conditions needed to make any country's economy expand rapidly. The key is to ensure that all the domestically incurred costs of whatever goods and services the economy produces which are to be sold on world markets are priced

Table 1.1   Comparison between the percentage growth rate per annum of Industrialised Countries and the Rest of the World between 1950 and 2010

	1950–1973	1973–1992	1992–2010
Western Europe	4.7	2.2	1.8
Western Offshoots	4.0	2.4	2.7
Japan	9.2	3.8	0.8
Rest of the World	5.1	3.4	6.3
Whole World	4.9	3.0	3.4

Source: Tables G-2 and C-16a in *Monitoring the World Economy 1820–1992* by Angus Maddison. Paris: OECD, 1995 and GDP Volume Measure tables in *International Financial Statistics*. Washington DC: IMF, 2011.

competitively. This, in turn, is almost entirely an exchange rate issue. The problem lies in persuading those in control to allow the appropriate environment to be created as Table 1.1 illustrates).

Competitiveness

What are the conditions which enable economies to prosper? How is an environment created which encourages expansion to take place? What can those responsible for the performance of an economy do to ensure that its record is as good as that achieved by the best performers in the growth league? It is often claimed that the solution for the problem implied by these questions is to concentrate on the supply side of the challenge to be tackled. The way to higher growth, it is said, is to improve efficiency by better education and training, by higher levels of investment and by enhanced productivity. Making domestic output more competitive will cause more growth to take place. The problem with this approach, however, is that improved efficiency will not necessarily produce lower prices and greater competitiveness. It depends on the price charged to the rest of the world for the economy's output. Nor does increasing productivity necessarily result in rising total output.

One variation on the supply side theme is to blame poor growth performance on production techniques and design sophistication which are not as advanced as those available elsewhere in the world, with ineffective salesmanship, late deliveries and inadequate after-sales service perhaps compounding the issue. This has certainly been a well-recognised problem in the past, especially in countries with high output per head but where growth has slowed down relative to new challengers. The car industry is a particularly obvious example, as all Western economies experienced severe difficulties in competing with the Japanese, but the same strictures could have been (and frequently were) applied to many others. Nowadays in the West, even with much greater awareness of the need to set high standards to compete internationally, the problem is that many Western countries are still incapable of producing many things that the rest of the world wants to buy at the prices at which they are on offer.

Though productive efficiency has *some* bearing on competitiveness, the actual amount is surprisingly little. The higher the level of productivity, the more efficiently goods and services will be produced, but it does not automatically follow that the goods produced will then be internationally competitive. High output per head may be closely associated with high standards of living, but it has no necessarily meaningful relationship with competitiveness. This is why there is no observable correlation between the growth rates of rich and poor countries. Yet it is true that in any expanding economy, productivity will be increasing, and many people thus conclude that concentrating efforts on raising output per head push up the growth rate.

Unfortunately, this conclusion is not correct. There are many examples of countries round the world where output per head is increasing relatively rapidly but overall growth in the economy is slow. The result is the rising unemployment and unused resources which are such conspicuous features of the European Union and, more recently, the USA. In the USA, however, where unemployment was long relatively low, rapid increases in productivity in some parts of the economy have produced a different problem. With effective demand insufficient to generate enough high-quality jobs for everyone but with rising productivity among some sections of the labour force, combined with a welfare system which forced many people into work for low wages, the result has been low or negative rises in output per head among large sections of the remaining working population.

Striking confirmation of these propositions is provided by comparing the position of the economies of the USA and the Far Eastern tigers economies, especially during the first few decades after World War II. In 1945 the US labour force was vastly more productive than the largely peasant workforces of Taiwan, Korea, Hong Kong and Singapore. The levels of training and education in the USA were far superior to those in most other countries, while high proportions of the labour forces in what later became the tiger economies were unskilled. The value of capital per head in the USA was many multiples of the tigers' almost nonexistent industrial capacity. Despite all these huge advantages the USA has been completely outpaced in the growth race with them since World War II.

Productivity, therefore, is not the key to making economies potentially capable of rapid growth. The key is competitiveness. What counts are the prices charged for the economy's output to buyers, both in the home and export markets, compared to those of foreign suppliers. How productive the domestic economy is hardly matters to competitiveness. How much its exporters charge the rest of the world for their output, whatever the level of productivity, is what is critical. Even after taking everything else into account – wages and salaries, taxation policy, social security charges and all other factors – prices are very largely determined by the exchange rate. Even if productivity is very low and everything is wrong with the economy's output, if a product is cheap enough, a fair proportion of it will sell. However high the quality of the output, if it is too expensive, market share will be lost. In the end, price balances out all the other quality factors. This is why the exchange rate is critically important.

Other things being equal, the lower the exchange rate, the less the domestic economy charges the rest of the world for its labour, land and capital, and the more competitive, compared with the rest of the world, the domestic economy will be. This condition bears directly on the three requirements identified earlier for increasing both productivity and output. First, for all those economic activities requiring capital investment to secure increase in output, the lower the associated labour and interest costs, measured in international terms, the higher the profitability of the capital investment, and the more of it will be undertaken. Second, the more competitive the output produced, the easier it will be to sell larger quantities at a profit, and the greater the capacity utilisation. Third, the higher the profits thus generated, the more those sectors of the economy engaged in producing internationally tradable goods and services will be able to attract the most talented people into management positions. Exceptional profitability will also enable them to employ and make best use of the most competent people available to staff at every level.

A company's competitive position is heavily disadvantaged if its costs are significantly out of line with those of the rest of the market, and the same is true for the whole economy. There is, however, one further important difference between companies and economies. If the exchange rate is too high, bringing it down is a far more potent way of cutting costs across the board than anything any individual company can do. All companies have fixed costs which are difficult, and sometimes impossible, to reduce significantly. While competitiveness could in principle be increased by reducing wage costs, there is always massive resistance to cuts in money wages making this option not generally viable. What is true of companies and wage earners, however, is not true of the economy as a whole. A changed exchange rate changes the cost of every domestic factor of production. No wonder countries with overvalued exchange rates suffer so grievously and those with undervalued exchange rates do so well!

The relationship between productivity and competitiveness is therefore the reverse of what is often supposed. Increased productivity does not produce greater competitiveness. Rather, greater competitiveness generates the conditions where increased productivity is most easily achieved – and achieved with the greatest advantage. This is not a trite conclusion. It has profound implications for determining the conditions which will make economies grow, and the policies which need to be pursued to make this happen.

The competitiveness (or lack of it) in any economy's export sector is thus crucial to its capacity to grow and to keep its labour force fully employed. The huge growth rates achieved by many of the Pacific Rim economies stem from the fact that they have managed to maintain this condition for decades. Economies which, for whatever reason, have allowed this sine qua non to slip away have paid a heavy penalty in slower growth and suboptimal use of the available labour force. The USA is a pre-eminent example of an economy in the second category, although much of the Western world now falls into the same class. For the whole of the period beginning shortly after the end of World War II, the output of the goods and services produced by US companies has not, on average, been sufficiently competitively priced in world terms. As a result, the share of the US home market taken by imports, particularly manufactures, has risen dramatically while simultaneously the share of world trade achieved by US exporters has fallen heavily. As late as 1963 the USA imported 8.6 per cent of the world's manufactures and exported 17.4 per cent of them. By 1994 its imports were 17.5 per cent of the world total, and its exports 13.1 per cent.[4] Total US exports, which by 2000 had shrunk to 12.3 per cent of the world total, slipped to 8.5 per cent by 2010.[5] The UK percentages exhibit a similar but even more pronounced tendency in the same direction.

As a result of these persistent trends, the West has forgone the direct benefit which would have been secured by having a larger proportion of its GDP devoted to manufacturing and related sectors of the economy where, in the right conditions, increases in output and rising productivity are relatively easy to achieve. Many Western economies have also been exposed to persistent balance of payments problems, which have constrained the capacity of successive administrations to expand the economy as rapidly as they might otherwise have chosen. It has therefore been impossible for buoyant consumer demand and high rates of investment to fill the gap left by sluggish foreign trade performance. The combined impact of these major influences provides the fundamental explanation for the relatively slow growth the West has achieved, particularly since the 1970s. The reverse conditions, applying at the other end of the spectrum to most of the Pacific Rim economies, explains how they have managed to surge ahead.

Facing international competition

The conditions favourable to economic growth are far from static. Movement and change are essential elements, not least because of foreign competition. Rapid economic growth, once established, has a strong capacity to reinforce itself. On the whole, therefore, fast-expanding economies tend to keep growing rapidly, but this virtuous circle of fast growth cannot be taken for granted. It can slow down or even stop altogether for a time, as has been the experience of much of Europe since the mid-1970s and, most strikingly, of Japan since 1991. It is important to be able to explain both what causes growth to accelerate to a fast pace and why it can slow down, stop or even go into reverse. It is crucially important, therefore, to be able to pinpoint the mechanisms involved in global trade that generate both the virtuous circle of import saving and export-led growth and the vicious circle of import-led stagnation.

One of the keys to understanding this issue is to appreciate a particularly important characteristic of a large proportion of the investment taking place in all countries in those parts of the economy which produce internationally tradable goods and services. This is the large increases in output which investment of this sort is capable of producing at relatively low run-on costs, as fixed expenses become spread over greater volumes of output. Indeed, this characteristic provides the main explanation for the enormous growth in international trade which has occurred over recent decades. The result is a special feature of the production costs of internationally traded goods and services. They almost all involve steeply falling cost curves. This means that the expense involved in producing the first batch of any new product or service may be high, but all subsequent output is much cheaper. The average cost of production therefore falls quickly as the volume of output builds up.

This characteristic of internationally traded goods and services is highly significant. Any country with macroeconomic conditions making it relatively easy to sell the output from this kind of investment – in particular, low interest rates, a plentiful supply of credit and a competitive exchange rate – will achieve rapid growth. Once the initial investment is on stream, low marginal costs of production lead to high sales and profits, which are then available to finance the risks involved in subsequent waves of investment. With high profitability also enabling these enterprises to attract and hold the most able people in management positions, the next round of investment decisions will be more likely be shrewdly judged and efficiently carried out. The low cost of production makes keeping plants fully occupied relatively easy, as higher output leads to even lower production expenses and the capacity for yet more competitive pricing.

This virtuous circle thus tends strongly to fortify itself. Higher sales and greater profitability make it easier to finance research and development and thus to keep ahead. They also provide the money needed to cover high selling costs so that new markets can be penetrated. The competitive position of successful enterprises is strengthened by better design, advertising and selling efforts and after-sales service, all of which are expensive. On the back of a large volume of profitable sales, however, they can be relatively easy to afford. Profits remain high, making increased output expenditure easy to finance. Both the savings ratio and the rate of investment as a proportion of national income tend to be much higher in economies with strong export sectors than when the reverse is the case.

Since with substantial rewards in successful enterprises go social status and political power, attracting and retaining the best talent becomes ever easier. It is impossible to overstress how important a contribution to achieving sustained growth is made by having a high proportion of the country's most able people involved in making and selling goods and services, especially those involved in foreign trade. Creating the right economic conditions for the virtuous spiral of import saving and export-led growth may be the precursor to economic success, but there is no substitute for the highest possible standard of efficiency at the level of the firm. This is where management quality is as critical as any other factor, perhaps the most significant of all. Sustained high growth rates can be achieved only by the difficult processes of making good judgements about increasingly complicated problems, managing more and more complex organisations, dealing with rapid and frequently intricate technical developments and assessing and sometimes accurately anticipating market trends, often trends involving the whole world.

The crucial question, then, is what makes it possible to break into the virtuous circle of import saving and export-led growth? What are the conditions which cause import-led stagnation? The exchange rate is the most critical determinant, for reasons which Table 1.2 makes clear. The table shows in schematic (but not unrealistic) form the costs and pricing options available to companies competing in international trade in three different economies: one with a parity in line with the world average, one with an exchange rate undervalued by 20 per cent and one with an exchange rate overvalued by the same percentage. The example shown here involves manufacturing, where the impact of high or low exchange rates is particularly pronounced, but similar results are obtained when considering internationally traded services.

Manufacturing companies' costs are made up of a number of components, some determined by world prices, some determined locally. In Table 1.2 raw materials and other intermediate products are shown as 20 per cent of international prices for the firm's output in the averagely competitive economy. There is a world market for nearly all commodities, but favourable

Table 1.2   Options available to companies producing internationally tradeable goods in economies with parities at varying levels

	Countries with Average Parities	Countries Undervalued by 20%	Countries Overvalued by 20%
Costs fixed in World Prices			
Material Inputs	20	19	21
Capital Depreciation	10	8	12
Total Internationally determined Costs	30	27	33
Costs fixed in Domestic Prices			
Labour Costs	60	48	72
Local Supplies			
Land & Premises			
Interest Charges			
Total Costs	90	75	105
World Prices for the Company's Output	100	100	100
Trading Profit or Loss at World Prices	10	25	−5

selling conditions for exporters tend to go with the efficient and low-cost raw-material and intermediate-product suppliers that are components of economies with a rapidly expanding manufacturing base. Economies with a strong export sector understandably tend to lack significant tariffs or other restrictions on raw-material imports, whereas economies with weak balance of payments positions are more prone to protecting their remaining industries with import constraints. Raw-material costs are therefore likely to be lower in highly competitive economies than in uncompetitive ones. The table's figures show a 5 per cent spread round the average.

Second, there are capital costs, which, when depreciated over output achieved in the average economy, are shown as 10 per cent of selling prices. These costs, however, are even more likely to be lower than raw materials in highly competitive economies and greater in those which are uncompetitive. Not only do fast-growing economies tend to have cheaper and more efficient suppliers for capital equipment than elsewhere, but they also benefit from potentially much higher levels of capacity utilisation. The result is that the cost of capital depreciation per unit of output tends to be much lower in companies in competitive economies than in those which have high domestic costs, a factor further reflected in the figures in Table 1.2.

Third, there are all the costs incurred locally. An overvalued currency implies that the average wage costs per hour, adjusted for local productivity, are necessarily above the world mean level by a proportion similar to the overvaluation. Indeed, the costs which the domestic economy charges the rest of the world for its labour, adjusted for productivity, substantially determine whether the currency is over- or undervalued in the first place. Since employee costs make up some 60 per cent of total charges incurred in developed economies, this factor makes a large difference to the average company's prospects. Higher wage levels, adjusted for productivity, affect not only the employee costs the firm directly incurs but also the labour component in the goods and services it buys from local suppliers. Moreover, in an economy with an overvalued currency, interest charges will also almost certainly be above average, and high interest rates tend to push up the firm's cost for land and premises, as well as borrowing for all other forms of capital expenditure. Taken together, all these locally determined costs account for 60 per cent of the selling prices for manufacturing companies in averagely competitive countries. These costs, however, measured against world prices for the firm's output, will be proportionately 20 per cent higher in economies with overvalued currencies and 20 per cent lower in those whose currencies are undervalued. Finally,

Table 1.2 shows the firm in the averagely competitive economy making a 10 per cent net profit on sales.

Now consider the options available to companies operating in the economy with the undervalued currency. If these companies sell at world prices, even with normal capacity utilisation, they make huge profits, because their locally determined costs are 60 per cent times 20 per cent less than the world average, giving them a 12 per cent cost advantage in addition to the 10 per cent net profit for which provision has already been made. An alternative strategy which would still give them a 10 per cent net profit on turnover involves their selling at prices some 15 per cent lower than the world average. This strategy, providing them an enormous competitive price advantage, would allow them then to use their capital equipment much more intensively, thereby reducing its depreciation charges as a percentage of selling costs by perhaps a fifth, the ratio used in the table. They could do so by relying on the large volume of orders obtainable at lower prices to achieve very high capacity working. In practice, the evidence from all the rapidly growing economies is that once reasonable profits on turnover are being made, companies which are already highly competitive tend to go for lower prices and higher volumes of sales rather than try to keep prices up. This leads to even more rapid export-led growth than would otherwise occur.

The companies in the overvalued economy, on the other hand, face very different prospects. Their higher domestic costs amount to 12 per cent of the world selling prices for their output. These excess charges are more than the 10 per cent net profit made by their competitors in the averagely competitive economies. Their higher locally incurred costs, if they sell at normal world prices, therefore wipe out all profitability for firms in countries with heavily overvalued currencies and leave them trading at a loss. They then have two choices. They can cut current expenses by paying lower wages and salaries, worsening employment conditions, cancelling investment projects and abandoning research and development programmes. Such steps may help in the short term but are fatally weakening for the future. Alternatively, they can try to sell at higher prices. If they do so, however – unless they are in a niche business not subject to normal competitive pressures – orders are bound to fall away, leading to lower-capacity working and higher depreciation costs per unit of output. To make a 10 per cent net profit on turnover while allowing for lower-capacity working, the firms shown with the cost structure in the table in the overvalued country would have to charge nearly 20 per cent above the world average. As it is clearly impossible to compete at such high prices, especially against aggressive companies in the undervalued economies, all they can do is withdraw from the market altogether or persevere with prices which are the best compromise they can find between total lack of profitability and holding on to some market share.

It is all too clear which of these three examples is closest to the recent cost-base experience of many of the producers in the more mature economies of the world, particularly in those sectors confronted with competition on consumer goods from newly industrialising countries, many of them in the Far East. Faced with the familiar problem of being uncompetitive, however, why cannot companies facing such conditions increase their productivity to whatever level is required to be competitive with the world average, as all those who advocate industrial strategies and wage restraint are essentially trying to achieve?

Some companies can and will succeed in doing so. These are the ones which will survive even in the harsh conditions portrayed in Table 1.2 for companies in uncompetitive countries. Critical, however, to economies as a whole is not the performance of exceptional companies. It is the average achievement which counts. The required change might be made if it were possible to engineer a sudden huge increase in productivity across the board, one competitors could not emulate, without any of the rise in output being absorbed in extra wages and salaries. One has only to look at these conditions, however, to see how completely unrealistic they are. It is far more difficult to increase productivity in slowly growing economies, with depressed levels of investment, low capacity utilisation and relatively poorly paid staff than in already fast-growing economies where productivity will inevitably be increasing rapidly. It is impossible not to share rises in output with the labour force to a substantial degree. What may be possible in isolated companies cannot be done across the board in all companies.

In economies with overvalued exchange rates, the more perspicacious managers of manufacturing companies do not persevere with attempts to improve productivity when they realise that they will never achieve sufficient increases in performance to be able to compete. They conclude that the safest, most profitable and most rational strategy is to abandon manufacturing in the domestic economy. Some of them decide to buy from abroad whatever their sales forces can sell, perhaps reinvesting the proceeds from selling off factory sites and installations into manufacturing facilities in other parts of the world. Others sell out to multinational companies, which they then use as ready-made channels to distribute their output. The less perspicacious plough on until their companies go out of business. One paradoxical reason why industrial strategies will always fail in economies with overvalued currencies is that the better the industry's management at seizing profitable opportunities, the faster the process of de-industrialisation is likely to be. This is why many companies with the best performance records in slow-growing economies are those which have closed down their manufacturing operations fastest and moved them as soon as possible to other countries where costs at the prevailing exchange rates are much lower.

Investment and productivity

It is sometimes assumed that because capital investment is subject to competition, it will therefore always earn about the same overall rate of return. As a corollary, it is often generally supposed that productivity increases, as they occur, are roughly evenly spread over the whole of any economy. Neither of these suppositions is remotely true. Taking the productivity issue first, Table 1.3 shows the experience of the USA, by far the largest and one of the most diversified economies in the world. For the 20 years between 1977 and 1997, a series of statistics on the same basis is available to provide accurate comparisons over a long enough period, covering both ups and downs in the trade cycle, for them to have high statistical significance. Far from productivity increases being evenly spread, they could hardly be more varied.[6] Output per head in agriculture increased at 5.7 per cent per annum over this period. Manufacturing, mining and wholesale trade all increased at around 3 per cent per annum. All the rest of the economy did much worse, with construction, government and services, in particular, showing significant falls in productivity over the period. The much-vaunted financial services sector achieved a cumulative annual increase in output per head over the whole of the two decades of only 0.4 per cent – a dismal result by any standard, although the high absolute output per head of those involved, reflected in correspondingly generous remuneration, should be noted. Worse still was the performance of the service sector, which employed an increasingly large proportion of the labour force. There, output per head fell by nearly 1 per cent per annum across the whole period. Some special reasons for the heavy fall in services in the US economy will be discussed later, but these do not change the general pattern, which is replicated in the statistics covering economies across the whole of the developed world. Increases in output per head are much easier to achieve in manufacturing and associated activities than they are in the service sector.

Table 1.3 Changes in output per head of the US working population between 1977 and 1997

	Output Value in constant 1992 $bn	Labour Force in Millions	Output per Head $000s	Output per Head Percentage Changes from 1977 to 1997	
				Total % Change	Annual % Average
1977					
Manufacturing	796.5	19.7	40.5		
Construction	213.8	3.9	55.5		
Mining	82.4	0.8	101.4		
Sub total	1,092.7	24.3	44.9		
Agriculture, Forestry & Fishing	61.1	4.1	14.7		
Transport & Utilites	346.8	4.7	73.6		
Wholesale Trade	201.0	4.7	42.6		
Retail Trade	364.5	13.8	26.4		
Finance, Insurance & Real Estate	742.7	4.5	166.3		
Services	712.5	15.3	46.6		
Statistical Discrepancy	37.3				
Not Allocated	–2.4				
Government	717.4	15.1	47.4		
1977 GDP	4,273.6	86.6	49.3		
1997					
Manufacturing	1,369.9	18.7	73.4	81.4	3.0
Construction	274.4	5.7	48.3	–13.1	–0.7
Mining	109.9	0.6	185.6	83.2	3.1
Sub total	1,754.2	24.9	70.4	0.57	2.3
Agriculture, Forestry & Fishing	127.6	2.9	44.5	201.78	5.7
Transport & Utilites	644.3	6.4	100.8	36.92	1.6
Wholesale Trade	532.0	6.6	80.0	88.04	3.2
Retail Trade	713.5	22.0	32.4	22.65	1.0
Finance, Insurance & Real Estate	1,286.0	7.1	181.4	9.08	0.4
Services	1,398.6	36.0	38.8	–16.66	–0.9
Statistical Discrepancy	–45.4				
Not Allocated	–25.0				
Government	884.0	19.6	45.2	–4.75	–0.2
1997 GDP	7,269.8	125.6	57.9	17.35	0.8

Source: Tables B.13, B.46 and B.100, *Economic Report to the President 1999*. Washington DC: US Government Printing Office 1999.

It is also highly significant that the sectors of the US economy showing the fastest productivity growth were those mostly involved in international markets. This, again, is a characteristic which manifests itself across the whole of the developed and developing world. This strongly suggests that any economy which wants to grow quickly would be wise to try to concentrate its activity in those sectors where large productivity increases are relatively easy to achieve. This can only be done by having the economy's cost base at a competitive international level, which the USA has failed to achieve over a long period. The resulting major reason for the very low increase in output per head in the USA between 1977 and 1997 – only 0.8 per cent per annum on average – is that so much of US economic activity is concentrated in sectors where productivity increases are hardest to achieve.[7]

These trends continued strongly into the twenty-first century. By 2010 only 7.6 per cent of the US labour force was employed in manufacturing, but productivity growth in US manufacturing accelerated to a remarkable 4.8 per cent per annum during the 2000s. Agriculture did even better, at 4.9 per cent a year. Meanwhile the whole of the service sector, having produced almost no increase in output per head between 1977 and 1997, contributed much less than manufacturing per head between 2000 and 2009, with a cumulative increase of 1.6 per cent.[8] As of 2012, manufacturing still provided a disproportionately large amount of the overall productivity increases which were only then slowly lifting US living standards because the proportion of the US economy devoted to manufacturing has been so low.

Returns on investment

One of the major reasons why the increase in output resulting from investment is so variable is that the return to the economy as a whole is much greater than the proportion which comes back either as dividends or interest to the individuals or organisations who put up the money to pay for it. The 'private' current return on investment, which investors typically receive, net of inflation, is seldom above about 10 per cent, even in those economies which are doing very well. However, it is by no means only investors who benefit directly from the projects for which they put up their money. Many others do as well.

The management and the employees in the enterprises where the investment has been made, whose productivity rises in consequence, almost invariably share in the benefits through salary or wage rises. The state also obtains a return through increased tax receipts. In addition, the consumer, who gets a better product or service, a lower price or both, is also a gainer. If the aggregate rather than just the private rate of return is considered, then across a wide swathe of much of the investment in fast-growing economies, the total return to the economy is much higher than 10 per cent. This is not a particularly difficult ratio to calculate from national accounts. For those familiar with the concept, it is the reciprocal of the ratio of incremental capital to output. It is often 40 or 50 per cent per annum, sometimes higher still.

From the point of view of the investor, the build-up period for an investment is not normally particularly important. This is the time between when the investor starts to forgo the alternative uses to which the financial resources could be put, and when the investment comes on stream, starting to produce output and income. It is the time taken to build or construct the project into which the money is being put. The investor's concern is that, once the project is in operation, it should be able to provide a sufficient return to cover the interest charges during the build-up period as well as producing a reasonable private return subsequently. For everyone else in the economy, however – indeed for the economy as a whole – the build-up period provides no return at all because the outlay for the investment is not yet producing anything. There is no additional output to defray the private rates of return or contribute to the total rate of return until the project on which the money has been spent is physically in use.

It is therefore extremely significant that investment projects typically found in rapidly growing economies combine the following characteristics: first, they have a high total rate of return; second, they have a short build-up period, often of the order of six months or less; and third, they tend to be used fully once in place, because of the high level of demand which fast growth entails. When these three factors are put together, a truly astonishing cumulative rate of return on investment projects of this type becomes relatively easy to achieve. Those which produce a total rate of return of 50 per cent or more in six months or less, if the return on all the new output thus created is saved and reinvested, can produce a cumulative total rate of return in excess of 100 per cent per annum. This makes it possible for the whole of that part of the economy where this type of investment is taking place not only to double its output every year but to generate all the savings required for this doubling to happen. This kind of increase can still be seen particularly in the light manufacturing sectors in, for example, China, Korea, Taiwan and Malaysia and was very evident during earlier periods in Japan. The huge returns on investment in the production of internationally traded goods and services and the tendency for them to be reinvested explain why rapidly growing economies have such high savings ratios and why their industries, if competently run, have relatively few financing problems.

These large rates of return cannot, however, be attained across the board. It is impossible to obtain 100 per cent returns on outlays in social infrastructure – housing, public works and the like – except in rare and unusual circumstances. Many private-sector investment projects do not meet these qualifications either. Anything which takes a long time to build, whether large-scale infrastructure projects or complex products requiring years of development, will inevitably have a lower cumulative total annual rate of return. These are not projects which produce fast economic growth. Those that do, however, are exactly those with which the most profitable and rapidly growing international trade is concerned. This is so because they have the same characteristic significant initial costs, with falling cost curves as production builds up and rising output per head comes through. Here, then, is another essential element in the strategy for achieving rapid economic growth: to pitch the exchange rate at a parity which enables fast export expansion and achieves import saving. This policy is needed not only because it creates and expands sectors of the economy where productivity growth will be very high. In addition, the total rate of return it can achieve is so large that it is capable of generating the whole of the saving required to finance its own expansion, even if this entails doubling its output every year.

Two important conclusions flow from these considerations. The first is that the lower the parity, the greater the chance of achieving both self-sustaining and self-financing growth at a high rate. The rise in exports thus likely to be achieved is more than sufficient to take care of any increased import requirements there may be. Since any import restraints will make the exchange rate higher than it otherwise would be, the case for tariffs being as few and as low as possible is reinforced. The second is that the large increase in productivity and output makes it much easier than might be supposed to deal with inflationary pressures caused by rapid growth. This important point is returned to in Chapter 3.

The hugely varying rates of return to the whole economy achieved by different classes of investment projects may also throw light on an important and puzzling economic growth paradox. Compared with the international average, the USA achieves a relatively high return on its comparatively low level of investment. This is why the growth rate of the American economy averaged a little over 3 per cent per annum over recent decades[9] despite its low reinvestment rate, which has averaged under 20 per cent per annum.[10] By contrast, many of the fast-growing economies in the Pacific Rim have scored relatively poorly in this respect. Much of their high growth can be accounted for by large amounts of increased inputs – labour, education and, particularly, high levels of capital investment. The explanation for the poor returns, particularly to investment, in many Pacific Rim countries surely lies in the mixture of investment projects undertaken. Korea, for instance, which has in the past spent, at government instigation, large sums of money on grandiose industrial schemes to produce ships, chemicals, cement and so on, has a large proportion of total investment producing low cumulative returns which, balancing the very high compound returns produced in the large Korean light industrial sector, produce an unimpressive average. The USA, with its proportionately far smaller government involvement in industry, has avoided these pitfalls. What could the US economy achieve if its internationally tradable sectors had the competitive advantages which Korean light industry has had, unaccompanied by the cronyism, corruption and waste which the Korean *chaebol* system brings in train?

2
The Exchange Rate

Rapid growth takes place in economies which are competitive in world markets and start with the advantage of costs at least as low as their competitors' (preferably lower). This advantage, by enabling them to expand exports without suffering excessive import penetration, provides them with opportunities to increase their share of world trade and to grow without the constraint of balance of payments problems. Internal demand can then be kept at a high and rising level, without undue inflationary pressures developing. These conditions were established and maintained for the USA during the nineteenth century and some of the first half of the twentieth, albeit behind high tariff barriers which had other disadvantages. They applied to most of the rest of western Europe – excluding Britain, which grew much more slowly – during the quarter of a century after World War II ended. The same conditions are to be found now in the fast-growing economies in the Far East. The reason why such sustained growth has been achieved, why living standards much more than doubled in the course of less than two decades, why inflation has in nearly all cases been relatively low and stable, is that the macroeconomic conditions have been right.

To achieve high exports, an economy has to sell at home and abroad the output of both its labour and its other factors of production, taken together, at competitive prices. If it does so, it will achieve import saving and export-led growth. If it fails to do so, especially by a wide margin, it will plunge into import-led stagnation. The only practical way of making any economy competitive is to position the exchange rate correctly. This is why the parity of the currency is critically important. There is no other feasible way for a country to change the price it charges for the whole of its output sufficiently to make the necessary difference.

The higher the proportion of a country's GDP involved in world trade, the more obvious it is that its exchange rate needs to be correctly aligned vis-à-vis its competitors. Perhaps one of the illusions under which the USA has suffered is that, because its foreign trade exposure is comparatively small, the impact on the economy of unmanageable competition from abroad may have appeared relatively slight. Whether the parity of the dollar on the foreign exchanges was appropriate for the interests of the domestic economy may therefore have been given less attention than it should have been. In fact, the exchange rate of the dollar against all other world currencies has been as critically important in determining the US growth rate as it has been to all economies exposed to any significant degree of international competition, as US economic history clearly shows.

In sum, for any economy, pricing its output at a competitive level by adopting appropriate macroeconomic policies is the key to expansion. The policy instrument available to any sovereign government to provide growth conditions is to position the exchange rate at a level which will enable its country's goods and services to compete successfully both at home and in world markets.

The theme which runs through this book is that history has been shaped to a much greater degree than most people realise by the exchange-rate policies which the governments of all the world's economies have pursued. Decisions taken on such matters as interest rates, the control of the money supply, the systems for regulating the creation and control of credit, and fixing the exchange rate have been crucial. Vital though these decisions may have been, however, they were often taken without any clear view of their likely impact. This is because governments have had remarkably little robust, reliable theory to guide them. As a result, to a remarkable extent, those responsible for economic policy in all countries during the last 200 years have been flying blind, often heavily influenced in the wrong direction by those with strong sectional interests. They have had to rely on conventional wisdom, much of it inadequate and some of it simply wrong. Political leaders who ran their economies more successfully than others did so mostly because they took the right decisions, even if for the wrong reasons or by happenstance, rather than because they were working within a coherent framework of well-conceived and articulated ideas about how the economies for which they were responsible really worked.

Changing the exchange rate

Is it possible for the exchange rate to be influenced by policy changes? Or is the parity entirely determined, as monetarists have claimed, by market forces over which governments have little or no control? If the market really controls exchange rates, leaving governments as power- less bystanders, then attempts by monetary authorities to position the foreign exchange value of the currency where they want it to be are bound to fail, unless they simply ape the market's wishes. If, on the other hand, government policy can have a powerful impact on the parity of the currency, then the scope for using exchange-rate policy to shape the performance of the economy generally is much enhanced.

One of the most important tenets of the monetarist school, reflected in varying degrees in the attitude of many policymakers, is that in all economies the exchange rate is very largely, if not entirely, fixed by market forces, so that no action government takes to change it will make any significant difference. Monetarists have built up an elaborate theory intended to prove that there is an equilibrium exchange rate towards which every parity tends strongly to return. The traditional form of this theory was known as the Law of One Price, and the modern form is sometimes referred to as International Monetarism. It states that if attempts are made by the authorities to move to a parity away from the one established as the equilibrium point by the markets, then differ- ential rates of inflation will soon pull it back to where it should be.

In particular, it is argued that any attempts to make the economy more competitive by devaluation will automatically cause a rise in inflation which will rapidly erode any increased competitiveness that might be temporarily secured. This will leave the economy not only as uncompetitive as it was before but with an inflationary problem added to its other difficulties. It is also contended that if, because of a temporary disequilibrium, the currency is overvalued, this will, by exercising a strong downward pressure on the price level, reduce the rate of inflation without sacrificing competitiveness, except perhaps in the short term. There is little doubt that many people believe this proposition to a greater or lesser degree. What is there to confirm that it is correct?

The reasons why devaluations do not always produce a corresponding increase in inflation will be reviewed in detail in Chapter 3. Suffice to say for the moment that the empirical evidence for the monetarists' contentions turns out to be extremely weak. On the contrary, there are good reasons, both theoretical and practical, for believing that on this issue they are wholly wrong. Furthermore, economic history shows beyond any reasonable doubt that monetarist contentions that exchange rates are entirely a function of market forces over which governments have no control cannot be correct. Governments can change and frequently have changed both the nominal and the real exchange rates of the economies for which they were responsible, sometimes by very large amounts. A conspicuous case was the huge rise in the rate for sterling which took place at the end of the 1970s and the early part of the 1980s. This was a direct result of the tightening of the money supply and the increase in interest rates which began under the Labour government of the time and was continued and reinforced by the incoming Conservative administration in 1979. As a result, the nominal value of the pound – excluding allowance for any differences in the inflation rate between sterling and other currencies – rose on the foreign exchanges from $1.74 in 1977 to $2.32 in 1980, an increase of 33 per cent, and against the Deutsche Mark from DM3.85 in 1978 to DM4.54 in 1981, an 18 per cent increase.[1] This happened despite far above average inflation in Britain over this period, thus enormously decreasing the country's competitiveness. In consequence the real exchange rate – allowing for varying inflation rates in different countries – rose by 25 per cent, with calamitous results for British industry.

Another telling example comes from the early part of the Reagan presidency, when the USA drove up the nominal value of the dollar by no less than 60 per cent against the Deutsche Mark (from DM1.83 to DM2.94) between 1979 and 1985,[2] although the inflation rates in the two countries were similar.

Governments can also bring down the external value of their currencies if they want to do so. Between 1982 and 1989 – albeit aided by the balance of payments surplus the Japanese economy was then accumulating – the nominal rate for the US dollar against the yen fell by an astonishing 45 per cent (from ¥249 to ¥138), while the rate for the dollar against the Deutsche Mark went down by 38 per cent (from DM2.84 to DM1.76) in just four years (1984–8).[3] Much more recently, UK authorities did nothing to arrest a fall in the trade-weighted value of the pound as much as 28 per cent between 2007 and 2009, though the rate since then has strengthened somewhat.[4] Of course, there is a limit to the extent to which governments can resist market pressures, as the USA discovered when the dollar was devalued at the beginning of the 1970s. There is still, however, considerable scope for monetary authorities in any country to choose whether they want to be at the high or the low end of the range of possibilities the market will accept.

Nor does a longer perspective do anything to improve monetarist theory's credibility. One of the most striking cases of a successful devaluation was that of France at the end of the 1950s. The government of Charles de Gaulle, faced with increasing competition from Germany as the Common Market became established, devalued the French franc twice, by a total of 29 per cent.[5] Inflation in France rose sharply for a few months but by nothing like as much as the devaluation. Within a year or so it had dropped back to where it had been. French competitiveness vis-à-vis the German economy was established. The result was a long boom which took the French average growth rate to 5.5 per cent per annum for a decade and a half, more than doubling the national income in 15 years.[6]

The evidence thus clearly shows that it is well within the power of a government to choose, from a spectrum of possibilities, where it wants the real exchange rate to be and, over the long term, to hold it there within reasonably narrow margins. There will be short-term fluctuations, but these are not important: the medium-term trend is what counts. There is without doubt a range of policies, all of which need to be used in coordinated fashion, that a government can pursue to change and then hold the exchange rate at or near a preferred level.

First, underlying all else, is the monetary stance adopted by the government. There is overwhelming evidence that tight money policies, and the high interest rates which go with them, pull the exchange rate up and that more accommodating monetary policies and lower interest rates bring it down. Study after study has shown that interest rates have a powerful effect on the exchange rate, significantly greater than other changes such as alterations in the availability or cost of oil and other raw materials. Nor are central bank base rates necessarily crucial. Nowadays bank rates may be very low, but the actual interest rates paid by most borrowers in the market tend to be much higher.

Second, the actions and stance of both the government and the central bank in dealing with the foreign exchange market have a major influence, given that expectations and opinion are almost as important as the underlying realities. If the government has a clearly expressed view that the exchange rate is too high or too low, the market will respond, as it did, for example, in the United States during the 1980s. The operations of central banks in buying or selling foreign currencies can and must be made consistent with other government policies.

Third, the government should have a clear strategy as regards foreign trade balances. In the short term, fluctuations are unavoidable, but in the longer term these can to a large extent be ironed out. If balance of payments surpluses are allowed to accumulate, as happened in Japan in the 1980s and as has been happening in China of late, there will be strong upward pressure on the exchange rate. The converse being clearly the case reinforces arguments for taking a liberal view on protection and in general avoiding impediments to imports. The balance of payments is also a function of the level of domestic activity. Deflation produces a larger surplus or smaller deficit and upward pressure on parity, and reflation does the opposite. The strength of domestic demand is therefore a further important determinant of the exchange rate.

Fourth, the government has a considerable degree of control over capital movements, with or without formal exchange controls. Any policy which encourages repatriation of capital and discourages capital outflows – particularly high domestic interest rates – will push up the exchange rate, and vice versa. The same applies to portfolio investment, which has none of the advantages of direct investment from abroad in plant and machinery. One problem which may occur if a policy of growth based on increased competitiveness is successfully pursued is that capital may be attracted in undesirably large quantities by exceptional investment opportunities. This may make it more difficult to keep the exchange rate down. The answer to this problem is likely to be lower interest rates, if these are feasible, or deliberately deciding not to fund the whole of the borrowing requirement to discourage an inward flow of money.

Domestic sources of capital funds can also be encouraged by economic policies which concentrate economic activity as far as possible in those parts of the economy, particularly light industry, which can generate their own savings and investment at a high rate. If there are enough domestic savings to finance all the economy's capital needs, there is no merit in stopping any surplus being invested abroad. If the exchange rate needs to be kept down, there are, on the contrary, positive advantages to capital exports. Such an approach is the opposite to the one pursued by the United Kingdom, especially over the last decade, in allowing large swathes of the British economy to be purchased by foreign companies. There can be no doubt that this policy contributed to the overvaluation of sterling during the first decade of the twentieth century.

Finally, allowance needs to be made for the well-known J-curve effect. If the value of the currency falls, there is a tendency for imports to stay at more or less their previous volume while the domestic revenue from exports decreases because the exchange rate has gone down. This produces a worsening in the balance of payments position until the volume of exports increases in response to lower prices.

If the value of the currency falls slowly, a succession of J-curve effects flows from each move downwards in the exchange rate. The impression that may then be given is that no improvement is in sight. The United States had something of this experience in the mid-1980s. The reverse tendencies are to be found if the exchange rate appreciates; then the false impression is given for a few months, until market forces work their way through, that making exports less competitive does not worsen the balance of payments position. Part of the reason for the J-curve, however, is importers' belief that any reduction in the profitability of their activities may shortly be reversed by an appreciation of the exchange rate caused by the authorities trying to reverse an unwanted change from the previous parity. If it is clear, however, that a radical change in policy on the exchange rate has taken place, and one unlikely to be reversed, it is possible to alter the behaviour of importers much more quickly.

Thus, with the battery of policy instruments available, governments can determine the exchange-rate level within wide limits. There is ample empirical evidence of government-instigated parity movements which have been successfully accomplished. Obviously it is impossible for all countries to move towards competitiveness with each other simultaneously, although it would be possible for the world economy as a whole to adopt more expansionist policies. The evidence nevertheless shows that it is practical for any individual country to decide where, within wide bounds on the spectrum of international competitiveness, it wants to be and, having chosen that position, to stay fairly close to its preferred location.

Is it true, therefore, that the markets can be bucked? They do not need to be. There are internally consistent policies which any government can adopt to hold the exchange rate at least at a level which allows the current account to be balanced with full employment and a sustainable rate of growth. These include low interest rates, an accommodating monetary strategy, keeping the economy open to imports competitive with domestic supplies and encouraging capital exports. Provided the markets are satisfied that government has adopted a policy stance with which it is determined to continue, stability can be achieved over a wide band of different degrees of exchange-rate competitiveness. It is not then necessary to buck the market. This is why, by choosing the right policy mix, if the will to do so is there, it is always possible to choose a macroeconomic stance which will ensure that external balance is combined with full employment and rapid growth.

Preferences for strong currencies

If there are very substantial benefits to be obtained from having a competitive exchange rate and the obstacles to achieving it are not very difficult to overcome, why is this objective seldom seen by most policymakers in the West – and by most ordinary people – as desirable? A major reduction in the value of the dollar, the euro and the pound against the Pacific Rim currencies is not a policy prescription found in newspapers, best-selling books about Western decline or the academic literature. It is not a plank in any major political party's manifesto. It may therefore be tempting to presume that were the monetary and exchange-rate changes proposed an effective remedy, they would have been much more generally recommended in the past. Before reaching this conclusion, however, it is necessary to review the following powerful reasons for believing that the remedy on offer, though effective, might be surprisingly difficult to see.

First, Western economies, whatever their deficiencies may be, have done extremely well for a long time. They have provided their citizens, on average, with a higher standard of living than is found elsewhere in the world, mostly by a large margin. They still comprise a major proportion of the world's economic output. Most major industrial and commercial developments have been pioneered in the West. Their economies, by world standards, operate far more efficiently than the average. Their culture, management techniques and values permeate and to a large extent still set standards for the rest of the world. With this record of achievement behind them, it is understandable that it has been hard to comprehend how vulnerable in some important respects the West's economies have become.

Nor have most countries which have challenged the West's hegemony over the past decades been successful in denting its apparent invincibility. In the 1950s and 1960s there were real concerns that the Soviet bloc might overtake the West in economic power and living standards, but this threat was steadily reduced during the stagnation of the years presided over by Leonid Brezhnev (1906–82), and it disappeared when the Soviet Union broke up following the era when Mikhail Gorbachev (1931–) presided over its disintegration. Then there were fears that Japan would surpass European standards of living and perhaps overtake the USA, at least in terms of GDP per head and even possibly in terms of its economy's total size. These have diminished dramatically since the early 1990s as Japan's fabled growth melted away. There is clearly now a threat from China, at least in terms of the economy's total size, but the average living standard in China is still far below what is commonly found in the West.

Second, it may well be that the sheer efficiency with which so much of the West's economies run has blinded people to their competitive weaknesses. Perhaps understandably, the terms productivity, efficiency and competitiveness generate vast confusion. It is very easy to assume that because the West's factories are much more productive than those almost everywhere else in the world – as in general they are – they must therefore be competitive internationally. This conclusion is, however, certainly not necessarily correct. Even if output per head is much higher in the West than in China, the average Chinese product may still be more competitive – indeed, it generally is nowadays, by a wide margin – especially if it involves reasonably straightforward and widely available production techniques. This has nothing to do with productivity, because Chinese output per head is far below that of the West in almost every branch of economic activity. Nor is it because Chinese wages are lower than those in the West, although this will of course have a major impact on the sort of production in which China has the most competitive advantage; notably, labour-intensive assembly work. It has everything to do with exchange rates and the cost base in China compared with Western countries for generally available production techniques. In the last analysis, wage costs per hour are what count, yet whatever they are, they can always be made internationally competitive or otherwise by picking the right or wrong exchange rate.

Third, there have been serious misunderstandings about the role and importance of manufacturing. It is true that as economies become more advanced and the standard of living rises, there is a tendency for the proportion of the GDP involved in the production of services to rise in relation to the ratio involved in manufacturing. This happens partly because of a price effect. Because productivity increases are so much more difficult to achieve in services, the relative cost of manufactured goods tends to fall, making them look less significant than in volume terms they really are. Yet it is also noteworthy that those with rising incomes spend more of their money on services. The result is first that it is easy to assume that as an economy becomes increasingly advanced, the proportion of its GDP devoted to manufacturing will always fall away exponentially and second that this is inevitable and does not really matter.

A vital theme running through this book is that this perception is misplaced. This does not imply that services are of no significance and that industrial output should always be given priority. It does entail, however, recognising that manufacturing and, indeed, all those activities whose outputs particularly lend themselves to international trading have a peculiarly important role to play in two critical regards. The first is that they comprise the parts of the economy where productivity increases are most easily achieved and hence are critical to the growth rate. The second is that since they provide most of the output to be sold abroad to pay for imports, it is crucially important that there should be enough available at competitive prices. If not, balance of payments problems, accumulating debt and all the other related constraints on economic expansion will inevitably ensue.

Fourth, a large majority of those who are most influential in forming opinions are now in the top earning brackets. In nearly all Western economies, the distribution of income has become markedly less even over the past quarter of a century, but this has not adversely affected the living standards of most of those who write books or newspaper articles, who appear on television or who get elected to political office. On the contrary, the rapidly increasing wealth and income of the most influential may have been responsible for creating a widespread illusion that almost everyone is much better off now than 20 or 30 years ago. Perhaps this is so because much wider access to higher education in the early post-war period left far fewer able people dissatisfied with their life opportunities and therefore inclined to identify their interests with the less fortunate in whose ranks they found themselves. Whatever the answer, however, neither in the USA nor in Europe is it true that the rich variety of life for the very well off reflects everyone else's reality. In the USA, living standards have stagnated for all but roughly the top 10 per cent of income earners during the last four decades, while during the 2000s particularly, those at the bottom of the pyramid saw their life circumstances significantly deteriorate.[7] In Europe, the increase in living standards has been higher than in the USA for those in work, but millions of people have either dropped out of the labour force altogether or have had major problems finding employment.

Fifth, although there have been a great many books published about the problems the West is perceived to have – some of them, particularly in the USA, best-sellers – coupled with a profusion of academic articles and publications on these and related topics, recommendations have been remarkably confusing and muted. Best-sellers 20 years ago were full of spine-chilling statistics about the advance of Japanese manufacturing techniques and anecdotes about relatively poor Western performance in response. Now with China the main threat, the recommendations as to how to overcome these problems still remain generally unconvincing if not plain wrong. Some advocate various forms of fairly straightforward protection, apparently without recognising that this is just a backdoor and relatively inefficient way of changing the exchange rate. Others favour a variety of confrontational, 'get tough' policies – really just protection in another guise. A different school has seen the solution in industrial strategies, concentrating resources on high-tech industries – mostly, it appears, without bothering to look up the statistics to see whether their recommendations have a foundation in economic reality. The notion that high-tech industries produce higher value added per employee is simply not correct. In the USA, for example, the average hourly earnings in 1997 of those in the long-established and relatively low-tech cigarette-producing industry (SIC 211)[8] were almost twice as high as those manufacturing electronic components and accessories (SIC 367) and 31 per cent higher than those producing aircraft and parts (SIC 372) earned.[9]

Nor has the academic economic world been much help, despite the vast number of practitioners in economics and all the effort which has gone into the debate on the causes of the recent financial crisis and the remedies to be applied to overcome it.[10] Pragmatists, whose major concern was making sense of the crisis as it unfolded and taking whatever practical actions seemed most appropriate in the short term to stabilise the situation, focused on the need for regulatory reform to prevent future financial meltdowns. Market fundamentalists, on the other hand, believed that the major cause of the crisis was government intervention, including maintaining low interest rates for much too long and thus fuelling housing booms, followed by what they saw as misguided policies to bail out banks. Institutionalists saw liberalisation, deregulation and poor regulation as the major factors behind insufficient action to curb the perennial tendency for booms to generate themselves in the housing and banking sectors and allow financial innovation to run riot. Keynesian collectivists, by contrast, tended to argue that the problem was one of demand deficiency and falling consumption resulting from a loss of household wealth, with only the government left to fill the demand gap. Structuralists saw the fundamental cause of the West's present malaise in widening inequality, which prompted governments to augment stagnant incomes by tolerating excessive borrowing by both consumers and the state. While there may be elements of truth in all these points of view, none of their adherents appear to understand the significance of exchange rates, which are hardly ever mentioned in the literature produced. It is hardly surprising, therefore, that their proposals seldom – if ever – claimed to provide coherent and realistic programmes for getting the West's economies to grow fast and sustainably enough to reduce unemployment and inequality and to generate a significant increase in living standards.

Sixth, perhaps most fundamentally of all, there are the many social and cultural forces which bear heavily on the framework of ideas shaping both public opinion and the menu of policy options that are viewed, by those whose opinions matter in the West, as being practical and acceptable. Ideology permeates economics, and establishment views heavily influence opinions on what choices are within and without the pale. Most countries in the West were for long broadly contented and proud even if they are much less so now than they were. Their social structures are still stable. The rich and established, who have done exceptionally well, generally do not want to see changes to policies which have served them satisfactorily. While those on the left might be happy to see a more equal distribution of income – perhaps provided that their own pockets are not hit – such is not necessarily the case with those of a more conservative turn of mind. Those on the political right might not be inclined to favour a change in policy which would make the poor richer, even if it did not make the rich poorer. There is also the fear of inflation to be taken into account. The monetarist creed, which appeals strongly to those in established positions because it produces a persuasive justification for the circumstances which suit them best, states almost as a catechism that expanding the money supply, reducing interest rates and lowering the exchange rate invariably produces more inflation. All the evidence suggests that all these canons of the monetarist faith are false, but many millions of people believe they are true all the same. As a result, expansionist policies involving depreciating the currency, with its supposed although illusory risks of inflation, are regarded as policies to be strongly avoided, rather than encouraged, whenever possible.

Nor is it just those the well off who may see significant disadvantages in a lower exchange rate. Everyone who goes abroad on vacation likes getting a good rate of exchange on their holiday money. Pensioners and others dependent on savings do not want to see the reduced interest rates associated with lower exchange rates. All the powerful interests involved in making money out of importing have good reasons to be concerned about their costs rising and profits falling. Finance always likes a strong currency, not least because of the leverage it provides in dealing with international capital transactions. Politicians and civil servants who, strongly supported by the media and academia, have spent decades trying to keep the exchange rate up are going to be hard to persuade that they have been aiming at precisely the wrong objective for all their working lives.

All these sentiments are wrapped up in the widely used rhetoric of exchange rates. When a currency's value is high, it is strong. When low, it is weak. When it depreciates, its value falls. When it appreciates, it rises. Loaded terms colour everyone's perceptions. The reality, however, is different. If a country's currency is too strong, its exports wither, its manufacturing declines, investment and the savings to pay for it fall, living standards for most people stagnate, life chances deteriorate, the foreign exchange and fiscal balances tend to go into deficit, and its relative power and position in the world falls away. This is a terrible price to pay for misconceptions which need to be exposed and which ought not to prevail.

Finally, it is surprisingly difficult to disentangle all the existing empirical evidence on the impact of exchange rates on economic performance. Table 2.1 sets out some telling statistics, which show how far from being clear-cut and obvious the evidence is. It is clear that between 2000 and 2010 exchange rates and the proportion of the economy devoted to manufacturing were not alone in determining growth rates. Russia and Saudi Arabia did very well out of high oil prices. Greece, Spain and Ireland benefited hugely, for a while at least, from the Eurozone. India, Brazil and the USA were helped by positive demographics. Japan was hindered by a high exchange rate, and Germany by the hangover from unification. Towards the end of the decade, the West was hit much harder than the East by the financial crisis. Disentangling the critical impact of exchange rates is therefore not easy. The really crucial point is that all the other factors which have clearly had an impact on the growth rates in Table 2.1 are largely if not wholly beyond any government's capacity to influence. The exchange rate is different. This is by far the most important determinant of economic performance over which any government and its central bank have a major influence.

Into the vacuum left by lack of adequate economic theory and by confusing economic data has marched an army of people with axes to grind. With no clearly defined reasons for choosing one policy rather than another, the scope for the furthering of sectional interests has abounded. This throws up another pattern which runs through the case set out in this book. As any of the world's economies began to prosper over the last two centuries, the centre of gravity of political influence started to shift. The tendency has been for first-generation entrepreneurs to metamorphose into second- and third-generation successors wanting to hold on to their wealth. As societies become

Table 2.1 Ratio change in share of world trade, growth in GDP per head and percentage of the economy devoted to manufacturing selected countries

	% of the Economy devoted to Manufacturing 2006	% Change in Share of World Trade FOB 2000/2010	% Growth in GDP 2000/2010	% Growth in GDP per Head 2000/2010
China	33.5	167	90	77
Singapore	29.2	8	88	71
South Korea	27.8	14	63	60
Germany	23.2	-3	13	13
Ireland	24.5	-35	40	33
Japan	21.0	-32	10	10
Russia	19.4	60	80	105
Switzerland	19.0	5	22	20
Brazil	18.4	55	49	43
Italy	18.1	-21	7	6
India	16.3	119	120	101
Spain	15.5	-8	29	25
United States	14.4	-31	23	21
United Kingdom	13.6	-39	20	19
France	12.4	-28	16	15
Saudi Arabia	9.5	37	45	35
Greece	9.5	-18	34	33

Source: IMF International Financial Statistics Yearbook 2011 – page 67 plus country tables; Manufacturing figures from Earthtrends website.

richer, financial institutions prosper – particularly banks, run generally by people with a marked tendency to give high priority to looking after their richer clients, responding as best they can to their clients' (if not their own) aversion to risk and demand for safe but relatively high returns. Political power then moves from new money to old, from industry to finance and from risk-taking entrepreneurs to the safe hands of company bureaucrats. With this shift of political power comes a change in macroeconomic policy which suits those with accumulated wealth. Unfortunately and no doubt unwittingly, the financial circumstances wanted by the now established groups in power tend to be those which produce exactly the wrong conditions for fast growth. Stable currencies, as free as possible from exchange-rate fluctuations, with low rates of inflation coupled, if possible, with relatively high real interest rates, provide precisely the conditions in which growth slows, manufacturing goes into a relative decline, exports languish and deflationary policies – seldom exceptionally painful for those in power – become the order of the day.

This largely explains another thread which runs through the history of the last two centuries. Major upheavals, whether caused by lost wars, internal revolutions or abrupt and drastic social and political changes, have tended to be precursors of much better economic performance.[11] This is the correlative of the tendency for the reverse to occur, as countries develop and maintain stable social fabrics which stifle new, non-conforming energetic people and produce a macroeconomic environment in which it is relatively hard for them to prosper and break through. This is why early adopters of the Industrial Revolution, with long, stable histories behind them – pre-eminently the USA and the UK – are currently so hard hit.

Protectionism vs. globalisation

Those suffering from price competition which they find hard to combat frequently urge that the way to create favourable conditions for growth is through measures designed to shield domestic producers from world competition. All countries tend to have vocal minorities demanding protection from the rigours of world trade. Agriculture – where arguably special circumstances apply, although there is a substantial body of opinion to the contrary – is heavily protected almost everywhere. So, also, in most other economies are many other sectors, such as shoes and apparel. Some of the protection is secured overtly with tariffs and quotas, but informal methods can often be just as effective, as is often claimed to be the situation in Japan. If the result is a severe trade imbalance – as has been the case, for example, in US trade with Japan and more recently with China – this condition can easily lead to pressure on export surplus countries to restrict their exports in such sensitive areas as cars and electronic components. 'Orderly marketing arrangements' and 'voluntary export restraints' are then put in place, and protectionism in a different guise materialises.

Buttressing these arguments are others which have been the common coin of economic debate for centuries. By imposing a tariff, the domestic economy can tax the foreigner to its advantage. Because those selling to the domestic economy will have to lower their prices to compete in its protected market, the terms of trade will improve. The domestic economy, which will then obtain more imports per unit of exports than it did before the tariff was imposed, is thus made better off. Furthermore, if the effect of imposing import duties is similar to reducing the exchange rate, having higher tariffs on some commodities than others may give the domestic economy advantages that would not be obtained by a devaluation. For example, if import duties are imposed on finished goods but not on raw materials, the domestic economy may be able to protect its manufacturers without raising their costs.

The arguments in favour of free trade, provided certain essential conditions are fulfilled, are nevertheless extremely strong. In modern conditions, there is an impressive and persuasive case against reverting to a protectionist approach – indeed, for moving further towards opening world markets to foreign competition wherever possible. The arguments for free trade and keeping all economies open to foreign competition are as important now as they ever were, provided they are not undermined by inappropriate exchange-rate policies, which can all too easily generate protectionism.

First, there are the traditional comparative-cost arguments for foreign trade. The costs of producing a wide range of goods and services varies from country to country. Countries gain from trading with each other if they swap domestic products whose relative costs are low for foreign products which could be made domestically only at high relative costs. It is important to note that the comparative-cost case for international trade is independent of absolute levels of productivity. Countries with such low productivity that they produce everything relatively inefficiently can still trade with advantage with countries which produce everything more efficiently. Variances round the norm are what make this trade worthwhile.

Second, there is the spur to efficiency produced by competition from abroad. Most people prefer a quiet life. They do not relish the prospect of having to adapt constantly to changing tastes and fashions, to new technology and methods of distribution. Provided it is not overwhelming, foreign competition keeps them on their toes. A copying process results as those behind the times replicate trends set by market leaders. They buy in or duplicate foreign technology and equipment, management techniques and sales methods. It is possible to achieve high rates of growth behind tariff barriers; Spain did so for a long period during the Franco regime, and Japan did so in different ways for decades. Output in these circumstances, however, tends to lack the quality of the goods and services available in countries which are more exposed to the world economy. Japanese manufactured goods may be superb, but much of the domestic economy in Japan, particularly in services, is a byword for inefficiency and wasteful use of people in low-productivity jobs.

The informal protectionism which is Japan's speciality has been, in some obvious ways, extremely expensive for its citizens.

Third, there are great advantages in producing competitive exports if all the raw materials, intermediate goods and other inputs which have to be brought in from abroad can be obtained at the lowest possible price. One of the problems with either import tariffs or quotas is that they generally increase the costs of domestic production. As supply chains between countries become ever more complicated and intertwined, drawing a clear distinction between raw materials and finished goods, with tariffs imposed on the latter but not the former, grows increasingly more difficult. If the key to long-term improved economic performance is to increase the competitiveness of domestic producers of goods and services at home and abroad, it does not help to increase their costs more than can be avoided or to restrict access to raw materials and components at the best available prices.

Fourth, tariffs or quotas are fundamental flawed if they are employed to deal with an underlying lack of competitiveness. The problem is that while it is conceivable that there should be relatively low import duties or a limited number of products subject to quotas, as soon as the height of tariffs passes a fairly low level – about 20 per cent – the distortions they bring become more and more difficult to justify. Administrative problems also mount rapidly when import restraints increase in complexity. It is not possible to keep on raising tariffs or tightening quotas indefinitely without dramatically diminishing returns setting in. Economic distortions get worse, evasion becomes an increasing problem, and complicated appeals procedures are difficult to avoid.

If the root problem, however, is as much a lack of export-market competitiveness as too much import penetration – the two go together – then either tariffs will have to be increased or quotas tightened beyond any realistic point. Alternatively, the real remedy needed, changing the exchange rate, should be adopted. Tariff protection will not increase exports, but a growing economy will need more imports. There is no way out of this problem short of autarchy, whereby the protected economy is forced to produce ever more of its needs in the home market even though buying them from abroad would be much cheaper.

The arguments, therefore, for maintaining economies as open as is politically feasible are strong, although there may be a practical case for some measure of protection because of difficulties ensuring that exchange rates are always correctly aligned. This is the justification for the North American Free Trade Area, for the European Union's Common External Tariff and for similar arrangements in South America, the

Pacific area and elsewhere. Achieving equality in competitiveness between economies within a customs union area may in practice, therefore, be easier to achieve behind a common external tariff high enough to contain an unmanageable volume of foreign competition. It has to be said, however, that this conclusion is strongly disputed by those who believe that regional trade blocs are an obstacle to more general free trade. In an ideal world regional customs areas would be unlikely to exist.

Nevertheless, in the real world some arguments for a degree of protection are difficult to resist. They are weaker for quotas than for tariffs, and the case for low rather than high tariffs is stronger. When there is unmanageable competition, there is always pressure for protection. The case to be made in these circumstances, however, almost invariably depends on exchange rates being in the wrong position in the first place. With protectionist policies all too inclined to become the justification for failing to correct exchange-rate fundamentals, there is no valid argument for a retreat into further protectionism as a major plank of economic policy. A much more effective way of dealing with the problems of major trade imbalance, for which tariffs and quotas are not the solution, is to make greater efforts to position exchange rates at the right level and to allow them to keep adjusting themselves as circumstances change and relative competitive advantage alters, so that the need for protectionist measures falls away.

The costs of overvaluation

Confusion about whether the exchange rate is best set high or low and about the impact on perceptions made by interest groups with the biggest short-term axes to grind, who generally favour the highest possible parity, need to be set against the huge and massively onerous impact on any economy of having too strong a currency, especially over a long period.

The first-round effect is that export competitiveness is lost and share of world trade diminishes. In all advanced economies, manufactured goods still comprise well over 50 per cent of exports of goods and services; thus, the manufacturing industry takes the brunt of the disadvantage caused by the cost base being too high. Export orders, especially at profitable prices, become harder to obtain while import penetration increases. In these circumstances, most companies engaged in exporting will find their profits squeezed. Inevitably, then, they tend to cut back on research, development and investment, weakening their future prospects. They also suffer from being unable to pay their work-force, at all levels, as much as the need to recruit the most talented people requires. Hardly surprisingly, in these circumstances, manufac-turing as a percentage of national income falls.

This immediately has two main impacts on the national economy, as well as several important side effects. As it is in manufacturing that the best prospects for productivity increases lie, the smaller the proportion of the economy devoted to it, the lower the growth rate tends to be. A second factor which exacerbates the problem is that lowered exports and increased imports worsen the trade balance. This factor makes it more difficult for the government to sustain a high level of demand for fear that doing so will widen the export-import gap. In addition, there will be further negative side effects. Areas of the country traditionally orientated towards manufacturing will find themselves in decline. The high-quality blue-collar jobs much more strongly associated with manufacturing than services will become harder to find. In addition, with the flagging level of demand that the economy can stand because of balance of payment constraints, unemployment is likely to rise, making it even harder to keep everyone who wants to work in employ-ment which stretches each individual's potential.

Worse is to follow, especially if the reaction of the authorities to a weak balance of payments position is to depress the economy to contain the trade balance rather than change the exchange rate. In these condi-tions, as the manufacturing base weakens, the trade balance is likely to worsen. All trade deficits have to be financed by capital receipts of one sort or another, mostly borrowing abroad or selling assets, and the bigger the deficit, the more borrowing and asset sales have to take place. The additional interest and dividend payments going abroad then weaken further the balance of payments position.

Nor is the trade deficit the only one likely to materialise as a result of the currency parity being too high. Before long, the impacts on the government's financial position will create a fiscal as well as a trade deficit. There are several reasons why this happens. A slack labour market tends to produce a sharp and also progressive increase in dependency. As fewer and fewer good jobs are available, more and more people rely on the state for employment, or financial assistance if they are not working, and government expenditures rise. At the same time, relatively depressed conditions decrease tax revenues. If to balance accounts the government then tries to reduce expenditure, economic growth weakens. If, as often happens, an attempt is made to buck the trend by adopting expansionist policies, deficits get greater. As is the case with the economy as a whole, a government's current account deficits have to be made up by capital receipts, usually financed by borrowing. The government then suffers from the same problem as the country as a whole, as interest charges get greater and overall balance becomes harder and harder to achieve.

As long as there are lenders willing to provide the loans required to finance these twin deficits, the situation remains containable. Crises occur when confidence in the country's or the government's ability ever to repay the money owed fails. Once the organisations – very often banks acting as intermediaries – that by this time are owed huge sums begin to doubt whether they will ever be repaid, they also begin to be concerned whether the counter-parties to the enormous number of financial transactions taking place all the time are liable to become insolvent if defaults take place. As confidence evaporates, the financial system tends to freeze up. Everyone who can hoards liquidity, and sources of further lending start to dry up.

It is all too clear that much of the Western world is now dangerously close to being in this position. Subsequent chapters trace the history of the last few decades, showing how the West got into this predicament. The last chapter discusses what steps the Western world needs to take to move back from the precipice to which it is now very uncomfortably close.

3
Inflation

Few topics are as loaded with ideological baggage as whether inflation, at least in moderation, is desirable or a scourge. It is also clear, at least in nearly all the Western world, which side has won this particular battle of ideas. It is now the conventional wisdom almost everywhere that one of the most significant objectives of economic policy – perhaps the most important of all – is to maintain the average increase in the price level at no more than or about 2 per cent.

There is, however, remarkably little reason to believe that an inflation rate as low as this is a particularly worthwhile goal if the interests of society as a whole are taken into account. In particular, there is very little evidence that it can be combined with other targets, such as full employment and a growth rate as high as, say, 4 or 5 per cent per annum. Of course, there are strong arguments against allowing very rapid increases in the price level to occur. Nobody wants hyperinflation. Yet this is an entirely different matter from tolerating some extra inflation to secure much improved growth and job prospects, if such a trade-off exists. In fact, very low price-level increases are uncommon in competently run, fast-growing, full-employment economies. Almost all have annualized inflation rates bunched around 4 per cent[1] – as did nearly all of western Europe in the 1950s and 1960s[2] – for good reasons and with few ill effects. An important study carried out by the International Monetary Fund in 1995 showed that there was no systematic evidence that inflation rates below about 8 per cent per annum caused enough disruption to slow growth or increase the number out of work.[3]

The widely exhibited determination in the Western world to keep inflation down to very low levels is not, therefore, a sign of economic wisdom. It is much more convincingly seen as another sign of the dominance in the West of the culture and outlook of banking and finance over manufacturing and industry. Low inflation – and the high real interest rates which go with it – favours old money vis-à-vis new; lenders as against borrowers; established wealth holders as opposed to parvenus; and the already successful vis-à-vis their challengers. All these powerful groups, typically with deeply conservative instincts, have a vested interest in treating inflation as a major affliction. In fact, in moderation – at 4 to 5 per cent, to allow something of a safety margin against shocks which might push it up to more dangerous levels – it is nothing of the kind. On the contrary, it is an almost entirely unavoidable but relatively harmless concomitant to any policies seriously orientated towards accelerating the growth rate and getting everyone back to work.

A particularly strong link in the chain of inflationary demonology has been firmly established in the public mind – and in the academic and policy-orientated literature – in relation to any downward change in the exchange rate. Fear that devaluations automatically generate inflationary pressures in economies where they occur is widespread. A long-standing major tenet of the monetarist position is that any benefits secured from depreciation will at best be temporary. Price rises in the devaluing country will soon wipe them out, it is argued, and the economy concerned, after a short adjustment process, will be left no more competitive than it was before, save that it will have added an enhanced level of inflation.

It is also widely believed that a devaluation necessarily produces a reduction in the living standards of an economy whose currency's external value is falling. Two reasons are usually advanced to support this proposition. The first is that if a country devalues, there will inevitably be an adverse movement in its terms of trade. That is, after the fall in parity, amount the imports of which can be purchased for each unit of exports is bound to fall, depressing the real national income. The second, which overlaps with the first, is that to make up for the reduced terms of trade, more room will have to be found for goods and services to be sold abroad. The only way of achieving this objective is to shift resources out of current living standards into exports, thus lowering average real incomes and depressing the real wage, even if substantial unused resources are still available.

There can be little doubt that the almost axiomatic strength of these monetarist arguments has persuaded large numbers of people that devaluations are inflationary, reduce living standards, disrupt business plans and discourage investment and that they ought to be avoided at all costs. This is the standard case for fixed parities. Even a brief look at economic history, however, shows that these views are almost entirely unfounded. There have been large numbers of exchange-rate changes in recent decades against which to test the validity of the widely believed monetarist case, a substantial number of the most prominent of which are set out in Table 3.1. Without exception, they show that even large exchange-rate changes generally make little or no difference to the rate of inflation, unless either the economy concerned was already operating at full stretch – as was the case in France at the end of the 1950s – or the situation was already catastrophic, as with Argentina and Iceland. Even in France, however, the sharp increase in prices, to which the double devaluations under Charles de Gaulle undoubtedly contributed, quickly abated, as did those in Argentina, after its major devaluation in 2002, and Iceland, following the insolvency of its major banks in 2008.

Furthermore, the average standard of living, far from falling after a devaluation, almost invariably rises, because all devaluing countries' GDP tends to increase significantly shortly after the currency has depreciated. Industrial output also has a marked tendency to rise sharply soon after a devaluation and to trigger increased investment. The experience of Japan, after the yen's major revaluation in the early 1990s, however shows the opposite outcome equally strongly. In most cases, the real wage also tends to rise shortly after the exchange rate falls. This is calculated in Table 3.1 as the difference between the change in average wage rates and the change in the consumer price level. The increase in the real wage is not so pronounced as the rise in GDP, because devaluations tend to increase employment, thus reducing the numbers out of work but also diluting average earnings. This bias can be seen in the US experience. The dollar fell in the second half of the 1980s as the GDP rose, but the number of people in work increased very rapidly. The table also shows the opposite results occurring in the major case of Japan's revaluation of the yen during the early 1990s. There the growth rate went down, the real wage stayed static, and unemployment began creeping up.

These may well be unexpected results to many people who have been led to expect a very different outcome. In particular, the figures in Table 3.1 provide no justification at all for the widely believed monetarist view that it is impossible to secure a permanent advantage in terms of competitiveness and growth by exchange-rate adjustments.

Table 3.1 Exchange rate changes, consumer prices, the real wage, GDP, industrial output and unemployment

	Year	Consumer Prices	Wage Rates	Real Wage Change	GDP Change	Industrial Output Change	Unemployment Per cent
Britain – 31%	1930	−6.0	−0.7	5.3	−0.7	−1.4	11.2
Devaluation	1931	−5.7	−2.1	3.6	−5.1	−3.6	15.1
against the	1932	−3.3	−1.7	1.6	0.8	0.3	15.6
dollar and	1933	0.0	−0.1	−0.1	2.9	4.0	14.1
24% against	1934	0.0	1.5	1.5	6.6	5.5	11.9
all currencies in 1931							
France – 27%	1956	2.0	9.7	7.7	5.1	9.4	1.1
Devaluation	1957	3.5	8.2	4.7	6.0	8.3	0.8
against all	1958	15.1	12.3	−2.8	2.5	4.5	0.9
currencies in	1959	6.2	6.8	0.6	2.9	3.3	1.3
1957/58	1960	3.5	6.3	2.8	7.0	10.1	1.2
	1961	3.3	9.6	6.3	5.5	4.8	1.1
USA – 28%	1984	4.3	4.0	−0.3	6.2	11.3	7.4
Devaluation	1985	3.6	3.9	0.3	3.2	2.0	7.1
against all	1986	1.9	2.0	0.1	2.9	1.0	6.9
currencies	1987	3.7	1.8	−1.9	3.1	3.7	6.1
over 1985/87	1988	4.0	2.8	−1.2	3.9	5.3	5.4
	1989	5.0	2.9	−2.1	2.5	2.6	5.2
Japan – 47%	1989	2.3	3.1	0.8	4.8	5.8	2.3
Revaluation	1990	3.1	3.8	0.7	4.8	4.1	2.1
against all	1991	3.3	3.4	0.1	4.3	1.8	2.1
currencies	1992	1.7	2.1	0.4	1.4	−6.1	2.2
over 1990/94	1993	1.3	2.1	0.8	0.1	−4.6	2.5
	1994	0.7	2.3	1.6	0.6	0.7	2.9
Italy – 20%	1990	6.4	7.3	0.9	2.1	−0.6	9.1
Devaluation	1991	6.3	9.8	3.5	1.3	−2.2	8.6
against all	1992	5.2	5.4	0.2	0.9	−0.6	9.0
currencies	1993	4.5	3.8	−0.7	−1.2	−2.9	10.3
over 1990/93	1994	4.0	3.5	−0.5	2.2	5.6	11.4
	1995	5.4	3.1	−2.3	2.9	5.4	11.9
Finland – 24%	1990	6.1	9.4	3.3	0.0	−0.1	3.5
Devaluation	1991	4.1	6.4	2.3	−7.1	−9.7	7.6
against all	1992	2.6	3.8	1.2	−3.6	2.2	13.0
currencies	1993	2.1	3.7	1.6	−1.6	5.5	17.5
over 1991/93	1994	1.1	7.4	6.3	4.5	10.5	17.4
	1995	1.0	4.7	3.7	5.1	7.8	16.2

Continued

Table 3.1   Continued

	Year	Consumer Prices	Wage Rates	Real Wage Change	GDP Change	Industrial Output Change	Unemployment Per cent
Spain – 18%	1991	5.9	8.2	2.3	2.3	–0.7	16.3
Devaluation	1992	5.9	7.7	1.8	0.7	–3.2	18.5
against all	1993	4.6	6.8	2.2	–1.2	–4.4	22.8
currencies	1994	4.7	4.5	–0.2	2.1	7.5	24.1
over 1992/94	1995	4.7	4.8	0.1	2.8	4.7	22.9
	1996	3.6	4.8	1.2	2.2	–0.7	22.2
Britain – 19%	1990	9.5	9.7	0.2	0.6	–0.4	6.8
Devaluation	1991	5.9	7.8	1.9	–1.5	–3.3	8.4
against all	1992	3.7	11.3	7.6	0.1	0.3	9.7
currencies in	1993	1.6	3.2	1.6	2.3	2.2	10.3
1992	1994	2.4	3.6	1.2	4.4	5.4	9.6
	1995	3.5	3.1	–0.4	2.8	1.7	8.6
Argentina –	2000	–1.1	1.2	3.3	–0.8	–0.3	14.7
72%	2001	25.9	–2.6	–23.3	–4.4	–7.6	18.1
Devaluation	2002	13.4	1.9	–11.5	–10.9	–10.5	17.5
against all	2003	4.4	22.0	17.6	8.8	16.2	16.8
currencies	2004	9.6	23.3	13.7	9.0	10.7	13.6
early 2002	2005	10.9	22.8	11.9	9.2	8.5	8.7
Iceland – 50%	2005	4.0	7.2	3.2	7.5	4.6	2.6
Devaluation	2006	6.7	9.8	3.1	4.3	8.4	2.9
against all	2007	5.1	8.6	3.5	5.6	5.2	2.3
currencies	2008	12.7	8.3	–4.4	1.3	7.0	3.0
2007/2009	2009	12.0	3.6	–8.4	–6.3	–5.9	7.2
	2010	7.1	4.7	–2.4	–4.2		7.6
	2011	4.0					

Note: All figures are year on year percentage changes except for Unemployment.

Sources: *Economic Statistics 1900–1983* by Thelma Liesner. London: *The Economist* 1985. IMF *International Financial Statistics Yearbooks*, *Eurostatistics* and British, Argentine and Icelandic official statistics and International Labour Organisation tables.

Perhaps the widespread conviction that devaluation will have the damaging results so frequently anticipated stems from the fact that many people would not be too unhappy if these predictions were well founded. Everyone with a stake in keeping interest rates high and money tight might be inclined to share such a view. All the same, it is extraordinary that so many believe these propositions to be true when there is so much simple and incontrovertible evidence easily to hand to show that the assumed relationships between depreciation, inflation and the standard of living are wrong.

If, as Table 3.1 shows, an industrial economy can devalue, especially when the economy has substantial unused resources, without paying a significant inflationary penalty, this is a very important policy matter. It means that long-lasting adjustments, which are highly beneficial in terms of growth, productivity and employment prospects, are in fact entirely feasible. It can then no longer be claimed that economies stuck in the doldrums lack any practical way out of their predicament. On the contrary, the way is open for any country which is having difficulty competing and keeping all its resources employed, especially its labour force, to remedy the position by making appropriate exchange-rate adjustments to allow demand to be expanded. Far from devaluation gains being only temporary and shortly to be eroded away by extra inflation, they tend to be self-reinforcing. This is not to say that inflationary problems can be ignored if parity changes continue to take place. Good management of the economy is required in all circumstances. The evidence in Table 3.1 makes it clear, however, that many widely held opinions about how devaluation, price rises and the real wage relate to one another are at variance with the facts and cannot therefore be well founded in theory. There is much evidence that the problems with inflation are more diverse and more manageable than is often recognised.

Devaluation and the price level

Those who believe that exchange-rate changes will affect prices are right in at least one sense. Any parity reduction is bound to exert upward pressure on the costs of all imported goods and services in the devaluing country. While the prices measured in the domestic currency of both imports and exports will almost certainly rise, the tendency for import costs to increase faster than export prices may worsen the terms of trade. In this sense, too, there is a direct cost to the economy. Furthermore, there is no value in a policy of depreciation unless it makes imports more expensive relative to home market production. A major objective has to be to price out some imports by making it relatively cheaper than it was previously to produce locally rather than in other countries. It follows that without price increases for imported goods and services, there will be no new bias towards production from domestic output.

The evidence presented in Table 3.1, however, indicates that other factors have to be taken into account. If, as is commonly supposed, only import prices were significant, then the figures in the table would show increasing inflation and declining living standards after a depreciation and not, generally speaking, the opposite. How then are the figures in the table to be explained? The answer is that devaluation's impact on the price level is more complicated than is often recognised. Many effects are disinflationary rather than the reverse and tend to increase national income rather than reduce it. Obviously, the more exposed an economy is to foreign trade, the greater the immediate impact of exchange-rate changes on living standards and the price level. Yet even in economies with comparatively small exposure to foreign trade, such as the USA's, it is still easily large enough to make the consequences significant.

First, one of devaluation's immediate impacts is to make all domestic production more competitive in both home and export markets than it had been. This is bound to lead to increased output, although there will inevitably be time lags before its benefits come through. There will therefore be some delay before domestic production, taking advantage of the new more favourable environment, rises, but any increase will help to reduce average costs as increased capacity works to spread overhead charges across more output. Production and service industries involved in international trade typically have falling cost curves, because for them the marginal cost of production is well below the average. Enterprises of these sorts cannot fail to benefit from a depreciating currency. Obviously, some of their input expenses, if they include imported goods and services or a switch to a domestic producer who has now become competitive, will rise. This is part of the price that has to be paid for devaluing. The increased volume of output which can now be obtained, however, is clearly a substantial factor weighing in the balance on the other side.

Second, some of the policies which have to be associated with bringing the parity of the currency down also directly affect both production costs and the cost of living generally. One of the most important of these is the rate of interest at which most borrowing is done, which almost invariably comes down with the exchange rate. Indeed, lowering the cost of borrowing is part of the mixture of policy changes needed to get parities reduced. High real rates of interest are a heavy and expensive burden on most firms producing goods and services. They are also an important component of the retail price index, particularly in countries where a large proportion of personal outgoings are on variable rate loans, such as mortgage payments. A substantial reduction, one designed to bring down the parity to a more competitive level, makes an important contribution to holding down inflation.

Third, rising productivity flowing from increased output not only has the immediate effect of reducing costs. It also makes possible meeting wage claims of any given size with less impact on selling costs. Nor is this just a factor which applies for a short period until those responsible for formulating wage claims adjust to the new situation and then increase their claims. International evidence strongly suggests that economies with rapidly expanding output have a better wage negotiation climate generally, and thus achieve rises in remuneration more realistically attuned to whatever productivity increases are actually being secured.

Fourth, one of the major objectives of reducing parity is to switch demand from overseas sources to home production. While the price of imports is bound to rise to some extent, the evidence that the increase in costs from exchange-rate changes is seldom passed on in full is strong. Foreign suppliers, calculating that what they lose on the margin they may make up by holding on to market share, are inclined to absorb some of the costs themselves. Furthermore, if demand is switched from imported goods and services to home production, this purchasing power will not be affected – at least not directly and in full – by the increase in import prices. It will benefit in cost terms from the fact that domestic output is now relatively cheaper than purchases from abroad.

Fifth, it is possible to employ the much improved fiscal position which higher growth produces to have a directly disinflationary impact, using the tax system. It is often argued that if there is a depreciation, the government of the devaluing country necessarily has to deflate the economy to make more room for exports. This argument cannot hold water, however, if there are large numbers of unemployed or underemployed people and considerable slack in the economy. In these circumstances, it is not difficult to combine increasing output, stimulated by a lower exchange rate, with an expansionary monetary and fiscal policy. It is then possible to structure tax changes to produce a positive disinflationary impact. Reducing taxes on labour, where possible, is particularly effective, because it both directly cuts production costs and encourages more employment.

Taxation policy may help secure a further crucially important objective to avoid price increases if there is a devaluation, not only immediately after parity has come down but subsequently as well. If the first-round effects of higher import prices can be neutralised by greater output, rising productivity and tax changes, then there will be no second and subsequent rounds of price rises flowing from the parity change. This is clearly an extremely desirable state of affairs to achieve, and one that makes it much easier to manage the economy in a way which forestalls erosion of the increased competitiveness flowing from devaluation.

When each of these disinflationary factors is taken into account, all of which apply in varying degrees whenever parity comes down, the figures in Table 3.1 become easier to understand. It is evidently not true that devaluation necessarily increases the rate of inflation. Still less is it true that it must always do so to such a degree that any extra competitive advantage is automatically eroded away.

At the cost of a few more calculations, it is possible to set out in quantified form why this should be the case. Suppose that the currency is depreciated by 25 per cent and that on average import prices rise by two-thirds of this amount, with foreign suppliers absorbing the rest. Assume that imports of goods and services make up around 30 per cent of gross domestic product – a fairly typical ratio in developed countries – so the impact on the price level from increased import prices in these circumstances is likely to be about two-thirds of 25 per cent times 30 per cent, which comes to 5 per cent.

On the other side, consider all the factors which work to reduce the price level when the external value of the currency falls by 25 per cent. First, the output of all enterprises in the domestic economy is likely to rise substantially on average. Suppose that the initial impact of a devaluation was to get the economy to grow by an additional 3 per cent. If two-thirds of this increase in output could be achieved in the period immediately following the devaluation by using the existing capital stock and labour force more intensively and efficiently, the benefits from economies of scale of this type would amount to around a 2 per cent contribution to reduced prices in year one.

Second, in 2012 the total money supply represented about twice the value of GNP across much of the developed world – a huge increase since 2000, when it was roughly half this amount.[4] All of it is essentially debt of one kind or another, and nearly all is interest bearing. While base rates are currently low across the Western world, actual lending rates are often much higher. Were variable borrowing costs reduced by, say, 1 per cent, a significant proportion of interest charges, though not all, would be affected. If half were reduced on average by 1 per cent, borrowing costs on the whole of the money supply, which is twice the size of GDP, would fall by about 1.0 per cent, producing a reduction of around another 1.0 per cent in the retail price index.

Third, one of the most important reasons for a depreciation is to switch demand from imports to home production. Suppose this happens to 10 per cent of all demand. Allowing for an import content of one-third, the remaining two-thirds of this new output would, broadly speaking, not be affected by increased costs as a result of the exchange-rate changes. Perhaps half of it, however, would only become economical to produce at rather higher world prices than applied previously. These ratios multiply out as 10% × 25% × 2 / 3 / 2. This factor reduces the inflationary impact by about a further 0.8 per cent.

Fourth, another major impact on the economy from reducing the parity would be to improve the public sector's finances, as tax receipts rise and calls on public expenditure for welfare benefits fall away. If some of this improvement were to be used to reduce taxation on items included in the consumer price index, it should not be difficult for the government to bring down inflation by a further 1 to 2 per cent by reducing taxes by this amount. Adding this to the other disinflationary factors set out in the preceding paragraphs produces a countervailing total of around 5 per cent, which equals the impact of higher input prices.

These calculations, made with a broad brush, are therefore inevitably subject to margins of error. They nevertheless show that the disinflationary impacts that can be garnered from a well-managed devaluation may be likely to counteract, quite possibly in full, the impact of higher import costs, even if depreciation is substantial. This is why a devaluation, as ample empirical evidence shows, is not necessarily inflationary at all, except perhaps when resources are already fully employed, as in the French example at the end of the 1950s or in the dire cases of Argentina and Iceland. This is clearly an extremely important conclusion and one with major policy implications.

It does not, of course, mean that inflation is no longer a problem. A well-managed devaluation may not accelerate price increases, but inflation may increase for other reasons. Leading sector inflation, external shocks, 'demand pull' price rises caused by bottlenecks and overheating, excessive growth in the money supply which may in particular lead to asset price inflation, and 'cost push' wage and salary increases outstripping productivity gains – all need careful management, but with competent policy execution all are containable. With many being closely related to other elements of the policies confronting all developed economies, the remaining sections of this chapter consider them in turn.

Leading sector inflation

While almost everyone agrees that, in general, lower rates of inflation are desirable, there is considerable evidence that very low rates of price increase are impossible to combine with a significant rate of economic growth. At some stage a trade-off between inflation and growth has to be faced. The higher the priority given to stabilising prices, the less likely the economy will grow rapidly. Certainly the notion that squeezing inflation out of the economy altogether is the way to prosperity flies in the face of universal experience. On the contrary, although there may be some inflationary price to pay for considerably higher growth, it is not likely to be a large or a dangerous one. Furthermore, recent developments, particularly the gains in efficiency from computers and increasing world competition, suggest that the risk that faster growth will produce price rises at unacceptable rates is even less than it was previously. Table 3.2 shows the rates of inflation and economic growth in ten OECD countries and the OECD as a whole during the 16 years from 1953 to 1969, a long period of continuous growth in world output, before their currencies were linked by the snake, the exchange-rate mechanism or the euro. This table indicates that during these years not one of these countries avoided a steady, albeit a relatively moderate increase in the price level. It also shows a tendency for those economies growing most rapidly to have rather higher inflation rates than those growing more slowly. Obviously other factors were at work than those solely concerned with the differing growth rates, but the correlation between higher inflation and growth is clearly there.

At first sight this seems the reverse of what one might expect. How did Japan achieve a cumulative compound growth rate of 10 per cent per annum if its rate of inflation was above the average for the whole of the OECD and well above the rate at which consumer prices rose in the USA, the UK and a number of other countries? Why did British exports not become more and more competitive with Japan's? Contrasting the

Table 3.2 Growth and inflation rates in ten OECD
countries between 1953 and 1969

Countries	Annual Average Growth Rate %	Annual Average Inflation Rate %
Japan	10.0	4.0
Spain	6.0	6.3
Germany	5.8	2.7
Italy	5.5	3.4
France	5.4	4.5
Netherlands	4.9	4.3
Switzerland	4.5	3.3
Belgium	4.0	2.5
United States	3.6	2.4
United Kingdom	2.8	3.4
OECD Average	4.4	3.0

Source: National Accounts of OECD Countries 1953–1969. Paris:
OECD, 1970.

period's slow British growth rates with the high performance of the
Japanese economy shows that this cannot have been so.

The paradox is easily resolved. In all the major countries of the developed world, productivity increases enabled sustained economic growth
to take place, and growth in turn generated rising output per head.
The increases, however, were spread evenly neither throughout any of
the individual economies concerned nor among them. In all countries
some parts of the economy had productivity growth that was slow, non-
existent, or even negative. If the number of children taught by a teacher
goes down, each child may be better taught, but the teacher's output
measured in economic terms falls. Really high rates of productivity
growth were found in those parts of industry – particularly manufacturing, agriculture and some parts of the service sectors – where mechanisation, falling unit costs with longer production runs, and much
more efficient use of labour were possible. The results were costs which
dropped rapidly in real terms, often in money terms too, even though
average prices in the economy rose. These sectors are the familiar gener-
ators of fast rates of economic growth.

This phenomenon was seen markedly in Japan, with one of the
fastest growth rates but also above-average increases in the consumer
price level. Now strongly evident in China, where many of the same
factors apply, it is caused by leading sector inflation. Employees in

parts of the economy with rapidly rising productivity secure large wage rises, which are offset by increased output. Those in jobs where such improvement in economic performance is unobtainable also press for and receive wage rises. The prices of the goods and services produced by these latter groups therefore have to go up. The faster the economy grows, the more marked these price increases will be. The overall inflation rate is a result of the averaging process taking place between the high- and low-productivity growth parts of the economy. In Japan the results were truly astonishing. Despite Japan's relatively large overall domestic inflation rate, for many years its export prices barely rose at all. Indeed, over the whole 1952–79 period, while the general price level in Japan rose by 364 per cent, the average price of Japanese exports rose by only 33 per cent. In Britain, over the same period the general price level rose by 442 per cent, and export prices by 380 per cent.[5] No wonder Britain kept losing more and more markets to Japanese competition.

Despite all the indications to the contrary and no supporting evidence from round the world, it is still said that price stability is the condition needed to maximise growth on a sustainable basis. Economic history provides no support for such a view. The lessons from international comparisons and economic history indicate that rapid growth is associated with price changes in all directions – some upward, particularly where productivity increases are hard to achieve, and some downward, especially where there are falling cost curves. With rapid growth – 8 to 10 per cent per annum – consumer-price-level rises tend to be above the world average, mainly because of leading sector inflation, but in most cases the rate at which prices increase is still relatively stable. As Table 3.2 shows, in the 1950s and 1960s the Japanese economy grew at 10 per cent per annum, with 4 per cent average inflation. In economies growing at 5 to 6 per cent per annum, the optimum combination of rapid productivity growth without too much leading sector inflation seems to be achieved. This was the experience of most countries in western Europe during the 1950s and 1960s: over a long period, inflation rates averaged just under 4 per cent, with similar nominal base interest rates. If the objective is to get the Western economies to grow faster, perhaps at 4 per cent or even more per annum, it is likely that we will have to expect price rises and interest rates similar to those experienced in other economies achieving growth results of this order.

Shocks to the system

Seen from the vantage point of the early part of the twenty-first century, the 1950s and 1960s look like a period of remarkable stability and growing prosperity in the Western world. At least until 1968, low and quite stable levels of inflation were almost everywhere combined with rapidly increasing standards of living. After the adjustments of 1949, there were few exchange-rate changes among the major economies of the time, the most significant being the double French devaluations in 1958, the British devaluation in 1967 and the German revaluation in 1968, followed by some consequential parity changes in other countries. By the standards of what was to follow in the last quarter of the twentieth century, price increases were low, although they attracted a good deal of concern at the time. All the advanced economies were helped by the falling cost of raw materials, many of which came from the Third World. The biggest shock to the system, albeit a temporary one, was the Korean War which, at the beginning of the period, led to a sharp increase in commodity prices. Prices quickly collapsed, however, as the war ended. Inflation then fell away as the long boom in the 1950s and 1960s got under way. No period of economic history of any length is devoid of inflationary shocks, however, and as the 1960s ended, a much more turbulent period began.

The rate at which prices increased in the world's mature industrial economies during the 30 years from the late 1960s to the late 1990s, following the calmer period preceding it, exhibited upsurges when major inflationary shocks materialised, followed by declines to more usual levels within two or three years. The end of the 1960s saw the average year-on-year increase in consumer prices in industrial countries peaking in 1970 at 6.3 per cent from the inflationary pressures generated by the Vietnam War and the implementation of President Johnson's Great Society programme, but the index was back to a 4.8 per cent increase by 1972. The next peak, at 12.4 per cent year on year, came in 1974, following the early 1970s boom and the quadrupling of oil prices, but the index had fallen back to an 8.0 per cent increase by 1978. At the end of the 1970s came the third major shock: the next oil price rise, causing a further year-on-year peak of 9.4 per cent in 1980, yet the index was back to 5.2 per cent by 1983.[6] These average figures, of course, mask a wide range of experience country by country. In particular, there was substantial variation involving overall rises in the domestic price level over this period between long-standing low-inflation countries and others which had long had much more difficulty containing price increases. Between 1975 and 1995 consumer prices rose 84 per cent in Germany, 183 per cent in the USA, 322 per cent in Britain and 640 per cent in Spain.[7]

Looking back over the whole period since World War II, the ups and downs which have taken place in inflation have clearly been caused by a wide variety of factors. From the world's point of view, only one of all the major inflationary events – that of the early 1970s – appears to have been the direct result of excessive credit creation, in this case initially in the USA during the late 1960s. With appropriate policies, the rest of the world could have avoided much of the inflation which followed, as indeed happened in some countries. Germany's year-on-year price rises in the mid 1970s never rose above about 7 per cent, compared with 24 per cent at peak in Britain.[8] In most of the developed world, the real money supply – that is, net of inflation – remained remarkably stable, although fluctuating much more than average in Britain and the Netherlands.[9] In the USA it has also been much less constant than elsewhere. The widest money supply measure, L, as a percentage of GDP, rose from 80 per cent in 1971 to a peak of 93 per cent in 1986 and then fell heavily to 77 per cent in 1994. By 1997 it was back to 82 per cent – still, historically a relatively low percentage.[10]

Other causes of price rises had little or nothing to do with changes in the credit base. All of them, however, because they caused higher inflation and thus increased the requirement for money, had to be accommodated by increasing the money supply if deflation was to be avoided. When the supply of money fell in real terms – as it did during the 1974–9 Labour government in Britain, when it was reduced by 27 per cent[11] – the deflationary effect was very powerful. Interestingly, during the Reagan era in the USA (1981–9), although interest rates rose to exceptionally high levels, restrictions on the money supply were modest. Much the heaviest squeeze came subsequently, particularly in the late 1980s and early 1990s. Both the M3 and L measures of the money supply fell in real terms every year from 1987 to 1994,[12] pushing the US money supply ratios down well below the international average. There is little doubt that this is one of the major reasons why the dollar was then so strong.

Since the 1990s, inflation has run consistently at lower rates than it did during the period of the big price rises, which started at the beginning of the 1970s. Ever-increasing competition from the Pacific Rim reduced the cost of many products while weakening labour's bargaining position, which had already been undermined by increasing unemployment in Europe and rising immigration in the USA. Slow growth in the West moderated the impact of leading sector inflation and reductions in the importance in GDP of raw materials, especially oil, reduced the impact of commodity price changes. The West, therefore, generally enjoyed a period – at least until the turmoil which started in 2008 – of modest growth with low inflation.

The history of the last 60 years has shown a remarkable ability by all countries in the developed world to absorb inflationary shocks, from wherever they came, despite the variety of different events which, over the years, have been responsible for initiating rapid increases in the price level. Once the initial cause of the inflation surge disappeared, the rate at which prices rose soon slowed, given an absence of further shocks and reasonably competent management of the macroeconomy. This ought not to cause surprise. Economic growth is powerfully effective at absorbing inflation. Indeed, except during the major twentieth-century wars and what increasingly appears to have been an abnormal period between the early 1970s and the early 1990s, inflation has never looked like being a major problem.

If this is so, however, it removes the underpinning for a major component of economic policy employed in varying degrees by almost all major Western governments since the 1970s. All have tended to assume that the best way to counteract inflationary shocks was to deflate their economies rather than to absorb the disturbances by increasing output. The monetarist argument – that all increases in inflation are caused by antecedent rises in the money supply and only monetary discipline will stop prices rising more and more rapidly – is only a more precise formulation of a view which underlay conservative economic policymaking for a long time before monetarism became fashionable. On the contrary, the international evidence shows that the resulting deflation has been damaging, destructive and not particularly effective at keeping inflation down below what it would have been anyway. If most of the events which have generated upsurges in inflation were not caused by anything to do with the money supply and the international experience is that rapid rises in the price level nearly always recede once the immediate cause has been removed irrespective of the monetary stance in the economies concerned, what is left of the argument that the money supply is both cause and cure for all inflationary ills? Moreover, the picture is even worse if the prospect for the coming period is one of continuing slow growth. The historical evidence suggests that economies which have used growth to dampen inflation have done at least as well, perhaps better, at restraining price increases as those which have used deflation. Table 3.3 shows the record for the major Western economies for the period 1973–8, when all of them were suffering in various degrees from the upsets of the 1970s, and for the following five years, 1978 to 1983. Japan, with much the highest growth rate at the time, was far the most successful in bringing down inflation. All the remaining countries, whose growth rates fell between the first and second periods, had similar or higher rates of inflation in the later period compared with the earlier one. This evidence reinforces the view that economies which have reasonably strong growth rates are better at absorbing external shocks than those which are growing more slowly.

Without doubt, the future will bring more random shocks and policy changes which will cause upsurges in inflation. But when they come, what is the best policy to pursue? Is it cautious deflation, or is the safest solution to keep economies growing to absorb pressures for rising prices with increased output? The evidence from international experience shows that in both the short and the longer term, a reasonable measure of boldness pays off. Restricting the money supply and deflating the economy is not the most efficient way to contain

Table 3.3 Economic growth and inflation rates in selected countries between 1973 and 1978, and 1978 and 1983

Country	1973–78		1978–83	
	Average Growth Rate %	Average Inflation Rate %	Average Growth Rate %	Average Inflation Rate %
Japan	3.7	12.8	4.1	4.2
France	3.1	10.8	1.4	11.8
United States	2.8	8.0	1.3	8.8
Italy	2.1	16.6	1.5	17.3
Germany	2.1	4.7	1.2	4.7
United Kingdom	1.7	12.4	0.7	11.2

Source: Economic Statistics 1900–1983 by Thelma Liesner. London, *the Economist*, 1985.

inflation. Rising output is at least as efficacious an agent for slowing increases in the price level, and generally it is more so. If this is the case, in large measure the poor job prospects for many people, the lost output and the social strains caused by the deflation and slow growth which so many Western economies have been through during decades past, primarily to fight inflation, have been unnecessary and could have been avoided.

Excess demand

If the Western economies adopted a more expansionist policy, one requiring a significant devaluation of their exchange rates vis-à-vis those of the rest of the world, particularly those of the Pacific Rim countries, it is not likely that the parity changes required would of themselves necessarily lead to any great inflationary problems during the early or later stages. The causes of inflation, however, are not only those already discussed. A further potentially substantial generator of price increases of a different sort is overexpansion of demand, so that overheating occurs. Once demand on any economy outstrips its capacity to supply, prices will start to rise. This is a prospect which must be taken seriously – and avoided.

'Too much money chasing too few goods' is the classic definition of inflationary conditions. While one of this book's central propositions is that the solution to this problem should, wherever possible, be to expand the supply of goods rather than restrict demand, there must inevitably be a point where too many local shortages and bottlenecks have an increasingly serious effect on the price level. This problem has almost never been significant in Western economies since the Korean War, but it could become significant in the future.

There are, however, good reasons for believing that these difficulties are likely to be relatively easy to contain. The vast reservoir of unemployment and underemployment and long years of low demand have taken a heavy toll on both European and American manufacturing capacity, but plant utilisation of what remains leaves room for significant increases in output before capacity constraints start to bite hard. Some labour will have rusty skills. Many plants and much machinery may not be as modern or efficient as they should be, thanks to relatively low levels of investment over recent decades. These resources, however, are much better than nothing, and there is no doubt that substantial extra output could be obtained from them.

While there is a significant reserve of unused or underused resources to draw on, these will not last forever. Once they are gone, the problems of sustaining economic growth without overstretching the economy will become more acute. One major disadvantage which decades of unmanageable competition have inflicted on the developed world is not just the closed plants and the fall in manufacturing employment, but the break-up of teams of people with design and production experience. The West has still managed to retain at least a partial lead in a number of newer industries, such as advanced uses of electronics and biotechnology, but there is still a wide swathe of production where foreign imports dominate the market – toys, giftware, household and hardware products – though many of them could and would be made in Europe or the USA given suitable exchange rates. Most are comparatively straightforward to manufacture – which is why the West could easily produce them competitively if it had the appropriate international cost base – but it still takes time and skill to achieve high standards of manufacture and marketing. Building a successful industrial operation is not the work of a day, and thus the damage done by the weakening of the West's manufacturing base is not going to be put right in a few months. These problems can, however, be solved over a reasonably short period of years, and meanwhile they can be contained or minimised.

First, we have seen that the more the economy's resources are deployed into sectors concerned with falling cost curves and foreign trade, the easier it is for self-sustaining growth to be achieved. The faster the Western economies are to grow, the more vital it is that wages and salaries in the import saving and exporting sectors of the economy should rise relative to those everywhere else. There will be a pressing need to attract the most talented people, capable of making good as quickly as possible the management deficiencies that are bound to exist after years of slow growth. The large returns on investment obtainable in these sectors should be able in turn to provide enough new output to finance all the additional investment required without calling on the resources of the rest of the economy. There is thus an extremely strong case for fostering this kind of self-sustaining growth and avoiding unnecessary obstructions to its taking place. There will also inevitably be pressure to expand expenditure in other directions. To avoid overheating, however, it is important not to allow poorly judged taxation or public investment policies to siphon too many resources away from those parts of the economy which are achieving large increases in output towards those which cannot do so. Fast growth comes by letting wealth be created before it is taxed too heavily and by allowing as much investment as possible to be concentrated on projects with short pay-off periods and high returns.

Second, for at least some shortages, there is considerable scope for importing inputs not available from home production. One of the strongest arguments against the strategy of reflating the economy behind the shield of import tariffs or quotas and against protectionist policies generally is that they reduce or preclude the availability of alternative sources of supply at competitive prices to cope with domestic shortages. This is not an advantage the West should throw away. Yet not all materials can be imported, nor, in particular, is the supply of skilled labour inexhaustible, much of it having been drained away from manufacturing by relatively poor wages, bad working conditions and uncertain prospects. Too many skilled engineers have now turned their hands to other ways of earning a living outside the industrial sector. They need to be attracted back with improved wages and conditions.

Third, any serious attempt to reflate the West's economies, one designed to bring the labour force back to full stretch again, faces a major training, retraining and educational task, particularly for all forms of engineering and technical work. One of the consequences of the decline of manufacturing in the West has been that a far smaller proportion of its university-level students take engineering courses than is true in other countries. A recent report showed the USA producing just over a third of the number graduating from comparable courses in China – 137,000 compared with 352,000[13] In Germany, with a population less than one-third that of the USA but with a much stronger manufacturing tradition, around 50,000 students, over 20 per cent of all students, begin university-level engineering courses every year.[14] This ratio is similar to Japan's, where around 100,000 engineering graduates are produced per annum, forming more than 20 per cent of all graduates.[15] In countries with a longer history of manufacturing decline, the position is typically much worse. In Britain only a little over 20,000 students graduate in engineering annually,[16] and a report in 2011 showed that, of this low number, nearly a quarter after leaving university were in non-graduate or unskilled jobs.[17] Training courses have little value if there is insufficient demand available to provide work for those who have been through them. They are, however, an important component of success once new opportunities for employment come on stream, since they can be supplemented by on-the-job training from employers needing to upgrade the skills of their workforce.

The unemployment figures in all of the Western economies would clearly be much higher if they were to include those not registered as unemployed, such as housewives and those who have been involuntarily retired early or who would like to work but view as hopeless the prospect of finding a job.[18] There is also a major problem with lack of skills among those who are unemployed in Europe or are in menial, low-output positions in the USA. Nearly all require at least basic skills, such as the ability to drive a motor vehicle or use a keyboard, and the scope for employment for those who cannot read or write properly will inevitably be limited. Long years of poor job prospects may have sapped the motivation of a generation of children, especially in deprived areas; often their educational attainments are poor and considerably worse than they were a few years ago. Similar problems of outdated or rusty skills apply to those who are older. The West cannot afford to fail, for either social or economic reasons, to get a high proportion of its unemployed or underemployed labour force into more productive jobs. Providing the training to enable them to hold down the better-paying jobs which could be created in the future is no more than their due. The experience of the years during World War I and particularly World War II shows that it is possible to find worthwhile employment for almost everyone, if sufficient will and determination are there.

Labour costs

In the end the most important determinant of inflation trends is the rate of increase in wages and salaries. Payments to labour represent an average of some 60 per cent of total costs in the world as a whole but tend to be considerably higher in the slower growing Western economies. In the USA and Britain it is nearer to 70 per cent, mainly because the savings and investment ratio is so much lower in countries which are growing slowly than in those expanding more rapidly.[19] If the wage and salary bill rises faster than output, the extra costs are bound to be reflected in higher prices. If an economy is run with a much greater level of demand, one intended, among other things, to produce a very substantial reduction in the level of unemployment, is it inevitable that high levels of wage inflation will be the consequence?

Before attempting to answer this question, it is worth looking again at the historical record and the current experience of countries in the developed world, particularly in the last third of the twentieth century, when inflation rose and then receded in the West. Inspection of the unemployment percentages for developed countries and across different periods, as an indication of the tightness of the labour market, and of the rates at which the consumer price level rose must surely undermine belief, even among the most convinced, that wage inflation is inevitable. Table 3.4 provides some of the relevant figures. Those for the earlier period, before the general increase in inflation in the mid-1970s, show a wide range of countries with low rates of unemployment and moderate rates of inflation. Since the beginning of the 1990s, countries as varied as Singapore, Norway and Switzerland have all managed to combine nearly full utilisation of their labour forces with low increases in the price level.[20]

Much of the argument about the level of unemployment in developed countries used to centre on the concept of the non-accelerating inflation rate of unemployment, known by its acronym, NAIRU. It was argued that, without sufficiently large numbers of unemployed people, the pressure for wage increases would tend to outstrip the growth in output which the economy could provide and necessarily lead to increased inflation. NAIRU, it was said, was higher in countries with more inflexible labour markets, with more rigidities in the form of restrictive practices, both in the way the workforce was deployed and in wage bargaining. The debate about NAIRU reflects modern-day views that the only way to reduce unemployment is by wholesale reform of the labour market. While it is recognized that training and improved economic performance have a role to play, the only fundamental solutions to the problem of unemployment, it is argued, are to reduce supply-side rigidities by making wage rates and the labour market more flexible, to reduce job security and to weaken the power of trade unions to fix wages unrelated to productivity gains.

There may well be substantial economic advantages for countries with non-rigid labour markets – offset, in many cases, by significant social costs – and there must be a point where there is a trade-off between fuller and fuller employment and rising inflation. Most Western countries, however, are a very long way from being in this condition. Even if unemployment fell to much lower levels, moreover, it is not clear that wage inflation would necessarily result. Evidently, it was possible

Table 3.4 Unemployment and inflation in ten OECD countries at selected periods between 1963 and 1993

	1963–73		1974–79		1980–89		1990–93	
	Unemployment Rate %	Inflation Rate %	Unemployment Rate %	Inflation Rate %	Unemployment Rate %	Inflation Rate %	Unemployment Rate %	Inflation Rate %
United States	4.8	3.2	6.7	8.5	7.2	5.5	6.5	3.9
Japan	1.3	6.2	1.9	9.9	2.5	2.5	2.2	2.5
Austria	1.7	4.2	1.7	6.3	3.3	3.8	3.6	3.6
Norway	1.3	5.1	1.8	8.7	2.8	8.3	5.6	3.0
Switzerland	0.5	4.2	0.5	4.0	0.6	3.3	2.2	4.6
France	2.0	4.6	4.5	10.7	9.0	7.3	10.0	2.8
Germany	0.8	3.4	3.4	4.7	6.8	2.9	7.3	3.6
Italy	5.3	3.9	6.6	16.7	9.9	11.2	11.0	5.5
Spain	2.5	4.7	5.3	18.3	17.5	10.2	18.1	5.8
United Kingdom	1.9	5.1	4.2	15.6	9.5	7.4	8.3	5.1
OECD Average	3.2	4.1	5.0	10.8	7.2	8.9	7.3	5.5

Source: OECD *Historical Statistics* Paris, OECD, 1995.

to combine relatively high rates of growth and low levels of unemployment with moderate inflation for 25 years after World War II in most of Europe, even more so in Japan, when supply-side restrictions of all kinds were at least as prevalent as they are now and often much more so. Why then should it not be possible to achieve low levels of unemployment now with or without radical change to labour markets? Getting there might take some time, but there is no convincing reason that returning to an unemployment rate around 3 per cent in the industrialised countries should not be achievable within perhaps four or five years, if appropriate policies were implemented, with almost the entire labour force in jobs which stretched their holders' talents and in most cases paid them much better than they now are. A great deal can be done to achieve this objective.

First, wage determination is, in the end, as much a political as an economic process. Wage increases for which people are prepared to settle are not decided by a totally mechanistic process. Persuasion also counts. Even more difference may be made by the prospect of a rational economic policy capable of delivering results and therefore seen to be one where some sacrifice of current wage and salary increases is worthwhile to obtain more in the future. Certainly a major objective must be to create a climate for wage negotiation which is conducive to average money increases at a level as low as possible, hopefully with the support of trade union leaders, to secure larger real rises as soon as is practical in the future.

A complicating factor in wage determination, if a transition is to be made towards accelerated economic growth, is that it will not be possible to have the same increases for everyone. A substantial relative adjustment will be needed. If talent at every level is going to have to be switched to those parts of the economy capable of producing high productivity increases and rapid investment pay-off periods, pay rises will have to be considerably higher in these areas of economic activity than elsewhere. To this end, aiming for relatively low general increases but with substantial wage drift at the level of individual enterprises seems the most realistic policy.

Another problem is that there are going to be shortages of certain types of skilled labour and also a pressing need for a considerable amount of retraining to enable the labour force to be adequately prepared for the new types of jobs which will become available. Government programmes will have a major role in providing training and retraining to enable a sufficient response to this challenge, supplementing what is carried out on the job. If skilled labour shortages and similar bottlenecks are to be avoided, the places where they are likely to occur need to be identified far in advance and training put in hand as early as it can be to provide the manpower needed at adequate skill levels. Generally, this will need to be fairly precisely orientated towards specific job opportunities. Improving general standards of education and motivation in schools is another vital component, one taking much longer to pay off. Preparing those already of working age – and particularly making sure that young people entering the labour market for the first time have the required skills and motivation – will almost certainly have to be given higher immediate priority.

There clearly is potential for wage pressure if these changes take place, and all the dampening effect of increasing output in absorbing whatever wage increases there are will be needed. There is no reason, however, why the major disinflationary influence of increasing production should not be supplemented wherever possible by government actions on the price level. Lowering interest rates, which has many other advantages, reduces the cost of living. If the economy needs reflating, several ways for doing so, ways which actually reduce costs, such as lowering taxes on employment to keep down the price level, have already been mentioned. All this should help to produce a more helpful wage climate in addition to acting directly on the cost both of living and of producing output of all kinds.

Faster growth makes larger money wage claims possible without inflationary consequences. Rising output in an economy run in a way which appears rational and sustainable makes a degree of wage restraint seem a sensible policy. Flowing from this comes something closer to a consensus. This should make economically unjustified wage claims look irrational and greedy, instead of the only way available to buck trends which never seem to end, as has been the experience too often in the past in the USA, Britain and other countries with a long record of slow growth. If some countries can operate with 3 or 4 per cent rates of unemployment, with the rest of their labour forces in jobs stretching their members' talents, there is no reason why others should not be able to do so, too.

Even if events were to prove this approach too optimistic, although the evidence does not suggest they would, if there were significant extra inflation as a result of downward parity changes and the Western economies grew much more quickly, there is still a strong case for believing that it would be worth it. The standard of living is, in the end, far more important than the cost of living. It would be worth paying a modest inflationary price to raise growth rates from their current level to the world average or beyond and vastly to improve the job prospects and productivity of the European and American labour forces. In any event, such an inflationary surge would almost certainly be temporary and quickly absorbed. This does not, however, appear to be the real choice. It is not necessary to choose between more growth with significantly more inflation and less growth and much lower price rises. In the short term, as well as the medium and long term, high rates of growth and manageably low rates of inflation can and should be made to go hand in hand.

4
Unemployment

Since about 1970, an extraordinary change has taken place across much of the developed world. It has been the huge growth in unemployment, matched by the inability of policymakers to do anything effective to reverse it. Unemployment in the European Union has hovered close to 10 per cent for most of the last four decades and in September 2011 it stood at 10.2 per cent. Twenty-three million people in the EU were actively looking for jobs.[1] For much of the period since 1970, US unemployment has been lower than Europe's, mainly because of its much harsher regime for those out of work. In October 2011, however, with 9.0 per cent of the labour force registered as being out of work, the US percentage had grown nearly as high as in the EU.[2]

On the scale in which unemployment is seen in many Western countries, it is surely right to regard it as a major evil, especially given the extent to which it is concentrated among young people. For everyone who wants to work and make a useful contribution to society and is denied the opportunity to do so, being without a job is a personal tragedy. With income suffering accordingly, it is also an economic disaster. Taxpayers, especially in countries with major welfare programmes, suffer, too, since they have to foot the bill for unemployment and related benefits. The indirect financial costs of having millions of people with no job is also very high. The unemployed are much more likely to need the assistance of health and social services and to require other welfare benefits than they would have if they were working.

Nor are the financial costs of unemployment simply confined to payments to those who have no jobs. In addition, the economy forgoes the output they could have contributed if they were working instead of idle. In 2010 the average gross value of the output of every person in employment in the USA was about $94,000.[3] In the EU it was around

$76,000 at the current rates of exchange.[4] Even assuming that the average output of those just coming back into a job would be somewhat less, the lost production of goods and services from having people capable of working out of work is clearly very substantial.

There is also a huge social cost to be taken into account. Innumerable studies show that crime, particularly theft, and high levels of unemployment are correlated. It is hardly surprising that it is difficult to get the more disadvantaged teenagers to concentrate on their studies if they have little prospect of a job when they leave school. It is thus equally difficult to avoid seeing a strong association, reflected in international comparisons of educational achievement, between poor job prospects and low levels of literacy and numeracy among a whole generation of young people, many of whom have never been employed at all.[5]

High levels of unemployment cause major fiscal problems, especially in countries with substantial welfare programmes. A large proportion of the taxable capacity of the EU member states is deployed into paying for unemployment and all its associated costs. At the same time, the tax base shrinks because millions of people who could be working and paying taxes are drawing benefits instead. The major reason why many EU governments have had problems in reducing the proportion of the national product spent by the public sector – and thus containing or diminishing the overall level of taxation, with the difference being made up by increasingly unmanageable levels of borrowing, has been the inexorable rise in the cost of social security payments, for which high levels of unemployment, directly and indirectly, are largely to blame. Furthermore, having millions of people who would like to work makes less and less sense when the demographics of developed economies are considered. The position varies from country to country, but there is a marked tendency everywhere in the developed world for the number of people of working age to decline, particularly in relation to the retired. This inevitably means that the burden of supporting non-earning fellow citizens is going to grow heavier for those who are in employment. Having large numbers of people of employable age who want to work but cannot because there is no work available for them makes no sense at all in these circumstances.

Nor do the published figures of the numbers out of work tell the full story. The headline unemployment rate measures only those who are actively looking for a job. It excludes all those who would like to work, if the opportunity for doing so existed, but have given up trying to find a job, temporarily or permanently, because the prospects look hopeless or because they would be no better off in than out of employment.

The ratio of active job seekers to those who could work but do not try to varies from country to country. The average for the EU as a whole, according to Eurostat figures, is that for every 100 people registered as unemployed, about another 50 would like to have jobs if they could.[6]

The total number of people who would prefer to work, given a reasonable opportunity to do so with acceptable levels of remuneration, is therefore far higher than the number of registered unemployed. International Labour Organisation figures show that there may be as many as 35 million people in the EU who could be drawn into employment if the conditions were right.[7] No doubt a substantial number are currently working in the black economy, so the potential gains may not be quite as large as appears possible at first sight, but they would still be very significant. So, too, would be the fiscal benefit from bringing them back into the tax system. Furthermore, there is considerable scope for increasing the amount done by those who count as employed but who work only limited hours and do not have a full-time job. Some people, especially those with families, may prefer part-time responsibilities, but there are many others who would rather work longer hours for more pay.

The number of jobs needed across the developed world rose considerably more quickly than the size of the population partly because of changes in the proportion of those of working age but much more significantly because of the increasing willingness of women to work. This change, more than anything else, created the requirement for substantial numbers of extra jobs per head of the population. In part, the USA had lower unemployment rates than the EU until recently because the it has a much less comprehensive welfare system, one which forces people who would otherwise be unemployed to take any job available, however low the pay. In turn this goes a long way to explaining the very poor output per head trends, especially in the service sector as shown in Table 1.3 in Chapter 1. Now, however, registered unemployment in the USA is only just below the EU level, despite the far harsher US regime. Unemployment, especially for young people – always the hardest-hit by declining job markets – is thus a desperately serious problem across nearly all the Western world.

Comparative experience

Unemployment has become an enormous problem in the West because productivity among those still working has risen faster than their nations' economies have grown. This happened particularly during the last quarter of the twentieth century. The level of unemployment then stabilised during the relatively successful early years of the twenty-first century before becoming much more of a problem following the 2008 financial crisis. Taking the EU as an example between 1973 and 1997, when chronic levels of unemployment became endemic in Europe, the annual EU compound growth rate was 2.2 per cent.[8] Output per head among those working, allowing for a 9 per cent[9] increase in the labour force over those 24 years, therefore increased about 2.1 per cent per year. Over the same period, registered unemployment in the EU rose from 2.5[10] to 9.9 per cent,[11] or an average increase in registered unemployment of a little under 0.3 per cent per annum. Allowing for all relevant factors, an annual cumulative increase in GDP around 3 per cent would have been required in the EU between 1973 and 1997 to keep unemployment around 3 per cent of the labour force, This would have implied an average annual increase in productivity of all those then working of about 2.5 per cent per annum. The shortfall in demand caused by the strength of Western currencies was directly responsible for the slow growth which led to so many people losing their jobs.

In contrast with the EU, whose total economy and population are roughly the same size as the USA's, during the last decades of the twentieth century the USA did considerably better at creating new jobs. Between 1973 and 1998 the employed US labour force increased by 54 per cent, from 85 to 131 million, as 46 million new jobs were created.[12] Over the same period, the then 15 EU countries saw the total number of jobs rise from 138 million to no more than 150 million, an increase of just under 9 per cent.[13] It is true that over this period, the US population increased by 28 per cent[14] and the EU's by only 8.3 per cent,[15] but the contrast in job creation performance is still striking. Job availability in the EU increased almost exactly in line with population growth, whereas in the USA it was much faster.

The US and EU economies nevertheless grew at almost exactly the same rate between 1973 and 1997 even though the former's labour force increased much more quickly – 1.7 per cent per annum cumulatively,[16] compared with 0.4 per cent.[17] The result in the USA was an exceptionally low rise recorded in output per head, or increasing productivity, averaging only 0.8 per cent per annum.[18] With such a rapidly expanding labour force, the US economy ought to have grown much faster than it actually did. It failed to do so because, just as happened in the EU, there was a substantial shortfall of effective demand in relation to the level needed to soak up the potentially achievable rises in productivity. Assuming a rough equality with the EU and allowing for a cumulative increase in output per head around 2.5 per cent per annum given reasonably favourable conditions, the shortfall in US demand turns out to be even higher than Europe's, mainly because the labour force was growing so much more quickly. To achieve full potential utilisation of the labour force, mainly because of its rapid growth, between 1974 and 1998 the missing US cumulative increase in demand appears to have been closer to 1.7 per cent per annum compound compared with 1 per cent for the EU. The US deficiency of 1.7 per cent each year is calculated as the difference over the last 25 years between the actual rise in labour force productivity, 0.8 per cent, compared to the potential increase, which, from experience in Europe, appears to have been at least 2.5 per cent.

After the big increases in unemployment seen during the last 30 years of the twentieth century, the comparatively prosperous years in the West at the turn of the century and up to the banking crisis of 2008 masked the problems of unemployment growth on both sides of the Atlantic. Unemployment in the EU fell to a low of 7.1 per cent in 2008,[19] while the USA, buoyed by its low interest rates and housing boom, did better still, with unemployment dropping to 4.6 per cent in 2006 and 2007.[20] Since 2008, however, the situation has deteriorated sharply in both sides of the Atlantic. Between 2008 and 2010 economic output fell by 3.9 per cent[21] in the EU and stagnated in the USA.[22] Unemployment correspondingly rose from 7.1 to 9.7 per cent in the EU[23] and from 5.8 to 9.6 per cent in the USA as shown in Table 4.1.[24] With little prospect of any significant economic growth in either area but with productivity among those still working continuing to creep upwards, the prospects for employment remain bleak indeed.

Wage freezes and work sharing have eased some of the strain. Those sections of the West's labour forces protected by powerful trade unions have managed to stave off job losses better than would otherwise have been the case but only by worsening the prospects for everyone else. The worst damage of all, reflected in appallingly high figures for youth unemployment, has been done to those trying to get into the labour force for the first time. The figures are bad enough in the UK and the USA, with, respectively, 20[25] and 18 per cent[26] of 16- to 24-year-olds out of work at the end of 2011, but in some places the situation is even worse. A staggering 46.2 per cent[27] of Spain's young people were jobless.

The only way to get unemployment down is to get the West's economies growing faster. Increases in productivity cannot be stopped. Increased demand is the only solution.

Table 4.1 EU and US unemployment labour force changes ratio

Area	Date	Population aged 15–64 mn	% Total 15–64 Population in Labour Force	Total Civilian Labour Force mn	Labour Force Factored for Population Change mn	Total Civilians Employed mn	Employed factored for Labour Force Change mn	Change in Number Employed %	Employed %	Unemployed mn	Unemployed %	Unemployed change to Labour force change
EU	1979–1983	203.8	64.4	131.4	131.4	123.8	123.8		94.3	7.5	5.7	
		212.4	63.8	135.5	130.0	121.5	122.7		89.6	14.1	10.4	
	Change		−0.6	4.2	−1.3	−2.4	−1.2	−1.9	−4.7%	+6.6	+4.7	82%
EU	1991–1994	242.0	68.3	165.3	165.3	151.6	151.6		91.8	13.6	8.2	
		244.1	67.6	165.1	163.7	146.7	148.1		88.8	18.5	11.2	
	Change		−0.6	−0.1	−1.6	−5.0	−3.6	−3.3	−2.9	+4.8	+2.9	26%
USA	1983	155.7	71.7	111.6	111.6	100.8	100.8		90.4	10.7	9.6	
	1988	162.8	74.7	121.7	123.4	115.0	103.9		94.5	6.7	5.5	
	Change		3.1	10.1	11.8	14.1	3.1	14.0	4.1	4.0	4.1	22%

Note: These calculations do not provide significant results over periods with small changes in unemployment because changes in the total size of the potential workforce and other factors then usually become too large in relation to changes in the level of unemployment for the relations under review to be seen. For all periods with big changes in the level of unemployment, however, in all developed countries, the same trend and roughly the same ratios are generally to be found.

Sources: Tables 0201, 0202, 0203 and 0301 in *Eurostatistics*. Luxembourg: EU, 1995 and 'Tables 2, 5, 5.1 and 6 in *Labour Force Statistics 1970–1990*. Paris: OECD, 1992 and Table B-35 in *Economic Report of the President*. Washington DC: US Government Printing Office, 1999.

Misguided solutions

Faced with the fact that much of the developed world evidently has serious difficulties providing large numbers of people with reasonably secure, well-paid jobs, almost everyone's instinctive reaction is to resort to essentially supply-side explanations. Many different reasons are put forward to explain the difficulties which advanced economies appear to have in allowing their workforces to compete successfully with those in other parts of the world. In consequence the remedies on offer range widely. It is not at all clear, however, that any of the explanations put forward at the popular or the more policy-orientated level to account for either the high levels of unemployment on both sides of the Atlantic or the low productivity growth in much of the US labour force have any real credibility. This being so, the solutions the explanations entail are unlikely to do anything effective to resolve the problem.

First, there is a widespread tendency to blame poor job prospects, especially for those on low incomes, on technical progress. Clearly, men and women can often be replaced by machines; which can do certain kinds of work far more quickly and accurately than any human can manage. Perhaps the greatest fears have been of computers, with their ability to replace armies of clerks, accountants and secretaries. It seems logical at first sight that if machines can replace human labour, the result must be fewer jobs and more people out of work. This argument, current since the beginning of the Industrial Revolution, when mechanisation started, is wrong because it depends on the 'lump of labour' fallacy – the assumption that the total demand for the output of the work force is fixed, so that if part of a given amount of work is done by a machine instead of by a person, lack of good employment opportunities will result. There is, however, no reason why the amount of output for which demand is available should be static. On the contrary, the history of the economically developing world has been one of rising demand ever since the Industrial Revolution began. Provided there is a steadily increasing amount of purchasing power available to buy the expanding output resulting from mechanisation and technical improvements, there is no reason why involuntary unemployment or underemployment should increase. The benefit from technical change will then appear as rising productivity and higher living standards. Problems will occur only if adequate purchasing power is unavailable to mop up all the new potential output.

Second, poor job prospects for low-income earners are not caused by the social and economic changes on which they are often blamed.

Neither more women in the labour force, nor more part-time workers, nor shifts from basic industries to light manufacturing or from manufacturing to services, nor any other alterations in working patterns are directly responsible for low incomes, though the indirect effects of some of these changes are a different matter. It is true that many of the new jobs which have been created recently in the industrialised countries have been part-time, especially in the service sector, and that women have been in some cases more willing to adapt to them and to work for lower pay than many men have found acceptable. It is also true that as the types of jobs available have shifted markedly from those where physical strength is required to office and service activity, older male workers have sometimes found their skills and experience difficult to match to modern conditions. This is because there are labour market mismatches between the skills and abilities employers seek and those a significant number of applicants have to offer. Overall, however, this cannot satisfactorily explain the current high levels of USA or EU unemployment. The changes taking place in today's labour market are not so different from those which occurred all over the developed world in the 1950s and 1960s, when no such problems were apparent, at least to anything like the same degree. The real reason is that there is not enough work to go round. In these circumstances employers will inevitably choose people who are most obviously suited to the employment they have to offer, who are most adaptable and who will work for the lowest pay. With insufficient jobs for everyone, those who are least obviously fitted for the available employment – whether because of location, skills, age or attitudes – will inevitably finish up with low-paid employment or no work at all. If there were a much higher demand for labour, these problems would largely disappear.

It is often argued that so many people, and particularly youngsters, are in dead end jobs or out of work because their educational skills are inadequate, they are poorly trained and lack technical capabilities, and they are not well motivated. There is little doubt that large numbers of younger people in the rich countries of the world lack good education and training. It is hardly surprising that many of them lack motivation if they are brought up in a culture where so many leaving school fail to find a steady employment with reasonable prospects. It does not, however, follow from this that they are incapable of holding down demanding jobs. As elsewhere in the labour force, the difficulty is that, not being those most obviously suitable for the employment on offer, they get left at the back of the queue. With there not being enough reasonably high quality work to go round, in these circumstances the least advantaged are the most likely to end up in poorly paid, low productivity jobs or out of work altogether.

A different line of argument is that the poor employment prospects for many people in developed countries is caused by their high wages, compared with wages in other parts of the world. It is assumed that EU or US labour forces cannot possibly compete with workers in China or elsewhere in the East, where the average standard of living is far below the Western level. It is, however, a fallacy to believe that work always goes where labour is cheapest. Another fallacy is believing that rich and poor countries cannot trade to mutual advantage and in overall balance, however different their wage rates and productivity levels. The critical factor is, not what labour is paid per hour, but its cost per unit of output, taking account of how productive it is and the rate at which it is charged out both to home and export markets. If the productivity of the labour force is high enough, it can compete comfortably in the world even though it is very well paid, as is clearly the case for Germany, Singapore and other countries. Wage rates for many Americans at the lower end of the income scales are not high by international standards, yet the companies they work for have problems competing in world markets – underlining the fact that the USA has in major low productivity problem in much of its workforce. It used to be said that cheap labour makes the Far East economies competitive. Now the tiger economies have per capita incomes approaching and in some cases exceeding those in the West, yet their economies are still growing fast. In 2010 Singapore had GDP per head of $43,117, and Hong Kong $31,514, compared with $46,860 for the USA and $32,537 for the EU.[28] This did not stop Singapore growing in 2010 by an astonishing 14.5 per cent and Hong Kong by 6.8 per cent.[29] Though 2010 may have been an exceptional year, for the whole of the 1999–2010 period the average cumulative annual increase in GDP in Singapore was 6.0 per cent. It was 5.3 per cent in South Korea, 5.1 per cent in Taiwan and 4.2 per cent in Hong Kong.[30]

Variations in the cost of producing different goods and services explain why rich and poor countries can trade to their mutual benefit, even if the poor country makes everything less efficiently than the rich one. Any country, whether rich or poor, will always produce some goods or services relatively more efficiently and cheaply than another will: These are those that they can sell abroad. For example, a low productivity Third World country may be a much cheaper place in which simple assembly work can be carried out. A rich country, in turn, may be able to design complex products at far lower cost than might be possible even for the poor country's lowest-paid labour. These so-called variances make it worthwhile for them to trade. Each gains, each is better off than it would otherwise have been, as a result of the exchanges which trade makes possible.

For trade of this sort to be to everyone's advantage, however, another important condition has to be met: the trade has to be in rough balance. In the modern world, where almost every country buys from and sells to every other, it makes no sense to try to make sure that trade between every pair of countries is in bilateral equilibrium. What counts is each country's overall trade balance with the rest of the world. If it is out of kilter, however, in that there are economies which are unable to sell enough to the rest of the world to pay for their imports, the inevitable results, absent parity changes, will be curtailment of demand to avoid balance of payments problems and increased unemployment. This is an argument, however, not for abandoning the advantages of free trade, but for ensuring that exchange rates are correctly positioned to enable each economy to hold its own with the rest of the world.

A different explanation advanced for high levels of unemployment, though not underemployment, and in consequence much more applicable to Europe than America is that generous state-run welfare systems have blunted the need to work. Large numbers of people do not, therefore, try to get jobs. It makes more sense to sit at home collecting benefits, the argument runs, than incurring the costs of being at work, especially if the pay is low. There is some truth in this assertion, especially for people on a low income. The effects of relatively high levels of income tax on low wages combined with benefit withdrawal can produce very high effective rates of tax on people at the bottom end of the pay scale. There are also particular problems for married couples, where one spouse working for low pay can reduce family entitlements by more than the income gained if the other remains out of work.

As a general explanation for high levels of unemployment, however, this argument is also implausible. First, large numbers of people who are out of work do not suffer from these kinds of income-trap problems. Second, at least some of these problems arise from the fact that there is so much unemployment in the first place. Many jobs are now on offer at low pay because large numbers of people are competing for the fewer unskilled jobs available. Third and perhaps most importantly, much of the income-trap problem directly results from the huge cost to the state of having millions of people involuntarily out of work. There is acute strain on the revenue and benefit system, largely because of the massive loss of income tax revenues from unemployment, combined with the heavy costs in benefits of having millions of people without jobs. The resulting high levels of assessments on those with low earnings causes much of the overlap between taxes and benefits for people on meagre incomes.

Productivity and competitiveness

A widespread perception of the reasons for poor employment prospects for low-income earners is that large numbers of people appear to be marginal candidates in the job market for the supply-side reasons set out in the previous section. It is therefore hardly surprising that the government's response, in almost all countries with apparently inadequate job opportunities, is to tackle supposed supply-side deficiencies. The objective is to make the economy more efficient and thus better able to secure enough of the world's purchasing power to keep a higher proportion of the labour force employed. This activity is frequently devoted to efforts to improve productivity in the hope that the economy will thereby become more competitive.

The scale of much of this activity is enormous. In the USA it is reflected in major current education and training initiatives,[31] though these are dwarfed by actions in some other countries. France, with unemployment rates of more than 12 per cent of its labour force a few years ago, peaked at spending almost 0.75 per cent of its gross national product on training schemes. Sweden and Denmark spent even more – over 1 per cent of their GNPs.[32] Nor do efforts to improve competitiveness cover only training. Higher levels of investment are also seen as a key factor, especially if investment can be orientated to producing products with high value added. This often shades into claims that high technology is the key to improving productivity and competitiveness, generating initiatives to move advanced economies away from relatively low-tech activity to the higher-tech end of the spectrum, where it is thought that competition with producers in less developed parts of the world will become easier.[33]

Because this approach generally requires substantial capital expenditure, another plank in the policy platform is encouraging more saving to finance increased investment, particularly in manufacturing industry. Since fast-growing economies reinvest a much higher proportion of their national incomes than the relatively slow growing economies of the West, it is assumed that an increase in investment will tend to lead to high rates of growth. It is now also argued on both sides of the Atlantic that the state has a major role to play in enhancing the infrastructure to make the economy more competitive. Improving the road and rail system and developing more advanced telecommunications, proponents of this type of investment claim, will improve the capacity of any country to export and to compete in the world.

Unfortunately, evidence for the overall efficacy of any of these policies is almost totally lacking. Of course, more training gets some people into jobs they might not otherwise have been able to secure, and wilting levels of investment, whether in infrastructure, plant or machinery, will certainly weaken any economy's capacity to compete in the future. This is a different matter, however, from being able to show that all these state-driven supply-side efforts to cope with poor employment prospects have been successful. On the contrary, the evidence strongly suggests that they have failed to provide the sought-for solutions in the advanced Western countries which have spent large sums of money on them.

These policies have failed to work because none of them begins to cope effectively with the real reason why there are so many people throughout the developed West with poor job prospects. The answer has little to do with supply-side problems. On the contrary, it has everything to do with insufficient demand for the goods and services Western economies are capable of producing. When looked at in this light, it becomes comparatively easy to see why all the huge efforts currently being put into employment measures, however valuable they might be if demand were increasing rapidly, are not going to work in the absence of changes in economic policies which will make sustainable increases in demand possible.

The fundamental problem with trying to use education and training programmes and increased investment to make a slow growing country more competitive is that it is much easier to run such programmes successfully in economies which are already growing rapidly. Advanced Western economies are not the only ones with education and training programmes. Every developed country has them, and so, too, do developing countries. Furthermore, in countries which are growing quickly, with buoyant tax revenues and rapidly expanding and profitable enterprises, high quality education and training can be afforded relatively easily, both in academic and on-the-job environments. The incentive for everyone to improve his or her skills is also clearly evident. In a tight labour market everyone can find a job, and so time devoted to training courses is seldom wasted. The effort and money spent on education and training has an immediate pay-off for almost everyone concerned.

In countries with sluggish growth, the cards are stacked the opposite way. First, it is impossibly difficult to raise the skills of the labour force as quickly in a slow growing economy as in one growing fast because the opportunities for using increased training are far fewer. Slow growing economies, progressively slipping further behind, become even less competitive. Second, with not enough work to go round, much of the education and training that takes place is wasted, since many on courses cannot obtain work where the new-found skills from their completed training can be put to use. Even if they can, all too often they only displace someone else, who then finds his or her way either to the dole queue or to another training course. This is much too close to being an expensive and dispiriting zero sum game.

Nor is the encouragement of investment any more of a panacea in the absence of overall economic changes. As with education and training, it is far easier to implement successful investment projects in economies that are already growing fast than in ones which are static or growing slowly. Profitability is much greater, making them easier to finance. Where wages and salaries are relatively high, enterprises can attract able entrepreneurs and managers, who are likely to make good decisions. When mistakes are made, which inevitably they will be, it is easier to pay for them. As wave after wave of investment takes place, the experience gained in managing hones the highly skilled process of organising a successful investment strategy. Succeeding against competitors who have accumulated this kind of expertise is extremely hard. Far from being easier in high-tech industries, furthermore, success is likely to be more difficult. Running a high-tech operation successfully usually involves accumulating years of experience in managing rapid technical change. The chances for a newcomer company moving into this field and, from scratch, and competing successfully are not good. Logic and experience strongly suggest that it is generally easier to compete in industries where the technology is well established and where the risks and skill requirements are lower, provided that the overall cost base is favourable.

Nor do high levels of savings and investment necessarily produce high growth rates. Rather, high growth rates produce high levels of savings and investment. The key to better economic performance is, not to subsidise and cajole reluctant investors into putting money into new projects they would not undertake if left to themselves, but to create the macroeconomic environment where high rates of growth are strongly encouraged by rising effective demand. Investment will then follow as profitable opportunities open up. The reason for relatively low levels of capital expenditure in much of US and European manufacturing compared with the that in the faster-developing areas of the world is that the prospects for making money out of new plant, machinery and factories in fast-growing economies tend to be much better than those in North America and Europe, which have much lower average growth rates.

There is, nevertheless, a broad issue as to what strategies are the right ones to pursue when there are millions more people available for work than the economy needs in order to achieve its current output. Does it not make sense to try to improve productivity in conditions where there are very large numbers of people with no jobs? Is there no alternative but to move towards the American solution, reflected now increasingly widely across Europe which is to generate welfare and employment conditions harsh enough to drive productivity down to a point where output per head is low enough to allow for employment of nearly all the potential labour force at the prevailing level of demand? This is where enthusiasm for deregulation and labour flexibility will eventually lead. Simply posing questions in this form, however, exposes how far many government policies in the Western world may have drifted away from providing effective solutions to pressing problems. They also point the way to some important and widely believed fallacies about productivity and supply-side remedies and the link between competitiveness, improved economic performance and better job prospects. If the question asked is, what needs to be done to improve growth rates in the West, the stock answer from most quarters is that the only solution is to raise investment, productivity, quality, innovation and value added. Is any of this true?

As has already been shown, productivity is not the same as competitiveness. If it were, the richest countries would always outstrip poorer ones, would compete more successfully in international markets and would grow faster. This is clearly, however, not the experience of much of the world today, nor has it ever been in the past. The reason is that, output per head has everything to do with the standard of living but almost nothing to do with competitiveness. It is the exchange rate – more accurately, the prices each country charges the rest of the world for the combined cost of all its factors of production – which determines whether the economy grows fast or slowly or not at all. Increasing productivity to make the economy more competitive will only work if it can be done quickly enough to reduce prices more rapidly than the world average without reducing profit margins. Achieving this objective from a position where an economy is growing more slowly than those of the rest of the world is an impossibly difficult task, and attempts to complete it are virtually bound to fail.

Of course quality and innovation are important. No doubt, the better the quality, the higher the price which can be charged. What can be done, however, if an economy starts from a position where quality is poor and the products sold are old-fashioned? Making them better is expensive; and besides, everyone else in the world is trying to improve product quality at the same time. The companies likely to succeed are those which are already profitable and expanding which, of course, tend to be found in fast-growing countries. Companies in economies which are expanding slowly are likely to be growing less rapidly and to be less profitable and to have lower levels of investment and therefore not be in a position to afford and implement improvements nearly so easily. This is why fast growth is the easiest and fastest route to product enhancement. To use increases in quality and innovation as ways of raising competitiveness and growth, rather than see them as by-products of an expanding economy, is again to set an impossibly difficult target, one which will almost certainly not be achieved.

Value added and productivity have similar characteristics. The total value added in any economy is equivalent to its GDP. If the economy does not expand, total value added will stay the same. If productivity then increases in some parts of the economy, it will have to fall in others. This is the root problem with trying to raise value added and productivity without tackling the macroeconomic environment. Even if it is successful in those parts where the policies are effective, with no overall output increase the result has to be a corresponding reduction in prospects in the parts which the policies have not touched. A rise in average productivity in some areas while the economy stays the same size only guarantees worsening job opportunities somewhere else. In particular, a productivity increase among those with already high output while the level of demand on the economy remains the same ensures that those already worse off are bound see their employment prospects deteriorating.

The truth is that the connections between productivity, quality, innovation, value added and improved economic performance are indeed significant but are different from those normally perceived. It is not improved productivity or any of the other quality measures of output which produces more growth. The direction of causation is the other way round. That is not to say that productivity and related measures of economic performance are unimportant. On the contrary, they determine the standard of living and are thus of vital significance.

It is the output per member of the labour force which multiplies up to the gross domestic product. Whether an economy has a high or low standard of living, however, tells nothing about the ability of its producers to compete in the world and whether, therefore, its total output – and with it productivity, quality, innovation and value added – will increase or not. The economy's growth is determined by an altogether different factor, which is whether its output is competitively priced in the home and export markets. This is an exchange-rate issue, not one where realistic policies for improving productivity, quality, innovation and value added, in isolation from macroeconomic policy changes, have a chance of success on their own.

As with many other economic matters, feedback makes it difficult to distinguish cause from effect. Here, as elsewhere, it is all too easy to confuse symptoms and root causes. Determining the direction of causation is, however, critical to formulating proposals which will work. Many billions of pounds, dollars or euros can be spent on supply-side policies designed to improve competitiveness and growth by increasing investment, productivity, quality, innovation and value added. Little or nothing will be achieved. No money needs to be spent, however, on implementing the policy which will achieve the results which otherwise appear so elusive. Bringing down effective interest rates, increasing the money supply and positioning the exchange rate so that effective demand is raised, all cost nothing. Much more rapid growth will then follow, bringing enhanced investment, higher productivity, improved quality, innovation and greater value added effortlessly in train as market forces drive the economy to expand. Job opportunities will progressively cease to be a major problem, especially for those on relatively low incomes. The experience of all the combatants' labour forces during the world wars, of Europe in the 1950s and 1960s and of the tiger economies was the same: once the labour market gets tight enough, training almost everyone becomes worthwhile. This is the only secure, certain route to increased productivity and wages among the less-well-off, increases otherwise so easy to advocate but so difficult to achieve.

5
Sustainability

Changes in policy which succeeded in increasing the rate of economic growth among Western economies would inevitably increase the pressure on the world's ecology. Higher output would raise consumption of raw materials and produce more waste. Raising living standards could, unless carefully handled, substantially increase rather than reduce the risk of destabilising the world's climate. Can, therefore, a convincing case be made that a policy orientated to producing better economic performance, as conventionally measured, is likely to be self-defeating? While this line of attack has always had a vocal constituency, there are strong arguments that this view is much too pessimistic. From all major perspectives, the prospects for a sustainable future – and increased human happiness – look to be much better if the developed countries of the world are stable and prosperous than if they are teetering towards financial disaster, with all the social and economic problems that such a scenario would bring in train.

There are many global risks which are going to have to be managed over the coming decades. Some of them, such as major outbreaks of disease or volcanic activity or widespread terrorist activity, are difficult to forecast, and most, on past performance, are also not very likely to occur on a world scale, even if they do cause serious local disruption. Trying to anticipate them is not likely to be fruitful. If they do materialise, history suggests that humanity will probably find a way of dealing with them. Other large-scale potential problems are much easier to foresee and to quantify and it is to these that the sections that follow turn. Those which are generally agreed to be much the most pressing are availability of sufficient resources of all kinds to support ever-rising economic output, the impact on the world's future of its still rapidly rising human population and of the migration pressures arising from them, and the changes in climate which are forecast to result from mankind's rising living standards.

Before reviewing resource, population, migration and climate issues, however, there is still the question whether trying to improve economic performance is a worthy objective, even supposing that the ecological problems involved in achieving this improvement can be overcome. Could it be that achieving more output – at least beyond a minimum level, which is well below what prevails in most of the Western world – does not improve happiness and is thus a pointless goal to pursue? There is now a significant literature showing that, on the vast majority of measures which can be used, most people do not seem to be much, if any, happier now than they were decades ago, when their living standards were substantially lower.[1] There are complex reasons for this state of affairs, with incomes relative to other people playing a substantially larger role than the absolute levels involved. It may well be that if living standards go on rising, other things remaining equal, the same results will generally go on being found. Even if this turns out to be the case – as seems likely – very important exceptions to the happiness thesis suggest strongly that better performance by the developed world would still improve rather than have little influence on the human happiness condition.

First, being unemployed involuntarily is a major cause of unhappiness, as is job insecurity.[2] Such being the case, running the economy with much lower levels of unemployment must improve the happiness quotient. Indeed, it may be the most important way in which economic performance can increase happiness, since so many other factors which affect people's attitude to life – family relationships, community and friends, health, personal freedom, personal values – are not related at all closely to levels of income.[3]

Second, if the major contribution which the economic world can make to human happiness is to provide satisfying work, there is great danger in allowing conditions of little or no growth to materialise, especially over a long period, because there is no reason to believe that these conditions would keep productivity from rising by something on the order of 2 per cent per annum – as it has done ever since the onset of the Industrial Revolution – among those still working, even with no overall growth. If this happens and if the same amount of output can be produced by fewer and fewer people, unemployment is bound to go up – exactly as has happened across the Western world. Thus, there are good reasons for believing that poor economic performance is very likely to reduce happiness, however measured.

Third, while happiness may not increase with living standards once a reasonable minimum level has been achieved, there are large numbers of people in the world whose income per head is far below this point. It is one thing not to feel more content with life when your income goes up but when you always have enough to eat, when you do not suffer from a disease for which remedies exist but for which you cannot afford to pay, and when you have somewhere tolerable to live. It is quite another not to gain in happiness from a rise in income when you live life in severe poverty. Whether in Western societies or the Third World, which depends heavily on the West for economic support, there are very large numbers of people whose condition would very obviously be improved by higher living standards.

Fourth, it may well be true that having ever more material goods does not make people happier, but there can be little doubt that, given the opportunity, most people would buy more goods and services than they do. Frustrating this desire may not have dire effects on an individual's well-being, but it may well have collective disadvantages if a sense of overall failure and degeneration overcomes the whole of a society.

Those who claim that increasing living standards past a certain point does not generally increase human happiness may well be right, but this is not an argument against making sure that economic policy contributes to contentment where it can.

Population growth

The greatest threat of all to the sustainability of human existence must be the number of people alive increasing to a point where intolerable strains are placed on the earth's resources. This situation is certainly likely to be made worse if it is accompanied – as it almost certainly would be – by widespread determination everywhere to increase living standards in parallel to the rise in the total number of people to be accommodated. There are therefore very pressing arguments for creating conditions to ensure that the total number of human beings plateaus at a manageable number. What sort of policies are most likely to achieve this objective?

At the turn of the twenty-first century, the world's population was 6.1 billion, up from 2.5 billion in 1950. The number of people alive thus more than doubled during the last 50 years of the last century. The peak rise in percentage terms was in 1964 – 2.2 per cent. Since then, the rate of increase has steadily declined, standing at 1.1 per cent in 2000[4] and expected to go on slowly dropping. The absolute number of people added to the world's population, 87 million, peaked in 1990, falling to

76 million in 2000, with a continuing downward trend.[5] Nevertheless, the number of people on earth is still increasing at the rate of a little over 200,000 per day,[6] although there are wide variations in different parts of the world.

There are two major reasons why the population has grown so fast over the last hundred years, compared with previous experience. One is the fall in mortality among the young, particularly children up to about five years old. The other is that the average age to which those who survive are living is much higher than it was. Average life expectancy in the developed countries is now about 80 years and 67 years on average for the world as a whole.[7] Before the Industrial Revolution average life expectancy at birth was seldom higher than 30 years anywhere and generally around an average of 24.[8] In the fourteenth century in Europe, during which the Black Death killed off about a third of the population,[9] it fell as low as 18.[10] As late as 1930, life expectancy in China was only 24 years, it is now 70.[11] Significant widespread improvements in the probability of survival date anywhere only from the nineteenth century and have been especially impressive since the end of World War II.[12]

While mortality has fallen dramatically across all age groups, the reduction in fertility needed to bring the rate of increase in population down to manageable proportions has taken considerably longer to materialise. In the early 1950s women in developing countries gave birth to an average of more than six children, compared to an average of 3.1 today.[13] The reason why the rate of population increase in developing countries, as opposed to the developed world, is still so high is that the steps taken to reduce mortality have turned out to be much easier to introduce than the changes in attitude and perception needed to reduce the number of children which parents decide that they want. It has been relatively easy and cheap to eradicate disease-carrying insects and rodents, to chlorinate drinking water, to carry out vaccination programmes and to introduce drugs and dietary supplements, all of which, combined with better personal hygiene and rehydration therapy, reduce infant mortality.[14] Changes in gender roles, attitudes towards authority, sexual norms and perceptions of advantage, leading to lower planned births, have been much more difficult to introduce.[15]

High fertility and low mortality produce a young population which, as it moves into childbearing age, generates a further increase in children being born. The momentum thus generated means that, even if replacement level fertility was achieved today in fast-growing population areas, big increases in the number of people to be accommodated would still exist because of the age structure.[16] Nor are these the only major consequences of changes in fertility and mortality. In many countries the dependency ratio – the ratio between those outside the normal working ages and those within them – is much higher than it used to be, generating major new redistributive problems. In countries with very high birth rates, such as many of those in sub-Saharan Africa, almost 45 per cent of the population is under 15 years of age.[17] In the developed world, by contrast, there are now far more people aged over 65 than there have ever been before as a proportion of the population about 18 per cent in 2011,[18] and this percentage is expected to rise steadily towards 24 per cent in 2050.[19]

With all these caveats in place, what can now be said about future population trends? The starting point is the work done by the United Nations, whose population division produces a biennial report with updated projections for the world as a whole and for each country. The current projections run to 2100, with varying population estimates, depending on different assumptions, for each country produced at five-year intervals between now and then. The projections are summarised under three main headings. The central estimate is called the medium variant. There are also low and high variants, which are essentially the product of varying assumptions about the lower and upper probable bands of fertility.[20]

The medium variant estimate in the 2010 revision for the world's population in 2050, by which time its growth is expected to flatten out, is 9.3 billion. The low variant total figure is 8.1 billion, and the high variant 10.6 billion, compared with the 7.0 billion people alive on earth in 2011.[21] The medium variant thus implies an increase in population between 2010 and 2050 of 33 per cent, the low variant 16 per cent and the high variant 51 per cent. Since these very large differences are mostly the product of different fertility rate projections, what actually happens to fertility trends over the decades to 2050 will be crucially important to the world's future. Not all of the increase in population, however, is tied to an increase in births. A significant proportion is based on the expectation that people will live longer. By 2045 to 2050, those in the less developed regions are expected to attain a life expectancy of 75 years, whereas in the more developed regions the projected level is 82 years, implying that the regional gap will narrow significantly.[22] Globally, the number of people over 60 is expected to more than triple between 2000 and 2050, rising from 606 million to nearly 2 billion, while those over 80 increase from 69 to 379 million. In other words, in 2050, for every child in the developed world, there might be two people over 60 – about a third of the population.[23]

This age transition, which is caused by the interaction of changes in fertility, mortality and migration, represents a shift from a very young population, in which there are slightly more males than females, to an older population in which there are more females than males. This shift represents a powerful force for social, economic and political change.[24] At ages 75 and over, two-thirds of the people alive in the USA are women. In Pakistan, the reverse is true, largely due to the low status of women there and correspondingly poor life expectancy, though the trend is moving in the other direction.[25]

Obviously, the earth cannot support an unlimited number of people. An assessment, therefore, has to be made about the extent to which the population can expand before one or another aspect of the world's carrying capacity is exhausted. Opinions on the exact numbers differ, but even the lower end of the UN projections for 2050 are pushing towards a tolerable limit. Beyond that, to have the population as much as 50 per cent larger than it is at the moment – which would happen if current fertility rates continue largely unchecked, reflecting the high variant projections – and still rising by the middle of the current century would put the future manifestly at risk. Generally speaking, it must be the case that the smaller the population the world has to sustain as the number of human beings plateaus or peaks, the likelier it is that humanity as a whole will have a sustainable future. What then can be done to keep the population increase as low as is feasibly possible? Not surprisingly, the mixture of policies which looks most likely to be successful is complex, not least because fertility – the key variable factor – is fundamentally the aggregate of millions of individual decisions which, being private, can be addressed by public policy only indirectly.

Unquestionably, however, the greatest single cause of high fertility levels is poverty. All the statistical data show a high correlation between low living standards and high numbers of children per woman in the population. Figure 5.1 shows how strong the relationship is between living standards and fertility. Births per woman start to fall sharply once annual GDP per head reaches about \$2,500 (measured in 2009 US dollars) and then continue to fall as it climbs to \$5,000[26] in almost all countries, whatever the religion or culture of their peoples. The figure also shows how resistant poor countries have generally been to all the many well-meaning initiatives which have been undertaken in the least developed parts of the world to reduce birth rates in the absence of rising living standards. The figures for the last 25 years of the twentieth century are particularly striking. Whereas the number of children per woman declined from

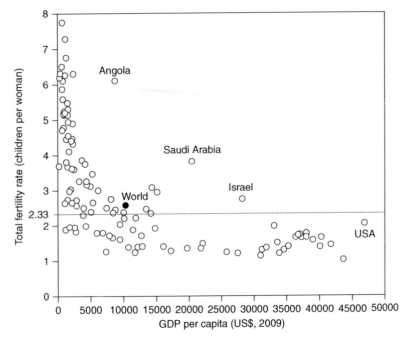

Figure 5.1 Total fertility rate (children per woman) plotted against GDP per capita (US$ 2009). Only countries with over five million population are included, to reduce outliers. The horizontal line shows the number of children per woman needed for a long-run stable population.

Source: Wikipedia Commons.

an average of 5.27 (1970–5) to 2.78 (1995–2000) in the less developed regions, it went down only from 6.60 to 5.47 in the least developed and thus poorest countries. It is equally noticeable that during the same 25 years, annual GDP per head for the world's population as a whole rose from just under $2,600 (measured in 2000 US dollars) to almost $5,400, whereas in the least developed countries it remained almost completely static, moving only from $1,613 to $1,661.[27] In many countries in the poorest category, income per head actually fell over this period, sometimes precipitously. In Somalia and Zambia it fell by nearly one third, and in Sierra Leone it was almost halved, although both countries' conditions have much improved recently as a result of rapidly rising commodity exports.[28] The whole world has a huge interest in ensuring that the poverty in these very poor countries is alleviated.

The key to ensuring that the world's population eventually plateaus at a manageable figure is thus inextricably linked with the rate at which those parts of the world with the lowest living standards can be brought up to a level where the demographic transition to lower family sizes occurs. Even then, it will take decades before the world's population stabilises. Crucial to raising living standards in poor countries is going to be the attitude not so much to aid but to trade in the rest of the world. The only way for poor countries to become richer is for their output per head to rise. By far the likeliest way to get this result is for them to develop trade relationships with the rest of the world that will enable them to follow the same export-led paths to prosperity as were shown to be viable by many of the Pacific Rim countries.

For this to happen, however, the rest of the world has to provide trade opportunities – which many countries have been loath to do. Protectionism – particularly involving agricultural products but also when adversely impacting industrial development – is much too prevalent. Reducing tariffs is never easy, as successive WTO rounds have shown, but the worse that economic conditions generally are, the harder it is to get tariffs removed. One of the strongest arguments for improving the economic performance of the Western world is that tariff reduction is the only way of providing the world with the opportunity it needs to contain the expansion of its population to a level which will be viable for the long-term future.

Resources

If far the best solution to the world's population problem is to raise living standards as widely as possible to bring down the birth rate, should the time when sufficient resources cease to be available to support the growth in economic output which would otherwise take place simply be brought forward? This has been a constant preoccupation at least since the publication of *Limits to Growth* by the Club of Rome in 1972.[29] With warnings of resource depletion having been taken up by many others has come the widely held view that increasing the growth rate, especially in the already relatively well-off West, even were it desirable, may not be feasible. A systematic review of the available evidence, however, suggests that this view is unsound.

Predictions of critical resource scarcity in the future are likely to be wrong for two main reasons: One is that a careful review of the resources on which the world depends shows that few of them, if any, should run short to an extent that will slow the rise in living standards; the other is the capacity of human ingenuity to solve problems – once the urgent used to do so becomes apparent and the required resources, generally driven by market forces, are brought to bear.

Turning first to resources they clearly come in a variety of categories; and a brief synopsis[30] of their availability indicates that our industrialised existence depends on remarkably few key raw materials. By value 80 per cent of them consists of seven raw materials: cement, aluminium, iron ore, copper, gold, nitrogen and zinc, all of which are in ample supply.[31] Of the remainder, 15 per cent consists of 16 more raw materials,[32] supplies of none of which will run out in the foreseeable future. Of the 5 per cent left, a study carried out in 1988, followed by further investigations, showed that of the 47 raw materials known to have significant applications, supplies of only one – tantalum, used for high-tech alloys and in some electronic applications – might run short. Particularly when account is taken of the scope for recycling and of the likelihood that reserves will be found as potential shortages appear and that improvements will materialise in the efficiency with which all raw materials are used, significant constraints on growth caused by lack of sources of supply of any of them seem unlikely. Reinforcing this view is overwhelming evidence that, as GDP per head rises beyond fairly low levels, the resource intensity of further increases in living standards rapidly diminishes proportionately to the raw material resources required to sustain them. This happens partly because of a shift towards a substantially higher proportion of increasing incomes being spent on services rather than goods. Worth noting, too, is that the total value of all raw material production represents only 1.1 per cent of world GDP.[33] Even if production costs were to rise significantly, they would therefore probably not put a serious strain on the world's growth prospects.

Second, will the world be able to produce enough food to feed 9 billion people, especially as the demand for better nutrition rises with higher living standards? The main reason for optimism is the astonishing rate at which food production has risen in quantity and quality over the past century. As a result, even though calorific intake has at the same time risen strongly, food prices have fallen dramatically, although with inevitable fluctuations. The main reason for the increase in food production has been the Green Revolution, involving higher crop yields, improved irrigation and water supply, ever more widespread and intensive use of fertilisers and pesticides and a significant increase in farmers' management skills. These trends will almost certainly continue. Technical advance is still taking place, not least in genetically modified foodstuffs, whose use will probably widen despite objections to them in some quarters. Given the huge gap between best and worst agricultural practices, large increases in output are still achievable. Improved communication and cheaper transport have enabled concentration of world food production in the areas best suited for growing each crop. There is also scope for bringing more land into agricultural use, particularly in Africa. The problem with providing everyone enough to eat does not, at least in principle, lie in producing enough food. Far more people are hungry because they do not have enough money to pay for the nourishment they need, and the best solution for that problem is to raise their incomes.

Third, will there be enough water? There is certainly no shortage of it in aggregate. Total rainfall capable of being captured is about 5,700 litres for everyone on earth per day.[34] The problem is with its distribution. Just to survive, a human being requires about two litres of water a day. This figure rises to 100 litres, however, if household needs and personal hygiene are included, and to anything from 500 to 2,000 litres a day if account is taken of the requirements for agriculture and industry. Globally, of all the water available, agriculture uses 69 per cent, industry 23 per cent and households 8 per cent. Taking seasonal variations into account, potentially almost 20 per cent of humanity is left short of water. There are, however, solutions. Desalination, although expensive, may be one. Avoiding growing highly water consuming crops in water-short areas is another. Much the most hopeful, however, is stopping the massive waste of water by pricing it more appropriately, particularly in agriculture, where most of the waste takes place. It is interesting to note that "water wars" have turned out largely to be a figment of copywriters' imaginations. The lack of warfare over water needs to be recorded alongside the no less than 3,600 treaties concerning international water resources which, as history shows, have been negotiated over the centuries.[35]

Fourth, what about energy? The average person in Europe now enjoys from non-human energy sources the equivalent of 150 times the power that the average human being could produce. In America the ratio is about 300, and even in India it is 15.[36] Of total energy consumption, oil represents about 41 per cent, gas 24 per cent and coal 23 per cent. At some future stage oil and gas reserves are going to become scarcer, more difficult to exploit and thus more expensive, but for coal this stage is very far off, and it may not be that much sooner for oil and gas, as surveying for new deposits intensifies and technology develops. Other obvious pressures for reducing the consumption of carbon-based energy supplies arise from fears of global warming. The issue is whether as the world's economy grows, other sources of energy can be brought onto the market, in sufficient quantities and at manageable prices, to fill the gap left as carbon-based fuels yield a declining proportion of total energy.

Doubtless, part of the solution will come from dramatically improved efficiency in using fuels of all sorts, especially as energy prices rise. Energy consumption per unit of output halved between 1971 and 1992.[37] Energy consumption's fall as a proportion of GDP as incomes rise to Western standards will also relieve pressure on resources. Nevertheless, alternatives to fossil fuels are going to be needed in major quantities. Renewable energy from wind and waves will no doubt fill some of the gap, although it is extremely expensive and not always reliable when most needed. Nuclear energy, despite its high cost and other well-known drawbacks, is another major possibility. Capturing the sun's heat may turn out to be a better medium-term bet. The heat the earth gets from the sun is about 7,000 times its current energy use.[38] The problem has been the costs of photovoltaic cells, but they are steadily falling. Just over 3.0 per cent of the Sahara Desert's area could supply the entire world's energy needs at present levels of consumption,[39] although distribution would clearly be a major problem. Finally, however, for all the importance attached to energy costs, they make up only about 2 per cent of world GDP.[40] Even were costs significantly increased above the present level, energy's impact on the world's economy would not be as substantial as is often supposed. If energy became, say, 50 per cent more expensive, at an extra cost of 1 per cent of GDP, a wide range of energy technologies would become economically viable. Energy, therefore, may well become more expensive relative to everything else in future, but running short of it in aggregate is unlikely.

Finally, the accumulation of unmanageable amounts of waste and pollution is another potential constraint on economic growth. Waste production tends to rise at least as fast as living standards – if anything, slightly faster. Recycling provides a limited solution, but its cost is fairly heavy, in both environmental and financial terms. Some form of land fill is left as the only alternative. This problem is clearly more acute in densely populated countries than in those with low densities, suggesting that moving waste round the world to underpopulated areas may be the best way to solve a problem which looks difficult but not insurmountable.

Pollution issues essentially break down into two categories of concern: air quality and water contamination. In terms of human health risks, air pollution is far the bigger problem, especially in underdeveloped countries. Major contributors are traffic fumes, open fires in poorly ventilated buildings, and industrial emissions. All these problems are largely solvable, however, by expenditure of enough money. As a recent World Bank survey showed, once living standards rise past $5,000 towards $10,000 per head per annum, the pressure to clean up the environment rises exponentially, ensuring that resources are made available to do it.[41]

Ocean-going oil tanker operations make up the single biggest cause of water pollution. They are now much more tightly controlled that they were, as are sewage discharges into the sea. Of greater concern is oxygen depletion in coastal areas, caused by agricultural run-off containing nitrates and phosphates, though the scale of these problems is limited in world terms. On balance, the UN recently declared, 'The open sea is still relatively clean'.[42] Rivers are a more serious problem, especially during the early stages of industrialisation. With the urge to improve the environment as living standards rise – evident all over the West – tending to ensure that sufficient resources will be deployed to overcome these problems, there is little doubt that outcomes will be similar in developing countries.

This brief survey of the constraints on growth strongly suggests that with reasonably good management, resources will present no insuperable hurdles to improving human living standards into the foreseeable future, whether the West takes steps to make its economies grow much faster or not. Looking just at resources is not, however, enough. Factoring in the capacity of humanity to adapt to new circumstances, via power or market pressures and the use of technology, is also very important. Fifty years ago, predicting the achievements of the Green Revolution in agriculture or the improvement in fuel efficiency of motor cars and aircraft would have been impossible. Something of a leap of faith that the improvements in technology and resource management which humanity has achieved over past decades will be repeated in the years to come may be required. To plan ahead on the assumption that no such repetition will occur, however, is surely too pessimistic. To assume that the ingenuity which has achieved so much since the Industrial Revolution began will no longer help people find solutions to resource and production problems would be an error of monumental proportions.

Climate change

There is yet another type of constraint to be considered regarding proposals to increase the world's growth rate, which entails improving the performance of the Western economies. Is it reasonable to discourage economic growth because of the impact of increased output on climate change and global warming, especially in the West?

Views about the extent of climate change's threat to the world environment differ, but there is a consensus on a number of aspects of increased industrialisation's impact on the atmosphere. Few dispute that certain gases – of which carbon dioxide is the most important, constituting about 60 per cent of the total – trap heat in the atmosphere although they can also reflect it back into space.[43] When observations started in 1960, the CO_2 concentration in the world's atmosphere was 315 parts per million. By 2011 it had risen to 392.[44] Thus, there is no doubt that CO_2 concentration has increased and is still rising because of industrialisation-related emissions. Also, no one disputes that average world temperatures have climbed over the last century and a half by about 0.8 degrees, although the rise occurred almost entirely over two relatively short periods, between 1910 and 1945 and between 1975 and 2000, with a plateau between 1945 and 1975.[45] There is less agreement on the mechanism by which concentrations of CO_2 and other greenhouse gases cause temperatures to rise, although all the climate change models based on empirical data show a strong connection. The main problem has been providing sufficiently detailed and accurate descriptions of how the world's climate works, particularly the cooling effect of particles and the effect of water vapour on temperature and weather. The impact of different sorts of clouds on the earth's temperature has been especially difficult to model comprehensively.[46] There is also disagreement about the extent that other factors, especially sunspot activity, influence the earth's temperature fluctuations, in addition to those having to do with increasing gas concentrations, especially over relatively short time-scales. Evidence suggests that the sun's brightness alone has increased sufficiently over the last 200 to 300 years to raise the earth's temperature by about 0.4 degrees.[47] If it is true that as much as 40 per cent of the increase in recorded surface temperatures may be due to this effect rather than that of greenhouse gases, the significance of the contribution of carbon dioxide and other gases to global warming may have to be correspondingly scaled down.[48]

Despite differences of opinion, however, the very broad scientific consensus is that emissions of carbon dioxide and other gases linked to economic growth have caused a rise in the earth's temperature and will continue to do so. Accepting, therefore, that increased economic activity accentuates climate change along the lines predicted by the UN, the world is looking at estimated increases through to 2100 clustering between 1.3 and 3.2 degrees, accompanied by a rise in sea level between 31 and 49 centimetres.[49] What impact should this have on proposals to increase the growth rate of Western economies?

A major difference between climate change and other considerations which bear on the pros and cons of increasing economic growth concerns the long timescales involved. Although cumulatively very substantial, the impact of increases in the average temperature of the earth is inevitably spread over a long period, generating questions of how much to discount benefits due to materialise far in the future compared with others more immediately available. Even if the Kyoto proposals, flowing from the 1992 Rio de Janeiro climate change conference, were implemented in full, they would put off only by about six years, at very high cost of output foregone, an increase in average temperature which would happen anyway.[50] Can curbing emissions as drastically as this be a rational approach when the alternative is a reasonable expectation that economic growth will continue over coming decades at roughly the same rate as over the last century, thus providing a huge flow of resources to deal with whatever costs climate change may bring? Most Kyoto targets can be reached at considerably less cost through a policy such as carbon taxes, which would let market forces encourage the use of energy sources which produce lower greenhouse gas levels.[51] If the earth still warms up as predicted, UN estimates indicate that the cost of offsetting the impact of climate change will be of the order of $5,000 billion, with roughly half the cost falling on the developed world. This is a very large sum of money but not one which is necessarily unmanageable, representing as it does 1.5 to 2.0 per cent per annum[52] of world GDP, a ratio which should fall as the world's economic output increases.

Even if global warming on the scale the UN predicts – unless vigorous action is taken to retard it – is regarded as too risky to ignore, it is not clear that trying to stop it by holding down economic growth, particularly in the West, will have the longer-term effects that its proponents hope for. If the economic condition of many Western countries is as poor and fragile as it appears to be, with resumption of at least some reasonable rate of growth being the only route out of current economic difficulties, blocking it off may plunge the world into a major financial crisis. Carbon emissions may drop in the short term, but probably not in the medium to long term, since a financial crisis in the West, with its almost certain major negative impact on economic conditions in countries where the birth rate is very high, will put off the time when the demographic transition there towards smaller families occurs.

A prolonged period of slow or negative growth in the world's developed countries is therefore all too likely to add to the eventual total number of human beings and make accommodating them in the world significantly harder than it would otherwise be. As all these people will, sooner or later, almost certainly want to have Western standards of living, the impact on the world's ecology and global warming will be correspondingly greater.

There are, moreover, other ways of combating climate change than letting it happen and paying the costs. There may be technological ways of offsetting the factors which drive global warming – so-called geo-engineering. Suggestions include fertilising the oceans with algae capable of absorbing carbon, putting sulphur particles into the atmosphere to help cool it and capturing carbon dioxide from fossil fuel combustion and returning it to permanent storage in appropriate geological formations.[53] These and other proposals are already under consideration. Their cost, while high, should be manageable in relation to the adaptation costs which might otherwise be incurred. It is also possible that the cost of renewable fuels will fall to below that of fossil fuels, in which case there is likely to be a major switch towards their use free of taxation or subsidies. Additional help may come from even greater improvements in fuel use efficiency than are currently anticipated, thus reducing greenhouse gas emissions. The ratio between GDP per head and fuel consumption has doubled about every 50 years in the developed world,[54] and hopefully this trend will continue. With assumptions of this sort in place, the central projections for temperature increases from global warming come in at considerably lower figures, suggesting a rise in temperature of 0.7 degrees by 2100, followed by a decline as renewable energy sources become more widely used. Even a somewhat more pessimistic scenario indicates a total temperature rise over the twenty-first century of no more than 1.5 degrees, followed by a slow decline.[55] Furthermore, not all impacts of climate change are negative. UN reports conclude, for example, that while there will be winners and losers, the overall effect on agricultural output should be positive rather than negative.[56]

Overall, therefore, the policy mix on climate change most likely to achieve the best results at minimum outlay is to constrain greenhouse emissions wherever it can be done at bearable cost, not least to minimise the risk of the world's reaching some kind of climatic or environmental tipping point. At the same time, however, we need to avoid the calamities which could befall us both in connection with Global Warming and in other ways if we fail to keep up the world's growth rate, among either developed countries or the Third World. This seems to be the most sensible way to minimise the risks from Global Warming, while putting everyone in the best position both to afford to make the contributions which will need to be made to counteract the costs of Climate Change and to do so without doing so prejudicing other important but much more immediately pressing objectives.

Migration

Migration has always been part of the human experience. As the world's population has grown, so too has the number of people migrating. From the eighteenth century onwards, 55 million Europeans went overseas, many to the USA, peaking at nearly 9 million arrivals in the first decade of the twentieth century. By the end of the first decade of the twenty-first, the total number of people worldwide – including legal and illegal international migrants and refugees – living in a country not the one where they were born was estimated to be about 215 million,[57] and its growth rate now exceeds that of total population growth.[58] The influx of migrants to Western countries approaches in absolute numbers the scale of nineteenth-century emigration. When Europeans migrated, however, they generally filled up territory with very few people. Today's migrants tend to go to places with relatively high population densities.[59]

Migration has positive aspects. Diasporas spread information and ideas and facilitate trade. They can and often do generate flows of remittances to poor countries. A recent study by Duke University showed that immigrants make up an eighth of America's population but have founded a quarter of the country's technology and engineering firms.[60] Generally, however, migration works best when the sending and receiving countries have roughly the same standard of living, not when there is a steep economic gradient to be traversed.

Hardly surprisingly, however, the flow is largely from poorer countries to richer ones. Migrants who move for economic reasons constitute by far the largest category. They move because they believe that they can better their life chances somewhere else, although the data consistently show that when families move, women's employment opportunities are apt to be less favourable than they had been.[61] The process of taking such decisions frequently involves leaving some family members behind, especially in poorer countries where remittances from the migrants to more developed economies represent a major economic benefit.[62] Sometimes a large degree of integration is relatively easily achieved. At the other extreme immigrants may experience almost total exclusion from the host society. Those who move often maintain substantial elements of their culture, including religious affiliations and language, at least for one generation.[63] The flow of Mexican migrants to the USA is now the greatest in the world, although their low educational levels have hindered assimilation.[64] The large-scale migration into and within the EU sometimes presents similar problems.

Who benefits from economically driven migration? Undoubtedly, the migrants generally gain from the process. The bigger the gap between migrants' earning power in their country of origin and in that to which they have moved, the greater their gains will be. With travel as cheap as it now is, movement from poorer to richer areas can be expected to increase in proportion to the size of the gap in living standards between developed and developing countries. The key issue, then, is whether on balance the overall gains from large-scale international migration, especially from poor to rich countries, outweigh the disbenefits. Much depends on the scale of migration and thus on the capacity of both host and donor countries to cope with its impacts – that is, on how easily migrants can be assimilated. What are the pros and cons of migration generally?

First, it is argued that there are large numbers of jobs in high-living-standard countries which the indigenous workforce does not want to do but migrants will. This may be true, but there are often other ways of getting necessary work done than by employing large numbers of unskilled people at low wages. Not surprisingly, there is evidence that large-scale immigration of people prepared to work for small sums discourages investment in labour-saving machinery and the productivity improvements which go with it. Furthermore, the losers in such a situation tend to be those competing with new arrivals. The evidence here is not wholly conclusive, however and some studies show much more pronounced effects than others.[65]

Second, it is maintained that immigrants are required to redress imbalances in the age structure of developed countries with low fertility rates and thus aging populations, particular cases in point being much of continental Europe and Japan. There are, however, two main problems with this approach. One is that immigrants get older, too. Sooner or later they will themselves become part of the dependency problem, even if – as usually happens – they have larger families than the indigenous population does in the meantime. The second is that the immigration required to fill the gaps in the population left by low fertility rates is on a completely impractical scale; the number of immigrants required to bring this about would be far greater than any estimates of the host countries' capacity to absorb them.

Third, it is maintained that immigration provides otherwise absent cultural diversity and that this is a positive good in itself. There is surely something in this argument, but it needs to be balanced against the resentment which large cultural and lifestyle differences can easily bring in train, especially if those involved are forced to live in close proximity to each other. Again, there may well be significant differences in perception among those who are well off – who, for example, enjoy dining out at a variety of ethnic restaurants – compared with those living on high-density housing estates with neighbours who cannot speak the host country language and who live their lives in different ways from the indigenous population.

Finally, it is argued that, because immigrants tend to be exceptionally hard working, positively motivated and entrepreneurial, they have a lot to offer. There is considerable force in this contention. In the British context, for example, although not all immigrant groups have done so well, Huguenots, Jews and Ugandan Asians are groups who have made conspicuously successful contributions, particularly to the business world but often more broadly, too. The obverse of this benefit, however, is the loss to the countries from which exceptionally talented and moti-vated groups come. All too often, it is the best educated and worldly-wise who migrate from poor countries which can ill afford to lose their skills.

In summary, therefore, while large-scale migration for economic reasons has some merits – especially for those who are already better off in the host societies and, in most cases, for the migrants them-selves, – the implications for everyone else are less obvious. Those in the developed world with a low income tend to find their earning capacity reduced while the pressure generated on housing, infrastructure and other social resources generally increases, especially in countries or urban environments where the population density is already high. At the same time the poorer countries from which migrants tend to come can ill afford to lose the skills and abilities of the sort of people who most want to migrate.

It is also clear that, as the scale of migration increases, the strains in all directions get greater and the tolerance of those in host countries, particularly poorer members, is stretched beyond the point of contain-ment. Thus, if migration is to be kept within reasonable bounds, there are two major requirements. One is that, as far as possible, the gap in living standards between poor and rich countries be kept as small as possible and reduced rather than increased. The other is that the living standards of the poorest countries be raised as quickly as possible to the point where the transition to smaller families takes place, thus reducing both the number of potential migrants and the pressure on them to move to being more manageable.

The major problem facing the world in migration terms, therefore, if the numbers of migrants is to be kept to containable proportions, is the low GDP per head in the poorest countries with the highest birth rates and the poorest economic prospects. The wider the gap becomes, the greater the pressure for large-scale migration for economic reasons will become. If the poorest countries are to become better off, it is even more important that the rich world does well enough to provide the trading opportunities and aid which poor countries need to raise their living standards. If the West falters, the result over coming decades is likely to be more, not less, migration. There are already signs that host developed countries have a limited capacity to absorb immigrants from poor countries before tensions rise to an intolerable level. At the least, it is in the developed world's interest to adopt policies which will raise the living standards in the world's least developed economies to a point where the birth rate starts to fall steeply, as happened everywhere else once the GDP-per-head tipping point was reached. Both developed and developing worlds have a huge interest in ensuring that pressures for economic migration are kept within bounds with which both donor and host countries can cope.

6
The Industrial Revolution

So far the case for major changes in economic policy priorities set out in this book have been largely theoretical. If they are to be a basis for deciding how to tackle some of our most pressing problems, it would help enormously if they could be shown not only to provide persuasive abstract theoretical constructs but also to be soundly based on empirical evidence. Apart from any merit that internal coherence and credibility may give them, is it possible to adduce evidence to validate them? If they can pass this sort of test, there would be much more solid reasons for believing that they can provide reliable guidance for future policymaking.

While it would be highly desirable to carry out definitive trials on the efficacy of different economic policies in order to provide unequivocal answers to matters in dispute, this option is not available. Prescriptions flowing from a subject like economics cannot be tested in the same way as are those from subjects where controlled experiments can be performed and theoretical concepts thereby proved or disproved beyond reasonable doubt. Methodology of this sort is generally impossible in economics, which is not a science in the way that physics or chemistry are. This does not, nevertheless, mean that there is no way of telling the difference between good and bad economic prescriptions and worthwhile and valueless theorising. A different way of assessing what is of value and what is not, however, is required. This has to be a way to test prescriptions and theories against what actually happens when the policies and practice which flow from them are applied in the real world, to see how well they explain the way in which events pan out as key turning points materialise and developments subsequently flow from them.

The next five chapters, therefore, are devoted to seeing whether the ideas set out in the previous five can provide a clear and convincing explanation which accounts plausibly and satisfactorily for the way in which economic history has unfolded since economic activity started and, especially, since industrialisation got under way in the eighteenth century. The challenge is to see whether these ideas can explain, persuasively and coherently, the reasons why, over a long period of time, the broad sweep of economic history has taken the path it has. They need to account for both good and bad outcomes. They need to supply a compelling and detailed explanation, in the light of actual historical events, why some economies have grown much more quickly than others and, in particular, why some which were doing exceptionally well then fell back and allowed others to lead in their place. They have to provide a clear account as to why unemployment, which, in most of the Western world had largely disappeared during the first quarter-century after World War II, has come back as a major plague, which current policies appear incapable of curing. Only if they test successfully against economic history's real achievements and failures should theories and prescriptions in economics be regarded as worth having. It is essential that they surmount this hurdle before it can be assumed they provide better explanations for economic history's most significant events and developments than others which fail to respond adequately to this challenge. Only when they have passed this test can prescriptions deriving from them for dealing with the West's pressing problems reasonably claim to be more soundly founded than those presently on offer and, therefore, more likely to meet with success.

This chapter starts with the historical background leading to the Industrial Revolution's onset. It summarises the key points in the world's economic history to the start of World War I. Subsequent chapters take the story forward to the end of 2011. The final chapter draws on both theoretical and historical sections of this book to put forward proposals for dealing with the severe economic difficulties currently facing most Western economies in the light of both the prescriptions it contains and their ability to account for actual experience

Pre-industrial history

Civilisation began some 11,000 years ago, shortly after the last Ice Age ended. Our ancestors, after hundreds of thousands of years of formative experience in foraging bands, began to form permanent settlements, as agriculture began and the very small number of types of animals and birds which are key to farming started to be domesticated. In about 8500 BC, in the Middle Eastern Fertile Crescent, wheat, peas and olives began to be harvested, followed by barley, lentils, chickpeas, flax and musk melons. Sheep and goats were evidently the first animals to be reared in captivity for food and milk, followed by cattle, then horses for riding and pulling. Similar developments began in China about a thousand years later.[1]

An interesting and important question is at what stage did anything resembling economic activity begin. It seems plausible that before there were any settlements, there were few significant transactions with any economic content. It is hard to believe, however, that as soon as farming and villages of any size formed, there was not a need for the division of labour, the exchange of goods and services and the establishment of some kind of recording of obligations arising from transactions which could not be simultaneous. When there was nothing resembling money – a much later invention – debts, the beginning of a credit system, were probably initially recorded largely in the memory of the settlement's head. This may well have been an important constraint on village growth at that time and may form an important part of the explanation for the long period from the dawn of civilisation to the emergence of towns and then cities.

The first recognisable states made their appearance, again in the Fertile Crescent, about 3700 BC. For them to function, a fair degree of economic organisation would have been essential, and indeed the evidence shows it had materialised.[2] Government was very much top-down, but it could not operate without significant division of labour. An elaborate system for recording debts and obligations was required, and there is ample evidence that baked clay tablets, entrusted largely to the priesthood, which formed the backbone of the state administration, were used. This system served as an important step towards the creation of money, since obligations recorded on the clay tablets could be transferred or assigned. These systems for keeping track of debts, owed by some and due to others, were not quite money yet, because both debtors and creditors were specific individuals or groups of people. It nevertheless provided a relatively flexible system for recording and discharging obligations, a system needed in an economy which was too big for everyone to know everyone else and where there were too many debts and payment obligations for any one person to be able to keep track of them all.

The next stage was the invention of money proper. Barter tokens were minted by the Chinese in the second millennium BC, but true coinage was invented in the Western world in the Kingdom of Lydia in Asia Minor, about 700 BC. Originally made of electrum, a local natural amalgam of gold and silver, the first coins were produced by the fabled Croesus of Lydia (d. 546 BC) in the sixth century BC.[3] As their value became separated from their intrinsic worth, they acquired the major advantage of not requiring the involvement of any personal debtor or creditor. Their value, backed by the state which issued them, lay in the trust of users that others would recognise and accept them. The invention of coinage greatly increased the scope for trade, and it is no coincidence that the explosion in exchange of goods and the later establishment of colonies within the Mediterranean occurred over the century or two after coins first appeared.

The ancient world, therefore, succeeded in developing the credit systems necessary to enable an extensive trade and commercial network to exist, to make it possible to establish large-scale states, to operate complex tax systems and to form, maintain and fund large-scale armies. At first sight, it might appear that the Roman Empire, in particular, had everything necessary to enable a beginning to be made on applying technology to the perennial problems of economic shortage. For nearly four hundred years after its consolidation under Caesar Augustus (63 BC–AD 14), it encompassed a large and varied area where peace and order generally prevailed. It had a relatively efficient and impartial legal system. The Roman Empire was plagued intermittently by inflationary problems, but they did not prevent substantial accumulations of capital. The Roman period is the only one when, until very recently, most of Europe had a single currency. Some industrial processes, such as smelting, were well known. A considerable quantity of theory about scientific matters, mostly developed by the Greeks, was available. Indeed, a steam engine of sorts, used as a toy, had been developed by the Greek polymath Hero (c.10 – c.70AD) in Alexandria, one of the centres of Greek learning.[4] There was a substantial artisan class, capable of contributing practical knowledge and experience to new ideas about production methods. The standards of education, especially among the more prosperous classes, were reasonably high. Both the Greeks and the Romans produced superb examples of civil engineering, from the Parthenon to the Roman road system. Yet despite all these potentially favourable circumstances, there was almost no technological development at all for hundreds of years. Why did nothing resembling the Industrial Revolution occur? There appear to be several reasons, and the more significant form an interlocking pattern. They all throw light on why the Industrial Revolution, when it gathered pace in Europe in the eighteenth century, although arguably the most important event in human history, was also one whose trajectory was remarkably difficult to forecast.

First, there was nothing equivalent to the body of scientific knowledge – a very different matter from the speculations of ancient Greek philosophers – that had accumulated in Europe at the time the Industrial Revolution got under way. It is true that many of the early inventions which got industrialisation started in Britain were developed by highly skilled journeyman engineers rather than intellectuals. Examples are the flying shuttle, invented by John Kay (1704–1779), which first appeared in 1733; the water frame (1769) from Richard Arkwright (1732–1792); the spinning jenny (1770) from James Hargreaves (1720–1778);[5] and the steam engines developed by Thomas Newcomen (1664–1729) as early as 1712 but greatly improved from 1769 onwards by James Watt (1736–1819).[6] The climate of opinion in which all these people worked had however undoubtedly been heavily influenced by the writings of Francis Bacon (1561–1626) and other proponents of what came to be called the scientific method, the system of experimentation and verification on which technical advance was to be built. It was a far cry from the methods employed by the most influential intellectual leaders in the ancient world, particularly the most important Greek teachers, Plato (427–347 BC) and Aristotle (384–322 BC), who relied much more on derivation of conclusions from first principles than on empirical experiments.

Second, the Industrial Revolution was not a complete break with the past, in the sense that new, practical inventions suddenly started materialising as never before. On the contrary, as an acceleration of a process which had been slowly gathering pace for hundreds of years, it advanced on a much more formidable basis than any that had existed in the ancient world. Along with the printing press, clocks, eyeglasses, lateen sails and other high-profile inventions, all of which were crucially significant, many other technological improvements had accumulated over the centuries or been imported from other parts of the world. Among them were the manufacture and use of gunpowder and paper, techniques for smelting many metals and processes for handling a wide variety of other materials, from glass and porcelain to sugar and tobacco.

Third, as well as technical knowledge, the Romans and Greeks lacked what may have been an equally crucial intellectual component: an adequate mathematical system. The whole of the ancient world used counting methods similar to Roman numerals. There was no true concept of zero. No calculations more complicated than an abacus could handle were possible. The universal modern numbering system, invented in India in the fourth century AD, took another 800 years to reach Europe via the Islamic Arab states. It was first publicised in the West by Leonardo Fibonacci (c.1170–c.1250), also known as Leonardo of Pisa, in his *Book of the Calculator* (1202), which rapidly led to the adoption of the so called Arabic – though originally Indian – notation first in Italy and then throughout Europe.[7] The new numbering system made it much easier to carry out relatively complicated calculations and allowed mathematics to develop far more complex ways of solving problems than had been possible previously. It is no coincidence that mathematics in Europe advanced rapidly once the new notation was introduced.

Fourth, another requirement for developing as complex a division of labour and, hence, as complicated an economy as the Industrial Revolution required was a highly sophisticated credit system. Until well into the Middle Ages, no true banks existed. Before then, merchants, who kept their stores of wealth in the form of gold coins, lent against their security. There were plenty of lenders and changers of money in the ancient world, many of them ex-slaves.[8] The inefficiency of the old mathematical systems, however, and the difficulties of record keeping before printing and paper manufacture were perfected both militated against sophisticated banking operations. The advent of the new mathematical notation, major improvements in paper production, the invention of double-entry bookkeeping and the subsequent rapid development of accountancy as a profession solved these problems. All added to the ease with which complicated records could be kept. The result was the appearance of true banks, first in Italy and then throughout Europe. Great banking dynasties established themselves – the Medici in Italy, the Fuggers in Germany – and many smaller-scale banking enterprises followed in their wake.

Fifth, even the development of banking proper left the economies of the time heavily dependent on adequate supplies of gold and silver for coinage to make the financial system operate. Financial instruments such as bills of exchange provided some leverage, but the scope was limited until the next major step forward, which was the development of paper currency. Although, again, there had been precedents in China, the issuing of notes began in the West at the end of the seventeenth century, led by the Bank of England, established in 1694 as a private corporation, a status it retained until it was nationalised in 1946.[9] Bank notes, not originally designed for general use, were issued in large denominations, mostly for financing trade. Essentially, they were bearer cheques, drawn in the UK on the Bank of England. Their impact, however, was to make it possible to separate still further the limited availability of gold and silver and the increasing amount of credit which the banking system as a whole could extend.

Sixth, even apart from the shortage of technical opportunities, the unconducive intellectual climate, the lack of appropriate methods of calculation and the undeveloped credit system, there may be an even more fundamental reason why the ancient world failed to industrialise. Its society was too regimented, too top-down, too stable and, despite the wrenching changes which periodically took place at the top, too stagnant and lacking in vigour to embark on the kind of free-thinking progress that the Industrial Revolution required. Technical progress may also have been held back by the widespread existence of slavery, which lowered the cost and social prestige of productive labour.[10] It is no coincidence that much of the early impetus in Britain and elsewhere came from dissident, independent people, who were excluded from the mainstream for religious or other reasons but were not precluded from trying new ways of doing things by convention or fear of retribution. The combination of their attitude of mind and the availability of the other components the ancient world lacked triggered industrialisation on an irreversible scale. It was to spread and transform the whole of the world.

Even if the ancient Mediterranean culture of the Greeks and Romans failed to give birth to industrialisation, it does not necessarily follow that it could not have begun elsewhere and before eighteenth-century Britain. Some of the factors required were available elsewhere; in some cases most of them. There were major unified states in China, India and the Islamic lands and, for a considerable period, in central Asia, too. There were also many smaller, reasonably stable polities, most with access to more technology than the ancient world possessed. In varying degrees they were in touch with at least some of the cultural and intellectual currents affecting Europe. The state which came closest to breaking through into industrialisation was fifteenth-century China, but the progress made was snuffed out by the country's leaders, who turned back to traditional ways.[11] India, on the other hand, showed no more signs of sustained industrial development than the Romans, despite the ability of the Mughal culture to build the Taj Mahal, its high point of excellence in design and execution. Nor were smaller nations elsewhere any better at producing sustained economic growth. It was in Europe, with its large number of relatively small states, that there began a cumulative increase in living standards, starting early in the second millennium, which eventuated in the Industrial Revolution and the transformation of humanity's prospects which it brought in train.

Early industrialisation in Europe

Thus, the Industrial Revolution, which began in Europe in the eighteenth century, rested on a foundation built over hundreds of years. Since at least the fourteenth century, Europe had seen a slow increase in output per head, set back from time to time by pestilence, bad government and war's devastation. Growth had come about partly from improved agriculture, partly from increased trade based on the availability of an adequate credit system, but mainly from the application of ideas, some based on novel technology, to a wide variety of production processes.

The advent of the printing press vastly reduced the cost of producing books and thus of disseminating knowledge. Developments in ship design and navigation greatly decreased the costs of trading and opened up access to large sections of the world previously unknown to Europeans. The resulting exchange of products enabled gains from never-before-available specialisation in the production of goods and agricultural products. The steady improvement in the working of metals provided the basis for the production of machinery. With the Renaissance and the Enlightenment came a ferment of ideas, some of which, fed through to industry, gave a clearer explanation of how industrial processes worked. Not least of these were advances in mathematics, mentioned previously, which made it easier for calculations relating to production processes to be done quickly and accurately. At the same time, the steady accumulation of practical knowledge acquired by increasingly skilled labour forces facilitated putting new ideas into operation.

During the eighteenth century, as the Industrial Revolution gathered pace faster in Britain than elsewhere, the British took over economic leadership from the Dutch. During the previous two centuries the Dutch had built up a formidable economy based on a combination of trade and commerce which provided them a higher standard of living than had ever been achieved elsewhere. As would happen frequently, however, the accumulation of wealth and financial power, which appeared to make the state strong, gradually became its undoing. As the Dutch economy's exchange rate rose, the comparatively higher costs of doing business in the Netherlands caused economic activity to drift away, not least to Britain.[12] The Dutch economy stagnated and lost its lead, though the reasons for this occurrence – essentially the same overvalued exchange-rate problem which became Britain's undoing in the nineteenth century and subsequently – were not appreciated then or for a long time to come.

In the meantime, Britain had moved further away from the medieval feudal system than most other countries in Europe. It had a more highly developed system of contract law and a generally less arbitrary system of government than were found on the continent. As a result of successfully developed trading patterns, it had a reasonably sophisticated banking system and accumulations of capital which could be mobilised for ventures involving risk. It had stable government. Above all, it had an entrepreneurial class, much of it, characteristically, excluded from mainstream political life as non-conformist, which was attracted to commerce and manufacturing. It also had major agricultural interests with much of the land owned by forward-looking landowners who were involved in exploiting new ideas in agricultural husbandry.

The Industrial Revolution, which got under way in textiles, pottery, mining and metalworking, was aided by improvements in transport such as the construction of canals. A combination of outworking and factories led to much increased output as production processes were broken into individual specialised functions, as Adam Smith (1723–1790) accurately noted in *The Wealth of Nations* (1776). This extremely influential book, published at a remarkably early stage of the Industrial Revolution, contained a powerful set of ideas about the changes taking place in the industrial and commercial worlds and about how government policy should be organised to take advantage of them. If the early pace in the development of economics set by Adam Smith had been maintained, the subsequent history of the world might have been very different.

Not only did the early Industrial Revolution involve rising living standards on average for the British people compared to those elsewhere, it also greatly enhanced Britain's power in the world. Britain was able to build and maintain a dominant navy and to deploy and finance the coalition of land forces which won them victory in the Napoleonic Wars. Thereafter, it enabled the British to control ever-increasing areas of the world until, three-quarters of the way through the nineteenth century, Britain ruled directly or indirectly about a quarter of the land surface of the globe. The accumulation of an empire on this scale undoubtedly provided Britain with ready access to raw materials and sources of supply of cheap food, as well as a partially protected export market. Earlier, profits from the slave trade had assisted the accumulation of capital, some of which helped to finance its Industrial Revolution.[13] The economy's relative decline as the territories Britain controlled grew in number, however, calls into question whether on the whole empire entailed a net benefit. Faster economic growth elsewhere strongly suggests that the effort and bias in policy involved in building up and running the British Empire and the cost of maintaining it were more than they were worth.

While France had a lower average standard of living than Britain in the early eighteenth century,[14] many of the other circumstances needed to get industry moving there were also in place. The French, however, were much slower to take advantage of new opportunities available in manufacturing. Partly this was the result of the arbitrary characteristics of the ancien régime, which lacked the contract legal system introduced shortly after the French Revolution (1789).[15] Partly it was a matter of social pressures, related to the sense of values of the pre-revolutionary period, which held industry and commerce in relatively low esteem. As a result, French industry tended to concentrate on the manufacture of individually produced items, some of them widely recognised as exceptionally high in quality, rather than move to mass production methods. French furniture, tapestries, china and jewellery were internationally renowned, but the cottage industry techniques used for producing them are not the stuff of which industrial revolutions are made. Germany also suffered from disadvantages, many of them similar to those in France, compounded by its patchwork of small states, each with its own tariff and economic policies. Europe's southern nations – Spain, Portugal, Italy and Greece – all much poorer, and some not yet united were in a weaker position to industrialise and remained so for a century or more. The Netherlands, which had grown rich during the eighteenth century, faltered as its trading and financial success undermined its domestic industry – a story to be repeated many times in the years to come. It was therefore Britain which made the running for a long time into the nineteenth century.

Nineteenth-Century Europe

Controversy over the value of the currency has a long history in Britain; the outcomes of policy disputes concerning it have heavily coloured the course of events. The conclusions reached not only had an impact on the policy decisions taken at the time but also framed how politicians, public opinion and the academic world thought about economic policy.

An important early case took place before the Industrial Revolution had really begun. During the reign (1689–1702) of William III (1650–1702), Britain's silver coinage had been debased by clipping.[16] The effect was to devalue the clipped silver currency in relation to gold. As a result, by 1695 the gold guinea, originally worth 20 shillings, was worth 30. Much of the era's international trade was conducted in silver shillings. What should be done? Let the silver coinage's value remain at 30 shillings to the guinea, or drive it up to 20? Leading contestants in the dispute were Sir Isaac Newton (1642–1727) for the former view and the philosopher John Locke (1632–1704) for the latter. The king accepted Locke's deflationary advice – a dismal and ominous portent for the future. The consequences, as Newton predicted, were falling prices and depressed business conditions. Newton nevertheless became Master of the Mint. In 1711 he fixed the price of the pound at £3 17s 9d per ounce of gold. Apart from suspensions during and after the Napoleonic Wars and World War I and two short breaks during the nineteenth century, caused by temporary financial panics, this parity remained intact until 1931.

The next major controversy over macroeconomic policy took place towards the end of the Napoleonic Wars. The strain imposed on the British economy during the long wartime period, stretching almost without a break from 1793 to 1815, had stimulated output. The economy was much larger and more productive at the end of the wars than it had been at their start. The high level of demand had, however, led to substantial inflation, which had nearly doubled the price level during the war years. Britain had gone off the gold standard in 1797 because the country banks of the time could not meet the demand for cash caused by the threat of an invasion. Too many holders of banknotes wished to change them into gold. The banks were therefore freed to increase the note issue without gold backing, in response to the increase in government borrowing to finance the wars, as well as the additional demand for money resulting from expanding national output. By 1810 prices had risen an estimated 76 per cent,[17] compared with 1790, and this rise was reflected in the price of gold, which had risen proportionately.

Had prices risen because the money supply had been increased? Or was extra money required to accommodate the growing need for cash as prices rose and the economy became larger, with the fundamental causes of inflation lying elsewhere? This controversy – still central to economic policy formulation – was the key issue addressed by the *Report from the Select Committee on the High Price of Gold Bullion* (1810), which set out the arguments between the 'currency school' and the 'banking school'. The currency school maintained that under a 'purely metallic standard', any loss of gold to or influx of gold from other countries would produce an immediate and automatic decrease or increase in the amount of money in circulation. The resulting rigid control of the money supply would provide the discipline to keep price rises at bay. With a mixed currency of metal and paper, however, this system could not operate satisfactorily unless it was managed as precisely as if it depended on the amount of gold backing the currency. Any deviation from this principle, it was averred, would lead to inflation.

The banking school, on the other hand, denied that a purely gold-based currency would operate in the manner the currency school claimed. Because of hoarding and other uses to which gold could be put, it was far from clear that the amount available to back the currency was as constant as the currency school claimed, and it was further contended that the currency school greatly overestimated the risks involved in expanding paper money. The banking school believed that the need for prudence in the process of competitive banking would exercise a necessary restraint on the issue of paper money. This approach would have led to a much more accommodating monetary stance and a lower exchange rate for sterling, but it was not to be. The committee came down in favour of the currency principle by advocating a return to the gold standard at the 1797 parity, despite the increase in prices which had taken place. The majority concluded that the price rises during the wars had come about because monetary discipline had slipped and that the only way to secure future financial stability was to get the pound back to where it had been previously in terms of its relation to gold. The views which prevailed in this report, setting as they did the tone of British financial policy for many years to come, were to have a profound impact on Britain's economic history to the present day.

Despite the reservations of the committee minority, which included David Ricardo (1772–1823), sterling was restored to its pre-war parity against gold when the Napoleonic Wars ended. This objective was achieved by methods with an all-too-familiar ring. The money supply was reduced, interest rates were raised and the pound strengthened against foreign currencies which had mostly left their parities against gold or silver where they were at the end of the Napoleonic Wars. It took six years (1815–21) to force wages and prices down sufficiently to enable cash payments in gold at the pre-war parity to be resumed. In consequence, there was a sharp depression as the post-war boom broke, leading to business failures, falling living standards, rising unemployment and great hardship for working people. Opposition culminated in a riot in Manchester in 1819 – Peterloo – which was broken up by a local cavalry force, reviving echoes of the battle which had brought the Napoleonic Wars to a successful end only four years previously. Trade unions were made illegal by the repressive Six Acts, passed into law at the end of 1819.[18] The final victory of the currency school, easily recognised as having views close to those of modern monetarists, was the Bank Charter Act (1844), which locked the pound into its high value measured in gold, a value finally abandoned only in 1931.

The resulting high cost of producing goods and services, compared with the rest of Europe, did not, however, hold back the British economy for long. During the first half of the nineteenth century, Britain was the only rapidly industrialising country. Thus, the costs of goods produced there fell rapidly compared with those elsewhere in Europe, making them very competitive despite the relatively high gold parity for sterling inherited from the outcome of the banking controversy. The British economy expanded by 2.8 per cent per annum on average from 1820 to 1851, when the Great Exhibition was held in London, marking the peak of British pre-eminence. From 1851 to 1871 growth slowed to 2.3 per cent.[19] Even so, the cumulative increase in wealth and the standard of living was without parallel anywhere, except Australia, New Zealand and, especially, the United States, far away on the other side of the Atlantic and heavily protected by tariffs, where high rates of growth were also being achieved.

Increasing confidence in its industrial capacity strengthened the case in Britain for trade liberalisation. The Industrial Revolution had started behind substantial tariff barriers, themselves a legacy of the mercantilist policies of self-sufficiency against which Adam Smith had preached in *The Wealth of Nations*. As an expanding population pressed the domestically produced food supply, however, necessitating increased imports of corn and other foodstuffs, the case for keeping down the cost of living by removing import tariffs and quotas became stronger. Free trade arguments were extended to manufactured goods, leading to the trade treaties negotiated in the 1840s and 1850s. By 1860 dutiable items coming in to Britain numbered only 48. By 1882 only 12 imported articles were taxed, and these purely for revenue-raising purposes.[20]

Unilateral free trade, however, acts like a revaluation of the currency: it makes imports relatively cheaper than exports. Adopting free trade policies, therefore, had the same effect as raising the sterling exchange rate, which was already very high. Free trade in consequence also contributed to Britain's undoing as the nineteenth century wore on. All over Europe, particularly in France, Germany and the Benelux countries, British manufacturing techniques began to be copied. The initial impulse came primarily from railways, construction of which got under way on a substantial scale all over Europe from the 1840s and 1850s onwards. This necessitated major developments in civil engineering and large investments in production facilities capable of turning out thousands of kilometres of rail, relatively sophisticated rolling stock and complex signalling equipment. In Britain all these developments had been financed by the private sector, but in France and Germany the state was heavily involved in railway construction from the outset, underwriting a considerable proportion of the high risks involved. Differing perceptions across Europe about the role of the state vis-à-vis the private sector have a long history.

British production techniques were soon copied in railways and in virtually all other fields. Other forms of communication were constructed, such as canals, which already had a long history in Britain. Mass production of textiles followed, initially in north-east France but soon throughout Europe. Iron and steel output – greatly stimulated by the development of railways but also providing the basis for the production of metal goods for a wide range of purposes – grew rapidly, particularly in Germany. The output of steel trebled there between 1840 and 1860 and again between 1860 and 1880.[21] Europe's economies became better able to compete with Britain for other reasons, too. Germany was united – first loosely under the *Zollverein* of 1834, later more tightly under Otto von Bismarck (1815–98), once Prussia secured its position of leadership. Everywhere – much more rapidly in some places than others – came improvements in education, the legal system, the organisation of the professions and the training of skilled workforces.

A major turning point came in the 1870s, as the worldwide consumer and investment boom caused by the American Civil War and the Franco-Prussian conflict collapsed when the wars ended, with a major fall in demand for armaments and a slowdown in railway building. For the first time, as Britain felt the full blast of foreign competition, its lead in industrial output was seriously threatened. The value of British exports fell from £256 million in 1872 to £192 million in 1879. Lower prices compensated in volume terms for much of this fall but not all. The 1872 export figure in money terms was not exceeded until 1890. As for manufactures, the ground lost was not recovered in terms of value until 1903, over 30 years later.[22] The British economy's growth rate stabilised at 2.0 per cent per annum for the last quarter of the nineteenth century. From 1870 to 1900 the economy in Germany grew by 125 per cent, in the Netherlands by 96 per cent, in Britain by 85 per cent, in Belgium by 82 per cent and in France by 56 per cent.[23]

The sources of increases in output differed between France and Britain, which were falling back, and Germany and other countries, which were pulling ahead. In Britain particularly, more and more investment went abroad. In the slower-growing economies a rising percentage of investment went into housing and infrastructure, and a relatively low proportion into industry. Total investment as a percentage of GDP in these countries fell or remained static. Where investments were made in industry, more went into widening rather than deepening the industrial structure. In Britain there was a vast expansion of the cotton industry and coal mining. Both were labour intensive, but where large additional productivity gains were difficult to achieve.

In Germany and, to a lesser extent, elsewhere on the continent, these trends were reversed. A higher proportion of investment went into new industries, such as the production of dyes and chemicals, sophisticated metal products and, later, motor vehicles and electrical goods. The significance of these industries lay in their scope for increased output and improved productivity. It was then much greater than in the industries to which Britain – trapped by the strength of sterling within the gold standard system – was moving. The circumstances which had given Britain the advantage in the early part of the nineteenth century were reversed. Germany and the Netherlands now had more competitive exports and were less prone to import penetration because of the strength of local manufactures and the protection they enjoyed. Influenced by Friedrich List (1789–1846), particularly by his *Das nationale System der politischen Oekonomie* (1837), the continental economies were much more willing to use tariffs to protect their rising industries. This made sense partly because they were much more nearly self-sufficient in foodstuff production so that free trade had a less general attraction. They could concentrate production where the growth prospects were highest, and they were in a position to reinvest productively a greater proportion of their national incomes in their own economies.

Thus, by the start of World War I, much of the income-per-head gap between Britain and the rest of north-west Europe had closed. Whereas in 1850 income per head had been twice as high in Britain as in the most advanced parts of the Continent, by 1914 the difference was only about a quarter.[24] Furthermore, Germany's industrial capacity was in many respects well ahead of Britain's. Its steel output had overtaken Britain's in the 1890s. By 1910 Britain was producing 6.5 million tons of steel per year, but Germany was producing 13 million.[25] Just before the war began, Germany had twice as many kilometres of rail track as Britain and generated six times as much electricity.[26] The high comparative value of sterling to the currencies of the Britain's competitors ensured that the price paid for this privilege – slower growth – was very high.

Economic power was seeping away from Britain, and with it the capacity of the British to continue dominating the world as they had for the previous hundred years. Between 1870 and 1913 the population in Germany grew a third faster than it did in Britain,[27] further strengthening Germany's military position. Rivalry between the great powers increased, and the Great War, with all its disastrous consequences for the world economy, came closer.

The US economy to World War I

When the first settlers arrived in North America from Europe, they brought with them immeasurable advantages over the indigenous population. The early colonists were by all historical standards exceptionally well endowed with their European legacy when they reached their destination, as indeed were many of those who followed them. Nevertheless, for a great many years the life of settlers in the USA was an arduous one. The country was enormous, and communications extremely primitive. Internal transport was difficult and expensive and with seaborne traffic the only practical solution to the movement of goods and people, there was a strong incentive for developing efficient sailing ships. The population was overwhelmingly rural. Even as late as 1790, when it totalled about 3.9 million, of whom almost 700,000 were slaves, only seven towns had a population over 5,000 and only twelve had over 2,500. In these circumstances, with internal transport problems severely limiting the size of the potential market, manufacturing on anything but the smallest of scales was impractical,. Almost all US export trade was in raw materials, primarily cotton, tobacco and wheat flour.[28]

The Declaration of Independence (1776), followed shortly by the Napoleonic Wars, in which the USA did not directly participate, and then the 1812 war with Britain, produced both opportunities and disadvantages. Trade was disrupted, but domestic manufacturing was encouraged, and exports grew dramatically, if erratically. Overall, the value of exports, which had been $20 million in 1790, grew to $52 million by 1815, while imports rose from $24 million to $85 million.[29] Part of the growth in output was attributable to the rapidly rising population, which had reached 7.2 million by 1810 and 9.6 million by 1820. But the really explosive US population growth started about 1830, when it was almost 13 million. By 1860 it was 31 million. Immigration peaked during this period in 1854, when 428,000 people moved to the USA.[30]

As early as 1820, the USA was among the richest countries in the world, judged by GDP per capita. Estimates show its living standard was then just over 25 per cent below Britain's, a little under 20 per cent behind those of the Dutch and Australians and about on a par with those of Austria, Belgium, Denmark, France and Sweden. By 1850 Britain was still well ahead of the USA, but the gap was closing.[31] The disruption of the Civil War slowed growth for a few years, but the US rate was poised for the rapid increase in output achieved between 1870 and 1913. During the 50-year period 1820–70, the US economy grew much faster than those on the other side of the Atlantic. Between 1820 and 1850 its cumulative growth was 4.2 per cent per annum, although the increase in output per head was much lower, 1.3 per cent, close to the Britain's 1.25 per cent for the period. This was now to change. During the 43 years from 1870 to 1913, the US economy's annual cumulative growth rate was 4.3 per cent. Allowing for annual compound population growth of 2.1 per cent, US GDP per head rose by 2.2 per cent per annum.[32]

A differential in growth rates either in GDP or GDP per head of 1 or 2 per cent per annum has a huge cumulative effect over a period such as the 43 years from 1870 to 1913. If two economies start at the same size at the start of a period this long, one growing 2 per cent faster per annum than its rival will be 134 per cent larger 43 years later. Even if the differential is only 1 per cent, it will be 53 per cent bigger at the period's end. The results of the differential growth rates of the USA and most of Europe in the late nineteenth and early twentieth centuries – reflected, of course, in what is happening now between West and East – presaged a seismic shift in world power. By 1913 the USA had overtaken Britain in living standards and left the rest of Europe well behind. Only Australia and New Zealand, with much smaller populations and GDPs, were still ahead. By this time the USA had both a high GDP per head and a large population to go with it. By 1890 the US population was 63 million; by 1913 it was 98 million.[33] The US economy was by then well over twice the size of its nearest rival, Britain, and more than four times that of Germany. Japan, which had grown by a respectable 2.8 per cent per annum during the previous three decades, had an economy only about 13 per cent of the US size in 1913.[34]

During the late 1800s and the early 1900s, gross domestic investment as a proportion of GDP was much higher in the USA than in other countries. It averaged nearly 20 per cent of GDP for the whole period, compared with about 12 per cent for Britain and 15 per cent for France.[35] Achieving a high investment ratio was as important in the nineteenth century as it is now. All these factors helped, but the key figures then, as now, were less expansion of the total economy than output per head. As the figures above show, large population increases kept American living standards growing much more slowly than the economy as a whole during the decades before World War I. It is noteworthy that Sweden and Denmark increased their GDP per head faster than the USA did over this period.[36]

Overall US growth in the nineteenth century was nevertheless unprecedented. By 1900 the American economy was about 25 times larger than it had been in 1820. By 1980, another 80 years later, the increase was only a little over 13 times the 1900 figure.[37] The key period for expansion of the US economy, however, started in the decade before the Civil War, when mechanisation and industrialisation really hit their stride. From 1830 to the beginning of 1865, manufacturing output increased nearly tenfold, while the population rose to about three times its 1830 figure. In the decade before the Civil War began, steam engine and machinery output increased by 66 per cent, cotton textiles by 77 per cent, railroad production by 100 per cent, and hosiery goods by 608 per cent. When Reconstruction got under way and new technologies that improved communications and the quality of manufactures were exploited, the economy took off. The US gross stock of machinery and equipment increased by almost 400 per cent between 1870 and 1890; by 1913 it had nearly trebled again.[38]

It is no coincidence that the advent of large-scale increases in industrial output triggered the rise in the US growth rate. The proportion of US GDP deriving from industry was on a strong upward trend throughout the nineteenth century. It employed 15 per cent of the labour force in 1820, 24 per cent in 1870, and 30 per cent by 1913.[39] The USA also used its investment more efficiently than the average, especially towards the end of the nineteenth century and the start of the twentieth, thereby gaining an important additional advantage.[40] This is still a characteristic of the US economy, although the proportion of its output derived from manufacturing is now much lower than it was, down to about 11 per cent in 2011 from the 27 per cent average achieved in the post-World War II era.[41]

It is often alleged that a stable financial environment is the key to economic growth and that low interest rates and low inflation are required to ensure high investment levels and output increases. It is hard to square this view of the world with the experience of the US economy in the nineteenth century, for most of which the USA had no central bank. The charter of the First Bank of the United States, which expired in 1811, was not renewed by the Jeffersonians then in power. The Second Bank of the United States, established in 1816, was shut down shortly after the re-election in 1832 of Andrew Jackson (1767–1845), who bitterly opposed its existence.[42] Until the establishment of the Federal Reserve system in 1913, there was no central control of the US money supply. Credit creation was in the hands of thousands of banks, spread all over the country, many of them poorly run, under-capitalised, prone to speculation and liable to fail.

It is hardly surprising that, in these circumstances, US interest rates, prices and credit availability gyrated from boom to bust all through the nineteenth century. In 1837, four years after the abolition of the Second Bank of the United States, came the most serious depression the USA had experienced, in some ways a crash worse than that of 1929. Prices fell 40 per cent between 1838 and 1843, railroad construction declined by almost 70 per cent and canal building by 90 per cent. Large-scale unemployment developed, and serious food riots broke out in New York City. The next upswing started in 1844, the next downturn in 1856 lasting until 1862. This pattern was to be repeated throughout the nineteenth century, accompanied every time there was a fall in economic activity by bank closures, bankruptcies and widespread defaults.[43]

Nor was the price level at all stable during the nineteenth century. Between 1815 and 1850, the wholesale price level fell by 50 per cent, with substantial fluctuations in intervening years. It rose by 50 per cent during the 1860s, peaking in 1866 because of the Civil War, with the impact of the California gold rush on the money supply causing much of the underlying inflation. Between 1848 and 1858 California produced $550 million worth of gold – 45 per cent of world output between 1851 and 1855.[44] After 1870 prices fell until, by 1900, they were 40 per cent lower than in 1870. They climbed again about 25 per cent in the years to 1913, mainly because the development of the cyanide process for extracting gold in South Africa led to another major increase in the world's monetary base, inflating the money supply and allowing prices to rise.[45]

Since World War II, promoting freer trade has been a major plank of US policy, in sharp contrast to the high tariff protection promoted by successive nineteenth-century administrations. Some import duties were imposed partly for revenue-raising purposes, as they were the major source of government income at the time, but industrial protection was also a factor from the beginning. The tariff of 1816 imposed duties of 20 to 25 per cent on manufactured goods and 15 to 20 per cent on raw materials.[46] Thereafter the tariff level fluctuated, with the trade cycle, as always, playing a major role. The panic of 1837 stimulated a new wave of protectionism, as American industrialists blamed high unemployment on cheap imported goods. The major shift to a much more protectionist policy came in 1861 with the Morrill Tariff, designed to make the importation of most mass-produced goods into the USA completely uneconomic. Import duties were not to be lowered again until 1913, under Woodrow Wilson (1856–1924), although even then they still stood at about 25 per cent. Wool, sugar, iron and steel, however, were added to the free list.[47]

A distinguishing feature of the US economy has always been the low proportion, by international standards, of US GDP involved in foreign trade. Exports averaged about 11.5 per cent of GDP during the period just before World War I, compared with 13.0 per cent now. Imports ran then under 8 per cent,[48] compared with 16.2 per cent at present.[49] Part of the reason for these relatively low ratios has always been the sheer size of the country and its ability to supply a high proportion of its needs from domestic sources. There is little doubt, however, that in the circumstances of the years up to 1913, the high tariff barrier helped US manufacturing industries develop unhampered by foreign competition. Goods which might have been purchased from Europe were produced at home. The high level of demand, albeit subject to severe fluctuations, generated by the unregulated credit and banking system, provided opportunities US manufacturers were quick to seize. Under the gold standard régime, which the USA joined in 1879,[50] when bimetallism was abandoned, it would have been difficult for it to have lowered its prices internationally sufficiently to hold off growing import penetration. The competitiveness of European exports at the time is amply demonstrated by the high proportion of their output which the European economies were capable of selling overseas during the nineteenth century and early twentieth. In 1900 about 25 per cent of all British GDP was exported and about 16 per cent of all of Germany's. Even in 1913 Britain was still exporting twice the value of goods and services exported by the USA, although its economy was almost 60 per cent smaller.[51]

The lessons to be learnt from the USA's economic history up to 1913 are as relevant now as they were then. If the economy is to grow fast, advantage needs to be taken of the ability of industry, particularly manufacturing, to generate high rates of output growth. By 1870 a quarter of the US GDP came from industry; by 1913 almost 30 per cent.[52] The increase in productivity in manufacturing – and agriculture – during this period was about 50 per cent higher than in the service sector – a ratio which has widened since then.[53] As the proportion of the US economy devoted to manufacturing rose, so did growth increase where it really counts: not in the size of national income, but in output per head of the population, which is what determines the standard of living.

Lessons from the gold standard era

Between 1820 and 1913, economic output is estimated to have risen in the 56 major economies of the world by just over 300 per cent, or cumulatively by 1.5 per cent per annum. The rise in output per head was 140 per cent, a little under 1 per cent per year.[54] These were much greater increases than had ever been seen on a wide scale in world history, demonstrating conclusively the immense power of the Industrial Revolution to change the prospects for humanity.

Could these ratios have been larger? Could the techniques used to garner the increased output obtainable from industrialisation have been spread significantly more widely, more intensively, more quickly than they were? In theory, no doubt they could have been, although there were many practical obstacles. In the first place, even the most perspicacious observers, such as Adam Smith, needed some time to realise what a momentous change in production methods was taking place. Second, the diffusion of knowledge about the Industrial Revolution did in fact spread rapidly, partly because of the popularity and success of *The Wealth of Nations*. Jean-Baptiste Say (1767–1832) published his own major work, *Traité d'économie politique* (1803), refining and extending Smith's work. Translations into languages other than French increased its influence. There was also a stream of visitors from both home and abroad to British factories, supplemented by the publication of learned and practical journals and exchanges of personnel and opinions in the relatively liberal world of the time.

The major practical constraints on spreading the use of the new industrial processes, then mostly being discovered in Britain, were those which had impeded the Industrial Revolution's start in other countries in the first place. Widely prevailing disparaging attitudes to industry, the disruption caused by wars – particularly the Napoleonic Wars, which lasted nearly a quarter of a century – the lack of stable government and enforceable contract law in many countries and inadequate capital and credit facilities were major obstacles. There was also a lengthy catch-up process which had to take place, even when copying of British techniques on a substantial scale began to happen. It took time to formulate plans, arrange finance, find and train suitable staff and make the necessary physical investments even when the will to do so had been established. Nor can an industrial base be created overnight. A process of accumulation has to take place, and the ability to move ahead often depends on accomplishing previous steps successfully. Expansion from a small or almost non-existent base, which cannot be achieved even in the most favourable circumstances at more than a manageable pace, necessarily constrains the size of the achievable total output for a long way ahead.

The more challenging question about the nineteenth century – indeed, the one to follow – is whether, despite all the delays inevitably surrounding the adoption of new ways of organising production, different institutional developments and economic policies might have speeded the process of diffusion and development, particularly since many of the basic constraints inhibiting progress had already been overcome. Could countries such as Britain, which slowed down, have maintained momentum and grown faster? If different economic policies, particularly those concerned with macroeconomics, had been adopted, would it have made a major difference?

The ideas set out in earlier chapters provide a framework for answering this question. They certainly suggest that significant and clearly identifiable policy mistakes were made in Britain. The re-establishment after 1815 of the pre-Napoleonic parity between sterling and gold not only severely depressed output for five or six years but also, much more seriously, locked Britain into a relatively high cost base compared with that potentially available to other countries when they started to industrialise. When Britain had world markets substantially to itself, this was not of crucial significance, but once foreign competition hit its stride, British vulnerability became all too evident. The adoption of free trade, by effectively revaluing sterling still further, then made a bad situation worse, as Britain lowered tariffs while competitors raised them.

Other countries were able to expand their economies largely unconstrained by foreign competition or balance of payments problems, but Britain was unable to do so. The British economy was therefore the major loser from inappropriate macroeconomic policies in the nineteenth century. Why did Britain allow this to happen? Partly, because the reasons for Britain's relative decline were not understood, there was no clearly articulated policy available for reversing it. Economic policy followed the classical precepts laid down by John Stuart Mill (1806–73). Building on the work of his predecessors in the same tradition, Mill's emphasis was heavily orientated to a minimalist role for the state, with low taxation and public expenditure, financial stability in so far as it could be secured by clearly defined central bank operations and free trade, with the maintenance of the gold standard as the underlying stabiliser. This mixture of policies suited well the growing strength and preponderance of the financial interests in Britain, exemplified pre-eminently by the City of London. In these circumstances there was no place for a determined and well-formulated series of policies to keep the British economy on a high growth track, although there was mounting concern about the extent to which Britain was falling behind its competitors. *The Final Report of the Royal Commission on Depression of Trade and Industry* (1887) is full of agonised concern about the state of the economy. In the end, however, there was little serious challenge to the conventional views of the time, and the result was that those with accumulated wealth dominated the way the economy was run, as against those striving to create new industries. With sterling too strong, imports were encouraged and domestic production discouraged. Too much investment went abroad. Too few talented people went into industry and commerce. Too many went into the professions, administering an empire acquired almost entirely as a result of Britain's earlier economic pre-eminence, and into academic life, the civil service, the church – anything, it seemed, so they could avoid industry and trade.

If an effective challenge to the policy status quo was to come from anywhere, it would have had to come from the intellectual world, but it was not to be. Mill and other mainstream thinkers and writers of the time, amplifying and endorsing the classical economic approach, built on a tradition with a heavy emphasis on markets being self-regulating and the role of the state being as non-intrusive as possible. Say's Law, propounded by the same Jean-Baptiste Say who had publicised *The Wealth of Nations*, held that a deficiency in demand was impossible, since the income from the sales of all the goods and services which were produced necessarily generated exactly enough expenditure to purchase all of them. This view, not seriously challenged until the advent of John Maynard Keynes (1883–1946), ruled out the possibility of any kind of systematic demand management. The most significant challenge to orthodoxy which did materialise, from Karl Marx (1818–1883), was designed, not to make the capitalist system work better, but to get rid of it altogether. The major nineteenth-century innovations in economics, from writers such as Auguste Walras (1801–66), William Stanley Jevons (1835–82), and Alfred Marshall (1842–1924), were mainly in microeconomics. They were primarily concerned with the formation of prices and marginal utility rather than macroeconomic issues, which generated little interest. Britain and the world in general paid a heavy price for this trend in intellectual fashion.

7

International Turmoil: 1914–45

World War I began as the result of a network of treaty obligations being called into play following the assassination of Archduke Franz Ferdinand (1863–1914) in Sarajevo on 28 June 1914.[1] Although few had anticipated the outbreak of war, its advent was greeted with a surprising amount of enthusiasm. Huge crowds turned out in Berlin, Paris, Petrograd (Saint Petersburg), London and Vienna, clamouring for military action.[2] By 1945 all such enthusiasm for war had been spent. Two ruinous conflicts had cost millions of lives, caused untold damage and set back the advance of living standards by an incalculable amount. Not only, however, had immense human and physical damage been done during the periods of open warfare. In addition, the network of international trading and financial arrangements which had allowed the world economy to function reasonably smoothly during the nineteenth century and the early years of the twentieth was catastrophically disrupted by the impact of World War I. The result was a period great instability and lost opportunities between the wars, as fragile booms in the 1920s collapsed into the worldwide slump of the early 1930s. Thereafter, there were sharp divergences, as some economies continued to decline while others made remarkable recoveries.

Throughout the period the record of most of those responsible for economic policy was confused and inadequate. The near-universal consensus among political and intellectual leaders up to the outbreak of World War I was that the state should see its role as holding the ring rather than being a major player. Clearly, however, this stance made no sense at all at a time of total war. Within a very short time, therefore, in all the belligerent economies, the proportion of output which went through the government's hands rose dramatically. In Britain it increased from 15 per cent in 1913 to an astonishing 69 per cent in

1917;[3] similar rises were seen in France and Germany. In the USA the peak, 36 per cent in 1918, was considerably lower, but even so it represented a dramatic change from pre-war days.[4] The outcome was that governments in all the countries involved in the war were presented with problems for which they were singularly ill prepared. While mobilising to produce vast quantities of guns, ships, aircraft and munitions and recruiting large numbers of people to be under arms was found to be problematic but achievable, securing these objectives without overstretching and destabilising the economy proved much more difficult. Even in the relatively understretched USA, prices rose by about 50 per cent between 1915 and 1918, but inflation's effect was felt much less there during the war than it was elsewhere. Britain's price level rose nearly 80 per cent, France's doubled and Germany's increased by 200 per cent.[5]

More than anything else, the disruption to the rough balance of competitiveness between the pre-World War I economies turned out to be the bane of the interwar period, compounded by the impact of the insistence by the victorious powers of payments of reparations by Germany, the major belligerent on the losing side. World total demand was depressed by the policies pursued by countries such as Britain, which, determined to restore sterling's pre-war gold parity, was willing to go through a period of severe deflation to do so. In Germany, until the advent of the Nazi regime, with very different ideas about how the economy should be run, a similarly cautious attempt was made to follow classical economic remedies, culminating in the cuts to unemployment benefit which, as much as anything else, led to Adolf Hitler (1889–1945) becoming Chancellor in 1933. In the United States, during the 1920s the economy was unconstrained by the balance of payments problems and the apparent need for deflation which afflicted most of Europe. The result was a major boom, culminating in a bout of speculation which left the banking and financial system heavily exposed to a downturn. When this came, the authorities were completely unprepared to deal with it. As elsewhere, vain attempts to balance a rapidly deteriorating fiscal position simply made an already catastrophic situation worse.

While the world's economies were languishing, work was being done by John Maynard Keynes and others which would lead, at least for a while, to much more stable conditions after World War II. The influence of those who realised that Say's Law was not correct and that it was possible for economies to suffer from insufficient total demand for years on end, however, was only marginal between the wars. Their thinking had some impact in Britain, Sweden and the USA, particularly on some of those involved in the New Deal, but only to a limited degree. Keynes's major influence on policy was to come later, as the institutions for the post-World War II period were established, although he also had a substantial impact on the way in which World War II was financed in Britain.

By the time of World War II, therefore, much had been learnt about how to control and finance total mobilisation, and inflation in all the main belligerent countries was less severe than it had been during World War I. Prices nevertheless rose steeply in those countries defeated and occupied during the war and in those on the losing side at the war's end. At the same time, there were a number of major advances in thinking about how to structure the post-war world, laying the foundation for the great advances in living standards in much of the world during the 1950s and 1960s. The period from the 1970s onwards, however, as world growth rates declined sharply, showed that still more needed to be done to develop policies which would combine reasonable rates of economic growth with other economic objectives, particularly fairly low rates of inflation.

The period 1914–45 is therefore an exceptionally interesting and important one, in terms of the impact it had on economic and political history and the development of ideas. Much was lost in terms of damage, foreshortened lives, unemployment, output foregone and the production of destructive military equipment, but important ground was gained in bettering understanding of some key requirements for improved economic management.

Europe's disastrous years

World War I was a catastrophe for Europe in every way. There was huge loss of life and immense material destruction. Even worse, the relatively stable and secure social and economic systems developed during the nineteenth century, which had stood Europe and the world as a whole in good stead, were disrupted, dislocated and dismembered. It took the passage of three decades and another world war before anything resembling the peace, prosperity and security of pre-World War I Europe would be re-established.

Approximately 10 million lives were lost prematurely in Europe as a result of World War I,[6] and a substantial additional number, harder to quantify, in the influenza epidemics which struck down a weakened population in the war's immediate aftermath. The damage to towns and factories, although much less than that in World War II, was still considerable. The national incomes of the countries of western Europe fell precipitously from the years just before World War I through the early years after, when the demand for war-orientated product fell away. France's industrial production dropped by over 40 per cent between 1913 and 1919, partly from the war's disruption and damage, partly from the post-war slump.[7] It was 1927 before German GDP rose again to its 1913 level.[8] Britain did less badly, its GDP staying more or less constant during the war, although it fell heavily, about 20 per cent, just after hostilities ended.[9]

Economic instability in Europe was greatly compounded by the Treaty of Versailles, negotiated between the victorious powers and the humiliated Germans. The Americans, who came into the war in 1917, insisted on repayment of the large debts run up by Britain and France for war supplies. Britain and France, in turn, required huge reparations of Germany, partly to pay the Americans and partly on their own account. None of these arrangements, negotiated by political leaders under immense pressure from electorates much more interested in settling old scores than facing new realities, bore any relationship to the Germans' ability to make the payments. Leaving aside the extent to which their economy was already languishing from the damage done by the war, the only feasible way for the Germans to pay the reparation bill was to run a very large export surplus. In the fragile state of the 1920s world economy, no country was prepared to tolerate a large German trade surplus, even if it could have been achieved. Payment of reparations on the scale demanded, whatever its electoral appeal or the US requirement that its debts be settled, was never a remotely realistic prospect.

Attempts to extract reparations, however, compounded with post-war political and economic disruption, caused havoc in Germany. The government was unable to produce sufficient tax revenue to meet the obligations it had undertaken to fulfil. It therefore resorted to the printing presses to create the money it could not otherwise raise. The result was the German inflation of 1923, which ended in hyperinflation and total collapse of the currency's value.[10] The Reichsmark had already lost two-thirds its value during World War I.[11] Now all those with savings in cash lost everything. This experience understandably scarred the German attitude to inflation and monetary rectitude, with reverberations still felt today.

Gradually, however, towards the end of the 1920s, some measure of normality began to reassert itself. There was a significant recovery in France, where industrial output doubled between the post-war low of 1921 and 1928, although even in 1928 it was only 10 per cent higher than it had been in 1913.[12] In Germany, too, industrial production also rose in the late 1920s, peaking in 1929 about 20 per cent higher than it had been in 1913; its GDP grew cumulatively between 1925 and 1929 by a respectable 2.9 per cent per annum.[13] In Germany in particular, however, the recovery was fragile. It depended heavily on large loans from abroad, especially the United States, to enable reparation payments to continue at the scaled-down rate agreed by the Young Plan in 1929, replacing the much harsher 1924 Dawes Plan. Nevertheless, in the late 1920s Germany's unemployment was falling and its living standards were slowly rising.

Britain remained depressed, mainly because of a repetition of what had taken place after the Napoleonic Wars. The link between the pound and gold had been suspended at the outbreak of World War I, and pressure on the economy during the war had led to considerable price inflation. Nevertheless, on the recommendation of the Cunliffe Committee, in 1918 it was decided to restore the gold value of the pound to the parity, $4.86, it had enjoyed in 1914. Attaining this objective meant forcing down costs in Britain, by imposing severely deflationary policies. The reductions achieved, particularly in labour costs, were nothing like sufficient, however, to restore Britain to a competitive position at the target parity. As a result, Britain spent the whole of the 1920s in an all-too-wearisomely familiar position, suffering from a lack of competitiveness both at home and abroad that led inevitably to domestic deflation and slow growth in output and living standards.

Europe therefore appeared to be very poorly placed to weather the depression which followed, beginning with the collapse of the US stock market in 1929. The most immediate effect of the American slump on Europe was the drying up of the flow of loans from the USA to Germany, plunging the German economy into a crisis of the same order of magnitude as the United States had experienced. Between 1929 and 1932 German GDP fell by almost a quarter. Industrial production dropped by nearly 40 per cent.[14] Unemployment, already at 9.3 per cent in 1929, rose to over 30 per cent of the labour force by 1932.[15] During this year it averaged 5.5 million, peaking at 6 million. In Britain GDP fell but less than in the USA and Germany. Industrial production dropped by 5 per cent, but unemployment, already 7.3 per cent in 1929, rose to 15.6 per cent in 1932.[16] Similar patterns were found in France and the Benelux countries. Mussolini's policy, keeping the lira's parity as high as possible, mirroring British ambitions, ensured that Italy's economy suffered similar disadvantages, although the proportion of Italy's GDP involved in foreign trade was much lower than that of Britain's.

The crucially important lessons to be learnt from the 1930s derive from the different ways that the major economies in Europe, particularly Germany, France and Britain, reacted to the slump which overtook all of them. In Germany the collapse of the economy, coming as it did on top of the trauma of the war, the vindictiveness of the Versailles settlement particularly the reparations clauses, the political instability of the Weimar regime and the hyperinflation of 1923, provoked a wholly counterproductive response from the Brüning government. In July 1931 and again in the summer of 1932, the amount and duration of unemployment compensation was reduced. Instead of attempting to reflate the economy, Chancellor Heinrich Brüning (1885–1970), supported by the SDP opposition, cut wages and benefits, worsening the economic situation and precipitating the German banking crisis of July 1931, following the Austrian Kreditanstalt collapse two months earlier.[17] The desperate attempts by well-meaning democratic politicians to maintain financial respectability were their undoing and that of the whole of Europe as the Nazis came to power. This mistake, on top of all the others, gave Hitler and his associates the opportunity to take over the German government in 1933.

The economic policies pursued by the new Nazi regime, however disastrous in leading Europe into World War II and however much racist and fascist policies are to be condemned, were nevertheless remarkably successful in economic terms. Unemployment, over 30 per cent in 1932, was reduced by 1938 to just over 2 per cent of the working population.[18] Over the same period industrial production rose over 120 per cent, a cumulative increase of 14 per cent per annum. The gross national product increased by 65 per cent, a cumulative annual increase of nearly 9 per cent.[19] A substantial proportion of the increased output but by no means all was devoted to armaments. Military expenditure, which had been 3.2 per cent of GDP in 1933, rose to 9.6 per cent in 1937. It then almost doubled to 18.1 per cent but only in 1938.[20] Between 1932 and 1938 consumer expenditure rose by almost a quarter.[21] Nor were these achievements bought at the expense of high levels of inflation. The price level was very stable in Germany in the 1930s. Consumer prices rose by only 7 per cent between the arrival of the Nazi regime in 1933 and the outbreak of war in 1939.[22]

How were these results achieved? Some of the outcomes could only have been accomplished by a non-democratic regime with access to total power. In particular, the pressure exerted to hold down wage increases and the policies imposed to restrict trade, so as to increase Germany's capacity to supply all its essential needs internally, would have been difficult for any democratic government to implement. Unquestionably, these policies also led to increasing distortions in the economy, with a price which would have to be paid sooner or later. All the same, plenty of new output was available with which to pay these costs.

The economy's expansion was made possible partly by vast increases in state expenditures, which nearly trebled between 1933 and 1938.[23] An increasingly high proportion of these were spent on rearmament as the decade wore on, but earlier most of it went for such civil expenditures as building a road system – one with significant military potential – far superior to anything seen before. A substantial proportion of the rest of the rise in output, however, went towards raising the German standard of living. Much of the initial expenditure was financed by large-scale borrowing, some through bonds, but much else from the banking system. Though there was a large expansion in the money supply, rising tax revenues, flowing from the greatly increased scale of economic activity and falling welfare costs, kept the regime's finances relatively easily in bounds and inflationary pressures subdued.

In Britain, the initial reaction to the advent of the slump was much in line with the economic policies previously pursued. The Labour Chancellor of the Exchequer, Philip Snowden (1864–1937), tried to persuade his reluctant cabinet colleagues that the only solution to the financial crisis overwhelming the country was to maintain a balanced budget by implementing the same sorts of cuts in expenditure which had been the undoing of the Brüning government in Germany. Eventually, there was a revolt. The overwhelming majority of the Labour MPs ceased to support the government and refused to back more cuts. They preferred to go into opposition, allowing a National Government to be formed with the support of the Conservative opposition.

The policies then implemented were a complete break from those previously in play. Sterling was allowed to be driven off its gold parity and to fall in value by 24 per cent against all other major currencies and by 31 per cent against the dollar.[24] Instead of making efforts to restore the previous parity, as it had after the Napoleonic Wars and World War I – the government dedicated its policy to ensuring that the new lower parity was retained. An Exchange Equalisation Account was established, with resources of 5 per cent of the gross national product, to keep the pound at its new competitive level. There was a very substantial expansion in the money supply, which increased by 15 per cent between 1931 and 1932 before rising a further 19 per cent during the first half of 1933.[25] Interest rates fell to almost zero. In 1933 three-month Treasury bonds paid an average interest rate of just under

0.6 per cent.[26] Protection, including a 15 per cent tariff on manufactured goods,[27] was added to reinforce the protective effects of the reduction in the exchange rate, adding significantly to the effective size of the devaluation. A recent study showed that the result was the creation of some 80,000 jobs in Lancashire alone.[28]

In Britain, as in Germany, the results were dramatic and positive. Far from living standards falling, as almost all commentators had confidently predicted would happen, they started to rise rapidly. Industrial production also increased substantially, if not as quickly as in Germany. In the five years to 1937, manufacturing output rose by 48 per cent, to 38 per cent above the 1929 peak.[29] Unemployment fell sharply, as the number of people in work quickly increased. Over the period 1931–7, the number of those in work rose from 18.7 to 21.4 million as 2.7 million new jobs were created, half of them in manufacturing.[30] Unemployment fell from 3.3 to 1.8 million. The previous decade's poor business prospects had left Britain bereft of investment in the most modern technologies. Now the ground was quickly made up, with new industrial capacity employing the latest technical developments, as also happened in Germany. Nor was inflation a problem. Contrary to all conventional wisdom, the price level fell heavily until 1933, partly reflecting the slump in world prices, after which it slowly rose.[31] The British economy grew faster during the five years from 1932 to 1937 – at a cumulative rate of 4.6 per cent per annum[32] – than in any other five-year period in its history, showing clearly, against what appeared a most unpromising background, how effective a radical expansionist policy could be.

Towards the end of the 1930s, the growth in the British economy began to slacken off, despite the increased expenditure on armaments in delayed response to the growing threat from Germany. A further round of exchange-rate changes was largely to blame. In 1934 the Americans had devalued the dollar by 41 per cent. In 1936 the 'gold bloc' countries – France, Switzerland, Belgium and the Netherlands – which their overvalued currencies had hitherto left in the doldrums with low growth and high levels of unemployment, followed suit.[33] Incredibly, given the experience of the previous few years, instead of devaluing with them to keep sterling competitive, the British agreed to support the new currency alignments with the Exchange Equalisation Account, thereby throwing away the competitiveness which had enabled its economy to recover quickly from the slump. In 1948 the Economic Commission for Europe estimated that sterling was as overvalued in 1938 as it had been in 1929.[34]

The French experience during the 1930s was the mirror image of Britain's. Until 1936, when, under the Popular Front government headed by Léon Blum (1872–1950), deflationary policies were at last abated, France, along with the other gold bloc countries, stayed on the gold exchange standard. French refusal to devalue depressed the economy further and further, reaping the inevitable consequences. French GDP dropped steadily in real terms almost every year from 1930 to 1936, falling a total of 17 per cent over these six years. Industrial production fell by a quarter. Investment slumped. Unemployment rose continually.[35]

A few telling statistics summarise what happened. French crude steel production fell from 9.7 million tons in 1929 to 6.1 million in 1938. In Germany over the same period, it rose from 16.2 to 22.7 million tons. France produced 254,000 cars and commercial vehicles in 1938 and 227,000 in 1938. In Germany output went from 128,000 to 338,000. British crude steel production rose from 9.8 million tons in 1929 to 10.6 million in 1938, while vehicle output went up from 239,000 to 445,000.[36] These figures show with crystal clarity how much the French economy weakened compared with Britain's and particularly Germany's over this critical period. Although other factors were involved, the results of the battles of 1940, during World War II's first full year, were significantly determined by whether, during the previous decade, the combatant countries had adopted policies which gave them the industrial capacity to manufacture the aircraft and other armaments they urgently needed once fighting started.

The contrast involving Europe's three largest economies in the 1930s could hardly have been more marked – the relatively successful results, at least in economic terms, in Germany and Britain versus the disastrously poor outcome in France and the other gold bloc countries. These lessons are still highly material. The really interesting exemplar is the British experience, at least until 1936, combining democracy with recovery. Thereafter, reverting to type, it threw away the huge advantage of a competitive exchange rate, rapid growth and falling unemployment it enjoyed in the mid-1930s. Still, 1931 to 1937 showed what could be done by a democracy faced with daunting economic problems when the right policies were chosen. Expanding the money supply, reducing interest rates and establishing the exchange rate at a competitive level were the keys to success. Creating conditions where exports could boom, the home market could be recaptured from foreign suppliers and industry could flourish had an enormously positive impact on the country's economic performance.

Boom and slump in the USA

It was not until 1917, three years after the start of World War I, that the USA became directly involved in the war as a belligerent. By 1918 the US economy had grown by almost 16 per cent above 1913 levels.[37] While the 1920s saw most European economies recovering from deep post-war slumps which left their populations with significantly lower GDP per head than they had enjoyed before the war, the US economy began to surge ahead. After quick recovery from a brief post-war setback (1919–21), a major boom was sustained during most of the rest of the 1920s. Between 1921 and 1929 the US economy grew by 45 per cent, achieving an average 4.8 per cent rate of growth during these eight years.[38]

From 1920 to 1929, industrial output climbed by nearly 50 per cent, while the people employed in achieving it hardly altered in number, reflected an enormous increase in manufacturing productivity, which rose cumulatively by nearly 5 per cent per annum as factories were automated.[39] The use of electricity in industry rose dramatically – by 70 per cent between 1923 and 1929.[40] Living standards increased by 30 per cent, although those on already high incomes gained much more than those further down the income distribution. Investment as a percentage of GDP rose from 12.2 per cent in 1921 to 17.6 per cent in 1928. Meanwhile, the price level remained remarkably stable, consumer prices being on average slightly lower in 1928 than they were in 1921.[41]

The confidence engendered by such economic success was reflected not only in an almost tripling of consumer credit during the 1920s but also on the stock market. A bull market began to build in 1924 and surged ahead with only minor setbacks for the next five years. The Dow-Jones industrial average, whose high was 120 in 1924, reached 167 in 1926, soared to 300 in 1928 and peaked at 381 on 3 September 1929, a level not to be exceeded for another quarter of a century. As speculative fever reigned in a largely unregulated market, much of the increase in the value of stocks was financed by increasingly risky but lucrative loans. As the boom gathered strength, those buying shares often put up as little as 10 per cent of the cost themselves, the balance being 'brokers' loans'. Initially these were provided by banks but later increasingly by corporations, which found the potential returns irresistible. Many of the major American companies invested ever more of their resources in speculation than in productive plant and equipment. Brokers' loans had been about $1 billion during the decade's early years but rose to

$3.5 billion by the end of 1927 and $6 billion by January 1929 and reached $8.5 billion by October 1929. The huge demand for such loans forced the interest rate on them up and up. By the time the stock market peaked in the late summer of 1929, 12 per cent interest rates were not uncommon at a time when there was no inflation.[42]

The initial falls from the stock market peak were modest, but by late October 1929 confidence was draining away. A wave of panic on 24 October was followed by Black Friday, 25 October, and a frenzy of selling on 29 October. In the first half-hour that day, losses ran at over $2 billion; by the end of the day they were $10 billion, as the Dow-Jones fell 30 points, reducing the value of quoted stocks by 11.5 per cent. Worse was to follow. Despite periodic rallies, the market moved inexorably downwards, until by July 1932 the Dow-Jones stood at 41, nearly 90 per cent below its 381 peak. Shares of United States Steel fell from 262 to 22, General Motors dropped from 73 to 8, and Montgomery Ward plummeted from 138 to 4.[43]

The collapse of prices on the stock exchanges had a devastating effect on the rest of the economy. The huge sums which had been lost caused a wave of bank failures from coast to coast, dragging down countless businesses with them. As both consumer and industrial confidence evaporated, sources of credit dried up, and demand disappeared for many of the goods and services which the US economy was amply capable of producing. Between 1929 and 1933, US GDP fell by 30 per cent. Industrial output went down by nearly half in the three years from 1929 to 1932. By 1933 a quarter of the American labour force was out of work. Nearly 13 million people had no job.[44]

The economy reached its nadir in 1933. Meanwhile, in 1932 Franklin D. Roosevelt (1882–1945) had ousted the hapless Herbert Hoover (1874–1964) as president in a landslide vote, initiating a so-called New Deal for the American people, one designed to tackle the slump. The policies implemented by the incoming Democratic administration fell into two main parts. The first involved a substantial increase in the role of the state. Financial help was provided to those hardest hit by unemployment. The Federal Emergency Relief Act provided $500 million in direct grants to states and municipalities. New agencies were established, some of them designed to act in a countercyclical way, increasing demand by using the borrowing power of the state to provide funding. The Tennessee Valley Authority provided regional energy and flood control. The National Recovery Administration assisted with industrial revitalisation. The Agricultural Adjustment Administration had as its goal the regeneration of the weakened farming sector of the economy.

These initiatives were probably aimed as much at increasing confidence that the Federal government was doing something to improve conditions as at having a specific effect, although expenditure on these schemes no doubt had some reflationary impact.[45]

Much more significant in reviving the economy were other steps taken on the macroeconomic front. In 1934 the dollar's devaluation by 41 per cent added to the substantial protection for American industry already achieved in 1930 by the Smoot-Hawley tariff, a major step towards the economic nationalism which was one of the curses of the 1930s. An early step of the Roosevelt administration had been to stabilise the financial system by declaring a bank holiday and then allowing the Treasury, under emergency legislation, to verify the soundness of individual banks before allowing them to reopen. Ten days later half of them, holding 90 per cent of all deposits, were back in operation. Thenceforth deposits exceeded withdrawals, as confidence in the banking system was restored, thus increasing the availability of credit. The Fed also encouraged recovery by allowing the money supply to rise as the economy picked up. M1 rose from just under $20 billion in 1933 to a little less than $30 billion in 1936, generating a major increase in the underlying credit base.[46]

By 1936 the US economy was in considerably better shape than it had been three years earlier. In these three years real GDP grew by 32 per cent, and unemployment fell by nearly a third, from 25 to 17 per cent. Industrial output rebounded, growing 50 per cent.[47] Corporate net income moved from being $2 billion in deficit to $5 billion in surplus.[48] There was little change in the consumer price level.[49] Despite these striking achievements Roosevelt, who, notwithstanding the New Deal rhetoric, had never felt wholly comfortable with borrowing to spend, became alarmed by the fiscal deficit, which reached $3.5 billion in 1936, and ordered a cutback in Federal spending.[50] This coincided with a reduction in the competitiveness of US exports as the gold bloc countries devalued and the deflationary impact of the promised new social security tax, another part of the New Deal, which was introduced at the same time. The consequence was a sharp recession. GDP fell by 4 per cent in 1937 and 1938, industrial output fell back nearly a third and unemployment rose from 14.3 to 19 per cent.[51]

By then, however, the imminent start of World War II transformed the prospects of the US economy. Although the USA did not become a belligerent until the Japanese attack on Pearl Harbor in December 1941, the lend-lease arrangements agreed with the Allied powers at the start of the European war rapidly provided a massive stimulus to US output.

Between 1939 and 1944, US GDP grew by an astonishing 75 per cent, a compound rate of almost 12 per cent. Over the same period, industrial output increased by over 150 per cent, while those employed in manufacturing rose from 10.3 to 17.3 million, an increase just under 70 per cent. The difference between these percentages reflected a huge further advance in manufacturing productivity, which rose cumulatively by some 7 per cent per annum. Prices increased on average less than 5 per cent a year, a far better outcome than had been achieved during World War I.[52] By the war's end the USA was in an extraordinarily strong position vis-à-vis the rest of the world. Most developed countries had suffered invasion and defeat at some stage in the war, and in consequence their economies had been severely disrupted, and in some cases devastated. Between 1939 and 1946 Japanese GDP fell by almost half, and Germany's by just over 50 per cent. Even Britain, which had avoided invasion and finished on the winning side, did nothing like as well as the USA. The British economy grew by only 10 per cent between 1939 and 1946.[53] No wonder that in 1945 the US economy looked supreme.

Keynes and demand management

The major contribution made by John Maynard Keynes to economic thought was his perception that demand and supply would not always be in balance at a level which would keep the economy at more or less full employment, as Say's Law claimed would happen. On the contrary, Keynes maintained, while the money spent by the nation on consumption always creates an equivalent income flow for producers, there is no reason why the same should be true for that proportion of income the nation saves. The corresponding expenditure in this case is by companies and the state on investment goods. There is no reason why, ex ante, these should be the same. If the economy has more ex ante saving than expenditure on investment, there will be an overall shortfall in demand, leading to deflation and unemployment. Furthermore, if, as economic conditions become more depressed, precautionary savings rise while investment falls as profitable opportunities decrease, the result may be an increasingly intense depression. As an accounting identity, investment and savings – more strictly speaking, investment and borrowing – have, ex post, to be identical in size.[54] It may well be the case, however, that equilibrium between them will be found at a level which leaves the economy as a whole well short of the total level of demand needed to keep everyone in employment, with a reasonable rate of growth being achieved.

The classical economist's response to the problem of unemployment had been to deny that it could exist, except in the case of workers changing jobs or out of work because of poor fits between skills and job opportunities, unless wages were too high or too rigid. The solution, if unemployment appeared, was therefore to ensure that wages fell until everyone was priced back into a job. As a further important contribution Keynes pointed out that this was not correct, but a fallacy of composition. What might be true of individual workers was not true of all the labour force taken together. If employers generally lowered wages at a time of unemployment, total purchasing power – aggregate effective demand – would diminish pari passu with the diminished wages, thus worsening the deflationary problem.[55]

Nor was it true, Keynes maintained, that lowering interest rates would necessarily improve the prospects for investment to act as a sufficient stimulus to pull the economy out of a depression. Worse still, lowering interest rates might increase savings and thus further aggravate the imbalance, as savers felt they needed larger cash investments to offset the lower returns they were likely to receive. The only solution was for the state to assume a much more active role to make up for the deficiency in demand in the private sector. If the economy was operating below full employment, the state itself should offset the excess saving in relation to investment by borrowing and then spending the money to increase overall demand.

Keynes also had strong views about the exchange rate's role in the performance of the economy. He had railed against Winston Churchill (1874–1965) when in 1925, as Chancellor of the Exchequer, he returned Britain to the pre-World War I gold parity, realigning sterling with the US dollar at $4.86 to the pound.[56] Speaking nearly 20 years later for the Coalition government in the Bretton Woods debate in the House of Lords (23 May 1944), the then Lord Keynes[57] said, 'We are determined that, in future, the external value of sterling shall conform to its internal value, as set by our domestic policies, and not the other way round. In other words, we abjure the instruments of Bank Rate and credit contraction operating to increase unemployment as a means of forcing our domestic economy into line with external factors.'[58] Keynes died in 1946, however, and British exchange-rate policy soon reverted to the norm.

Nevertheless, Keynes had great influence on economic policy in the post–World War II period. Along with the Americans, for whom Harry Dexter White (1892–1948) took the lead, he was heavily involved in designing the post-war international settlement's architecture.

Planning started in 1942 and culminated in the Bretton Woods agreement of 1944. Common ground between the British and Americans was the perceived need to avoid both competitive trade restrictions and floating exchange rates, both of which, as interwar experience had shown, could be manipulated to secure unilateral advantage at heavy multilateral expense.[59] Floating exchange rates were also believed to encourage inflation in allowing politicians an easy escape from overheating their economy to enhance their popularity. Securing consensus over timing was more difficult. It was agreed that some barriers to short-term capital movements would be required, at least in the immediate post-war period, but the Americans were also keen that trade restrictions be removed as quickly as possible. The 'dollar gap', which manifested itself for some years after the war's end, showed that British caution was well justified. The problem was that, with trade barriers removed, the demand from Europe and elsewhere for US exports was far higher than their dollar earnings could sustain.

Buttressed by the establishment of the International Monetary Fund (IMF) to deal with short-term international financing needs, the World Bank to manage longer-term development loans and, in 1946, the General Agreement on Tariffs and Trade (GATT), the Bretton Woods system, as it finally emerged, had several key characteristics. The centrepiece was agreement that exchange rates in future should be fixed and that all participating countries had to establish a par value for their currencies in terms of either gold or the US dollar. These par values could be changed only to correct a 'fundamental disequilibrium' in their balance of payments. Each country was expected to hold reserves to support its fixed exchange rate, which could be supplemented by the IMF's resources. Agreement was reached on procedures for liberalising world trade by removing trade barriers and progressively lowering tariffs.[60]

The period of high growth and relative stability during the 1950s and 1960s which followed the setting up of the Bretton Woods system, once the initial dislocations of the immediate post-war period had been overcome, was unquestionably impressive and a vast improvement on the record of the interwar period. From 1950 to 1970 the world economy grew by 157 per cent, compared with 97 per cent from 1913 to 1950.[61] Nevertheless, the arrangements agreed suffered from deficiencies, which became increasingly evident as time wore on. The major problem was that they contained no built-in mechanism for stopping economies which started doing better than the average from accumulating greater and greater competitive advantage. Under the gold standard, any country which accumulated a balance of payments surplus automatically had its monetary base expanded by the influx of gold. This tended to push up its price level, redressing, at least in part, the balance with its competitors. Under Bretton Woods no such mechanism operated. The onus for adjustment therefore tended to fall almost wholly on the less competitive countries, forcing them to protect their balance of payments position with deflation or devaluation. There was no corresponding pressure on the more successful economies to share their competitive advantage with others by revaluing their currencies.

The result was that a country such as Britain, whose exchange rate soon after the war was evidently much too high, had no easy way of securing international agreement to lower it to a more realistic level. Germany and Japan, on the contrary, whose exchange rates had been fixed at artificially low levels after the war, were in a strong position to resist revaluation. Towards the end of the Bretton Woods era, the USA began suffering from the malaise which Britain had, in more acute form, experienced almost continuously since 1945, culminating in the devaluation of the dollar in 1971 and the break-up of the system of fixed exchange rates shortly afterwards.

The consequence of this bias in the system was that countries with competitive exports and strong balance of payments positions could grow very fast, while the less competitive countries were held back by balance of payments constraints. The result may have been to hold back overall growth from being as high as it would have been, but nevertheless not by much as during most of the immediate post World War II period only a small number of countries, primarily Britain, were affected. Between 1950 and 1970 the world economy's cumulative expansion averaged 4.9 per cent.[62] The driving force was a combination of Keynesian policies at national level and relatively minor disequilibria in competitiveness between the major international trading nations, thus allowing nearly all economies to expand rapidly with full employment. With comparatively low welfare-dependency levels, since almost all families had breadwinners, most countries had easily containable pressures on their taxation and expenditure systems, helping to keep inflation at bay.

As long as these conditions held, rapid growth could continue. When the Bretton Woods system broke up, however, the world economy began to perform much more poorly. In the early 1970s, with world leaders deprived of the restrictions and discipline of the Bretton Woods constraints, within which they had worked for a quarter of a century, there was initially an unsustainable boom fuelled by monetary laxity.

A long period followed during which most of the world's major economies grew significantly more slowly, exhibited much higher levels of unemployment and suffered far more severe bouts of inflation. As will be seen, new guidelines were forthcoming as intellectual fashion moved towards monetarism, led by Milton Friedman (1912–2006) and his associate, Anna Jacobson Schwartz (b. 1915), in their seminal book *A Monetary History of the United States, 1867–1960* (1963). Though the book's ideas proved exceptionally appealing to many people, they were also extraordinarily ineffective at dealing with the fundamental objectives economic policy ought to be concerned with, particularly in Western countries. Between 1973 and 1992 the cumulative rise in world output slowed significantly, falling from 4.9 to 3.5 per cent per annum and to just under 2.9 per cent in industrialised countries[63] at the same time as their unemployment and inflation figures also deteriorated markedly. Nor has the recent record been much better. Inflation has fallen, but there is little sign of unemployment diminishing. Between 1992 and 2010 world annual growth was 3.5 per cent, but it was only 2.1 per cent in advanced economies.[64]

The world still urgently needs a framework of international economic policies which can enable recovery of the dynamism of the 1950s and 1960s without the burden of the fixed-exchange-rate regime which in the end undermined the Bretton Woods system. Post–dollar devaluation history shows how much was lost in 1971 because no adequate replacement was available to carry the Keynesian legacy forward when the Bretton Woods construct, which worked better than anything the world had yet seen so far reached the end of the period when it was viable.

8
Post-World War II

World War II was an even worse disaster for the world in loss of life and material destruction than was World War I. Many more people were killed in the hostilities. The increased destructiveness of the weapons used, particularly those involving aerial bombardment, caused far more damage to railways, houses and factories than had occurred during World War I.

Of the major European economies, Germany's was by far the worst affected. Constant bombing by day and night for the last half of the war had reduced most German cities to ruins. Coal production, which had totalled 400 million tons in 1939, fell to just under 60 million in 1945. Crude steel production, nearly 24 million tons in 1939, fell to almost nothing by the war's end.[1] The currency collapsed again, and many transactions were conducted by barter or by using cigarettes as a temporary substitute for money. During the period immediately after the war, there was not only a desperate scarcity of industrial raw materials of all kinds but also a serious food shortage. The standard of living plummeted to a fraction of its pre-war level, as the German people eked out a living as best they could in their shattered country.

France, too, suffered severely, but not as badly as Germany. French GDP fell 17 per cent in real terms between 1938 and 1946, and industrial production by about the same amount. Britain did a good deal better. Its industrial output grew by about 5 per cent between 1938 and 1946, while total GDP rose 16 per cent.[2] Paradoxically, however, the British emerged from the war in many ways much worse prepared for the peace than the Continental countries, almost all of which had suffered defeat at some stage during the preceding years. Britain's world pretensions were still intact, whereas those of the Continental countries were greatly reduced. Germany, in particular, was allowed no more than token defence forces, whereas there were millions of British citizens still under arms, deployed all over the world. Britain had also run up substantial debts with supplier countries during the war, despite the large quantities of materiel provided by the USA, much of it shipped across the Atlantic without payment being required. Britain had sold substantial quantities of foreign investments to pay for supplies, but large debts remained. Paying off the so-called sterling balances – debts, denominated in sterling, run up mainly to Commonwealth countries – was a major commitment for Britain, unmatched by comparable obligations of the Germans or French.

The post-World War II settlement for Europe, after some initial aberrations, was generally a great deal more reasonable and considerate than the provisions of the Versailles Treaty after World War I. The Americans, in particular, showed outstanding generosity with Marshall Plan aid, which, peaking at 3 per cent of US GDP, poured into all the economies of western Europe, underpinning the recovery which was beginning to take place. Currency reform in Germany in the summer of 1948 was followed by a substantial, and as it turned out, largely unnecessary 20 per cent devaluation in 1949. In the same year, an excellent harvest did much to solve the food shortage, suddenly leaving West Germany in an extraordinarily competitive position. Even though manufacturing in 1948 was still at only half its pre-war level, and output per head was even lower as a result of the large influx of refugees from the east, over the next 15 months production rose 57 per cent to 87 per cent of the 1936 level. Exports more than doubled from 19 to 43 per cent of the pre-war figure.[3]

The French economy, which also emerged from the immediate post-war period in a much more competitive position than it had had pre-war, began to expand rapidly. Starting from a higher base than the Germans, increases in output were still impressive. The French economy grew by 42 per cent between 1946 and 1950. While some of this increase reflected recovery from the war years' dislocations, much of the rest resulted from heavy investment in new industrial facilities triggered, as in Germany, by rapidly rising exports and home demand.[4] In Italy and the Benelux countries, too, there was a much swifter recovery from the war than had been predicted. Export growth and industrial output surged, as all the erstwhile devastated economies of Europe began to recover much more quickly than the British and Americans had thought they would. By contrast, the British economy, whose wartime output peaked in 1943, did not regain this level of performance until ten years later, in 1953.[5]

Several factors left the British, in particular, heavily exposed, especially the rapidly increasing competitiveness of the Continental economies, war debts, worldwide defence obligations and a major domestic commitment – the creation of the welfare state by the Labour government elected in 1945. Loss of income from foreign investments, caused by sales of assets to pay for war supplies, left Britain having to pay a much higher proportion of its import costs than previously with export sales. This proved to be an impossible task during the early years after the war, despite the government's strenuous efforts. Britain was caught in a double pincer. On the one hand, a major balance of payments deficit with the USA caused a big dollar gap. On the other hand, British exports were unable to hold their own against competition from the reviving export industries of Europe. The dollar gap problem was largely solved by devaluing sterling in 1949 from $4.03 to $2.80, but as much of the rest of Europe devalued at the same time, continental producers retained a competitive edge vis-à-vis British exporters.[6]

Britain's problem was worsened by the outbreak of the Korean War in June 1950. Its efforts to maintain its coveted if not wholly reciprocated special relationship with the USA led it to embark on a major rearmament drive, pre-empting industrial resources from exports and adding to inflationary pressures. The Continental economies, on the contrary, largely exempt from these commitments, continued to expand both their domestic and foreign markets.

The Continental economies were thus poised for the enormous expansion in output which they achieved in the 1950s. Driven by highly competitive exports and aided by high levels of investment and modest rates of inflation, between 1950 and 1960 France's economy grew by 56 per cent, Italy's by 80 per cent and West Germany's by 115 per cent. The British achieved a much more modest 30 per cent. France's industrial output over the same period grew by 89 per cent, Italy's by 131 per cent and West Germany's by 148 per cent, while Britain's grew by only 28 per cent.[7] Significantly, this was a lower percentage than the growth in the British economy as a whole, presaging problems which would be shared by the other erstwhile successful economies in future decades.

The results of the differential performance of the major European economies during the 1950s was a massive shift in their relative rankings, reflected in share of world trade, income per head and, not least, in self-esteem and self-confidence. Britain, which in 1945 had seemed to be much the most successful country in Europe, gradually began to have doubts about its economic strength and its military and diplomatic position in the world. The Continental economies, on the other hand, saw each other in an increasingly favourable light, as the traumas of World War II faded in peoples' memories. Discussions about some sharing of transnational sovereignty had started shortly after the end of the war, culminating in the Treaty of Paris in 1951, which established the European Coal and Steel Community. Now seemed the time to embark on a more substantial and far-reaching venture.

European recovery and the Common Market

It is difficult to exaggerate the extent to which the history of Europe since World War II has been dominated by the determination of the generations which had lived through two devastating wars to make sure such a calamity never occurred again. From this source have sprung all the post-war supranational institutions in Europe, though inevitably, once in place, the organisations established developed a momentum of their own. The key issue, from an economic standpoint, is the impact which this integration had on the achievement of growth, high levels of employment and sustainable rates of inflation.

The European Coal and Steel Community was the first major consequence of the vision of Jean Monnet (1888–1979) and his associates of a Europe not only at peace with itself but bound by increasingly integrationist and federal arrangements. From the beginning, it was made clear that the intention was not just to link the countries of Europe by expanding the commercial bonds between them but to build supranational political structures which might eventuate in the framework for a United States of Europe. The rise in power of the United States and the Soviet Union and the division of Europe into East and West made it seem prudent to create a polity to counterbalance the two superpowers. Furthermore, despite the successful rate at which the western European economies were growing, remarkably high tariff barriers still divided them. Most of these countries had long histories of protectionism but in the light of inter-war experience accepted that there were powerful arguments favouring freer trade, with the creation of a customs union as a first step towards closer integration.

Britain, offered membership in the European Coal and Steel Community, rejected it. The ECSC was set up to support production, research and development, and the restructuring needs of the coal and steel industries in the countries which participated in its establishment – the same six countries which subsequently came together to form the Common Market. It fulfilled its function as a supranational body, as for the first time the participating states showed a willingness to give up some sovereignty for a common purpose, yet in other ways it was less successful. The ECSC was essentially a cartel. Its primary function was to keep prices up to assist its members. As with any other cartel, the benefits to its constituents in enhanced revenues were clear enough. The cost to everyone else in the countries covered by ECSC, in the form of higher prices for coal and steel than might otherwise have prevailed, were not so obvious. The benefits to the coal and steel industries were bought at the expense of their customers, some of whom, competing in international markets, were severely disadvantaged by higher raw material and energy costs.

Nevertheless, the experiment with ECSC was sufficiently promising to encourage the participating countries to convene the Messina Conference in 1955. The main agenda was to consider integration on a more comprehensive scale. The outcome was the Treaty of Rome, signed in 1957, which brought the Common Market into being on 1 January 1958. The treaty's immediate objective was to establish a customs union, although its preamble spoke of those setting up the customs union as 'determined to establish the foundations of an ever closer union among the European peoples'.[8] There is no doubt that many of those involved saw the Treaty of Rome as the first step towards a much more substantial political goal.

Britain, much the largest and most important European economy not included among the original six, was asked to participate at Messina. The British, still sufficiently confident in their world role, the Commonwealth and their supposed special relationship with the Americans, declined to join the new organisation. An alternative British proposal, to set up an industrial free trade area in Europe without the political overtones of the Common Market and without the Common Agricultural Policy regime, was decisively rejected by the Common Market founders. They were not interested in just an economic union. As with so many of the decisions which shaped the way the European Community developed, Britain's rejection of membership was taken largely on political grounds with little thought being given to the economic consequences. In this respect the British mirrored their German, French, Italian and Benelux counterparts. The motivation for setting up the Common Market was almost entirely political, as was Britain's refusal to join. In both cases the economic arguments were treated as secondary and subordinate – a potent and very unhappy precedent for the future.

The case for setting up a customs union in Europe was never as clear-cut as its proponents claimed. Nevertheless, a plausible justification could be made for it on the grounds that the conditions required for the advantages to outweigh the disadvantages were probably, on balance, fulfilled. The Treaty of Rome did not, however, just establish a customs union. It also set up a number of other subsidiary organisations, of which much the most significant was the Common Agricultural Policy, which was part of a deal between France and Germany. France was willing to provide duty free access to German goods in its heavily protected market only if French agriculture was protected from world competition.

The Treaty of Rome stipulated that the tariffs between the economies of the Common Market at the beginning were to fall to zero over a transitional period of ten years, starting in 1959 and ending in 1969, while a common external tariff was established. The abolition of internal tariffs was completed 18 months ahead of schedule, in 1968.[9] Whether the formation of this tariff-free zone was in the best interests of the constituent countries can be assessed by their growth rates during the period before and after its establishment. Table 8.1 shows the comparative figures for the eight-year period prior to the start of the Common Market and for six years after it came into being.

There was a small fall in the growth rate for the six countries taken together. Most did better in the earlier period than the later, at the expense of the German annual average growth rate, which fell from 8.6 to 5.8 per cent. Yet the most significant major influence on the relative competitiveness of the Six over the 15 years covered by the figures was

Table 8.1 Growth in the original member countries of the Common Market for the fifteen years spanning its establishment in 1958

	1950–57		1958–64	
	Total % Increase	% Increase Per Year	Total % Increase	% Increase Per Year
France	38	4.8	46	5.5
Germany	78	8.6	48	5.8
Italy	53	6.2	59	5.9
Belgium & Luxembourg	24	3.1	39	4.8
The Netherlands	38	4.8	44	5.3
Average of the Original Six Countries	54	6.3	47	5.7

Source: Derived from OECD National Accounts.

the double devaluations of the French franc at the end of the 1950s. These reduced the parity of the franc against the Deutsche Mark by a quarter, following five smaller devaluations of the franc since 1949, evening up the competitiveness of the French and German economies, particularly in relation to their differing inflation rates. Thus, the early success of the Common Market can be traced to a significant extent to the exchange-rate flexibility which enabled the constituent countries to grow at similar rates. Each preserved a broadly equal level of competitiveness, without some countries running into balance of payments problems vis-à-vis others. Maintaining these conditions was one of the vital keys thrown away in the 1970s, when attempts began to be made to lock Community currency parities together.

During the same periods as those in the table above, the British economy had grown respectively by 20 and 29 per cent, with average annual growth rates over each of the two periods of 2.6 and 3.7 per cent,[10] not much more than about half the average achieved by the Six. The contrast between the performance of the British and the Common Market countries' economies was all too striking, provoking in 1961 Britain's first application for membership, which was rebuffed by Charles de Gaulle in 1962. A second British application in 1967 fared no better with the general, whose distrust of British attitudes and intentions remained undiminished.

The logic, as opposed to the emotion, behind Britain's membership application was, however, not easy to follow. It was widely assumed that by joining a union of fast-expanding countries, Britain's growth rate would be lifted to something closer to the average of those to which it was attaching itself. Exactly how or why this should happen was not explained. Critics of Britain's application remained concerned that the root problem behind its slow growth rate – its lack of competitiveness – would be exacerbated rather than improved by exposing Britain to more competition inside the customs union. Between 1963 and 1973 the total Common Market GDP rose by 58 per cent, a cumulative annual growth rate of 4.7 per cent, whereas the British GDP, protected by significant tariffs, had grown by only 39 per cent, or 3.3 per cent per annum.[11] These sceptical arguments failed to win the day, however, leading to Britain's third, this time successful, membership application in 1970. The European Free Trade Area, comprising Britain, Ireland, Switzerland, Denmark, Sweden, Finland, Austria and Norway, established in 1960, had failed to provide the dynamism which Britain sought. Britain became a Community member at the beginning of 1973, bringing with it Ireland and Denmark, both major

British trading partners, but not Norway, which opted to remain outside.

Up to 1973, therefore, the Common Market had been able to maintain most of the momentum established during the post-World War II recovery period. The growth rate had slowed a little since 1957 but not much. There had also been some convergence in economic performance. Unemployment throughout the years to 1973 was very low, averaging little more than 2 per cent over the period in all Common Market countries. Inflation, varying somewhat from economy to economy in the Community, was maintained at an average of a little less than 4 per cent.[12] Pride in the achievements of the last quarter of a century was understandable and considerable. There had been an enormous increase in wealth and living standards. At the same time, generous welfare systems had been established, progress had been made towards making post-tax income distribution more equal, vast improvements had been made in housing and education, and political stability seemed assured. Few people, therefore, foresaw the nature or scale of the problems which were about to unfold.

US experience post-World War II

The years immediately after World War II saw a substantial slackening of demand on the US economy as war effort–based government procurement fell away. US GDP fell over 17 per cent between 1944 and 1947. Unemployment rose from 1.2 to 3.9 per cent. The peak wartime output level achieved by the US economy in 1944 was not regained until 1951.[13] Still, the US economy was in an extremely strong position after 1945. Partly because of the dominant position in which the USA found itself post-war, however, it faced a number of problems which tended to sap rather than reinforce growth performance in the decades to follow.

First, its victorious position left it with heavy international commitments, which greatly increased US unilateral transfers abroad. The most substantial was expenditure on major military presences in Europe, the Far East and elsewhere. This cost increased sharply with the advent of the Cold War. The Korean War, which broke out in June 1950, generated an additional peak. Significant sums were also paid out to various international programmes, not least the Marshall Plan.

Aid programmes also went some way towards helping to deal with the second problem with which the USA had to contend, which was trade imbalances. Although there was a large potential demand for US exports, which would have helped boost the US economy, the rest of the world was extremely short of dollars with which to pay for them. Marshall Plan aid helped fill the gap not only by assisting recovering economies directly with aid on soft terms but also by providing subventions in dollars, which they in turn could use to buy American goods and services. There was still, however, a substantial dollar gap, which could be filled only when the recovering economies had got themselves into a strong enough position to trade on equal terms with the USA. This was a prerequisite for achieving one of the major US post-war policy goals which was removal of artificial barriers to trade and international payments, which would allow the world to return to something closer to nineteenth-century conditions than to those of the inter-war period. Although American tariffs prior to World War I had been very high, US authorities now recognised that, in the interests of the world as a whole, protectionism was not the way ahead. Freer trade and multilateral payments were not, however, achievable unless all the economies concerned could participate on manageable terms.

These considerations led to the third problem, the one that in the long term proved the most serious. After the war the victorious Allied powers were anxious that the defeated nations should not indefinitely require succour and subsidy. Greatly underestimating their erstwhile enemies' capacity for revival, the Allies took active steps to ensure that the economies of those countries had a chance of speedy recovery by providing them with exceptionally competitive parities for their currencies. This affected both the Deutsche Mark, following the 1948 German currency reforms and the 1949 DM devaluation, and the yen, where similar financial reforms carried out in Japan by the administration of General Douglas MacArthur (1880–1964) gave the Japanese economy an exceptionally competitive cost base.

Germany and Japan, therefore, soon surged ahead with remarkably rapid recoveries. At the same time, other developed nations overrun during the war also began to perform much better than previously. Some improvement was due to recovery from wartime devastation, but other causes were important, too. Nearly all these countries' leaders, learning from the mistakes of the inter-war period and fortified by the doctrines of Keynes and his associates, were determined to run their economies more successfully. As old elites, discredited by wartime failure or collaboration, were swept away, the field was freed for fresh talent. Opportunities created by rapid growth during the post-war recovery sucked able people into manufacturing and exporting, the parts of the economy where the scope for productivity gains was greatest. Strong and influential social and political groupings, determined to safeguard industrial and trading interests, were established. Its very different recent history was a major reason why, during the 1950s and 1960s, the US economy's annual growth, 3.6 per cent, was slower than that of continental Europe, Japan or the world as a whole, which was 4.8 per cent.[14]

Again, it is important to remember that differential growth rates, which may seem small viewed a year at a time, have a huge compound effect over any reasonably long span. During the 20 years between 1950 and 1970, the ratio of the size of the British economy at the end of the period compared with the beginning was 1.7:1; for the USA it was 2.0:1; for the western European economies, 2.6:1; and for Japan, 6.8:1. Allowing for population growth, the disparities in the changes of living standards caused by these growth rate differences were even more marked. By 1970 another massive alteration in the distribution of world economic power had taken place. Whereas up to 1945 the underlying trend had been to increase the relative strength of the US economy vis-à-vis the rest of the world's, for all of the first quarter-century after World War II the USA was in relative decline, a trend which has continued.

During the late 1960s the American economy's prospects began rapidly to darken. A major cause of these upsets was the combination of escalating expenditure on the Vietnam War with the rapidly rising costs of implementing the Great Society programme, which the Democratic president, Lyndon Johnson (1908–73), had close to his heart. Successive reports from military commanders in Vietnam, particularly General William Westmoreland (1914–2005), each suggesting that a further comparatively modest increase in expenditure and troop strength would move the outcome decisively in the USA's favour, had turned out to be false. As a result, the cost of the war had steadily mounted. Total defence expenditure rose from $51 billion in 1964 to $82 billion in 1968, an increase as a proportion of GDP from an already high 7.4 to 9.4 per cent.[15] The Great Society was both a cherished big government Democratic programme in its own right and a response to the civil rights campaigns of the 1960s, which in turn had drawn in other disadvantaged groups. Its cost, however, was high. Expenditure on income support, social security, welfare, veterans' benefits and family assistance, which had been $38 billion in 1964, had risen by 1968 to $63 billion, an increase from 5.7 per cent of GDP to 6.9 per cent.[16] The combined cost of the war and rising social expenditure therefore involved an increase in expenditure of 2.6 per cent of GDP in three years.

A shift of this magnitude might not have been a problem had taxes had been raised to pay for it. Federal receipts as a proportion of GDP, however, stayed the same, 17.6 per cent, between 1964 and 1968.[17]

The highly reflationary result was that government expenditure, financed largely by borrowing from the banking system, rose rapidly and generated a fiscal deficit peaking at $25 billion in 1968.[18] Though when this occurred, the US economy was booming, gross private fixed investment as a proportion of US GDP rose during the 1960s only to just over 15 per cent,[19] a very low figure by international standards. By the end of the 1960s, the average age of US plant was 18 years, compared to 12 in West Germany and 10 in Japan.[20] Overall the economy grew progressively more overheated, and its output less internationally competitive. Consumer price inflation, averaging 1.3 per cent per annum between 1960 and 1965, reached 5.7 per cent in 1970.[21] In 1969 the surplus on goods and services trade achieved every year since 1945 shrank to $91 million and in the 1970s it moved heavily into deficit.[22] Imports of motor vehicles and parts alone rose from $0.9 billion in 1965 to $5.9 billion in 1970, a real increase of nearly 450 per cent. Over the same five years imports of consumer goods, excluding vehicles, rose from $3.3 to $7.4 billion, almost doubling in real terms.[23]

When President Richard Nixon (1913–1994) entered the White House in early 1969, he therefore faced an increasingly difficult economic situation. The Vietnam War was winding down and government expenditure had been cut, but inflation persisted despite rising unemployment. The wage and price control programme he introduced helped bring the rate of increase in the consumer price index down from 5.7 per cent in 1970 to 3.2 per cent in 1972[24] but at the cost of unemployment rising to 5.6 per cent by 1972, up from 3.5 per cent in 1969.[25]

On the external front the situation was also deteriorating. Having moved back into surplus in 1970, the balance of trade showed a $1 billion deficit in 1971, followed by $5 billion in 1972.[26] It being clear that the dollar was seriously overvalued, in 1971 a conference was held at the Smithsonian Institution, in Washington, DC, at which the USA announced that the link between the dollar and gold, which had underpinned the Bretton Woods system, could no longer be kept in place. The dollar was then devalued, and the Bretton Woods fixed-exchange regime dissolved. With the dollar no longer available as an anchor reserve currency, all the major currencies in the world began to float against each other.

By 1972 the dollar had fallen 16 per cent against the yen, 13 per cent against the Deutsche Mark, 4 per cent against the pound sterling and around 10 per cent against most other currencies.[27] As a result, by 1973 the US balance of trade showed signs of recovery. The absence of exchange-rate constraints for the first time in decades, however, left policymakers all over the world without familiar landmarks to guide them. Shorn of accustomed restraints, most countries began to reflate simultaneously. With credit controls relaxed, the money supply greatly increased, partly fuelled by an increasing pool of Eurodollars, themselves the product of the US deficit. World output soared, growing 6.7 per cent in 1973 alone.[28] The impact on commodity markets was dramatic. After years of falling prices caused by excess capacity, demand suddenly exceeded supply. Many raw materials' prices doubled or trebled. Then, in 1973, the Yom Kippur War broke out between Israel and the surrounding Arab states. It ended with a resounding victory for the Israelis but at the cost of the West seriously alienating the Arab states, many of them major suppliers of oil to the Western nations, particularly the USA, which had supported Israel in the conflict. Shortly afterwards OPEC, the oil producers' cartel, raised the price of oil from around $2.50 to $10 per barrel.[29]

The consequences of all these events for the developed world were disastrous. Oil's increased cost, although representing only about 2 per cent of the West's GDP, presented importers with a new and highly unwelcome blow to their balance of payments. Almost all tried to shift the burden elsewhere by a process of competitive deflation. At the same time, the quadrupled price of oil, accompanied by the doubled and trebled cost of other commodity imports, greatly increased inflationary pressures. Growth rates tumbled, unemployment rose all over the world and inflation moved to unprecedented levels. Far from growing, the US economy, mirroring similar developments in other advanced economies, shrank by 0.6 per cent in 1974 and 0.4 per cent in 1975.[30] Unemployment rose to 8.5 per cent in 1975,[31] and the year-on-year increase in the consumer price level peaked at nearly 11 per cent in 1974.[32]

The severe economic difficulties and disruption facing the whole world – not just the USA – in the mid-1970s did not, however, affect only rates of inflation, growth and unemployment. They also had a profound effect on the intellectual climate. The consensus around the ideas of Keynes and his associates, which appeared to have guided world economic policy successfully in the 1950s and 1960s, was shattered. Demand management did not appear to provide any satisfactory solutions to the problems confronting those who now had to cope with severely unstable conditions. Into the vacuum thus created moved an old economic doctrine in a new guise to replace the discredited Keynesianism. Monetarism arrived on the scene in the USA and elsewhere as the intellectual underpinning of economic policy formation in a world which had lost fixed exchange rates and the discipline they provided as the anchors for taking decisions.

Mixed fortunes in Japan

Asia's countries comprised the largest part of the world economy in 1820, with nearly 70 per cent of the world's population and nearly 60 per cent of its GDP.[33] There was not then a huge disparity in income levels among the region's countries. By 1992, however, GDP per head in Japan was over six times the level in China, more than 14 times that in India, and 27 that in Bangladesh.[34] How did the Japanese manage to secure this achievement?

The turning point came when the arrival of the US Navy in Tokyo Bay in 1853 forced an end to the more than two centuries long Japanese policy of almost total isolation. In the 1630s the new Tokugawa shogunate, established at Edo (now Tokyo), prohibited all travel abroad. All foreigners were expelled, except for a small colony of Dutch East India Company traders on Deshima Island, near Nagasaki, who were allowed to receive one ship a year from Indonesia. Christianity, introduced by Saint Francis Xavier (1506–52), was suppressed.[35] Thus, when the Americans arrived, the Japanese economy was in an exceptionally backward condition. Living standards were roughly on a par with that of Europe's in the late Middle Ages.

While the economy was undeveloped, however, Japanese political and social institutions were considerably more flexible and robust than might have been expected. As a result though trade concessions were extracted by the Americans and extended to the French, Dutch, Russians and British, and treaties were forced on Japan in 1854 restricting its commercial and fiscal autonomy, the Japanese were able to respond far more positively to the challenge presented by Western intruders than their Asian neighbours had done. This was, partly because the Japanese, having borrowed important elements of the Chinese and Korean civilisations, were not ashamed to copy a Western model which had demonstrated its superior technology so dramatically.[36] The Tokugawa shogunate, humiliated by the challenge from abroad, was overthrown in 1867, and Emperor Mutsuhito (1852–1912) assumed full powers, adopted the title Meiji, which means 'enlightened rule', and launched a policy of swift westernisation.

The results were dramatic. Within a remarkably short time the previous rigid stratification of society was abolished. Land could be bought and sold freely. Primary education became compulsory, and new textbooks were written with a Western orientation. Large numbers of students went abroad to receive technical and higher education. Tariffs were fixed at no more than 5 per cent, so that the economy was open to Western imports. The Japanese army and navy were reformed and rearmed using Western technology. The government then launched a programme of economic development, much of it with a heavy military orientation. Though it had no parallel elsewhere in Asia, it was not dissimilar to developments elsewhere in the world where militaristic regimes were in control.[37]

The result was a steady expansion of the Japanese economy, which grew at a cumulative rate of 1.4 per cent per annum between 1870 and 1885, accelerating to 3.1 per cent between 1885 and 1900 and then slowing to 2.5 per cent between 1900 and 1913.[38] World War I saw the Japanese economy grow rapidly; by 1919 Japan's GDP was over 40 per cent more than it had been in 1913. After a sharp post-war recession, the economy continued to expand during the inter-war period, checked only by a comparatively minor drop of 7 per cent in 1929 and 1930. As in Germany, the advent of a militaristic regime determined to drive the economy forward produced a much higher growth rate. Between 1930 and Japan's entry into World War II at Pearl Harbor (1941), its economy grew cumulatively at 5.4 per cent per annum.[39] By then GDP per head was approaching the level of the poorer western European countries, though it was still only half the German level and 40 per cent of Britain's.[40] Close to half of all employment in Japan, 43 per cent, was still in agriculture, forestry and fishing.[41]

Though its military ventures – including during the 1930s the invasion and occupation of Manchuria and parts of China, followed in 1940 by French Indo-China – had stimulated the economy, World War II was a total disaster for Japan, as it was for Germany. Between 1941 and 1945, Japanese GDP fell by more than half.[42] By 1946 industrial production was down to 20 per cent of its 1941 level, and steel production had fallen 92 per cent. Two-thirds of its large cotton textile capacity had been destroyed.[43] In 1945 Japan – before long to be car maker to the world – produced only 8,200 cars and commercial vehicles.[44] Besides the damage done by atomic weapons in Hiroshima and Nagasaki, US bombing raids had left all major cities in ruins. Inflation was rampant. The Japanese were humiliated and destitute.

When the American occupation, headed by General MacArthur, began, its major objectives were, first, to reform Japanese political institutions and extirpate the militaristic legacy which had caused so much harm and, secondly, to get the economy back on its feet and stop it being a drain on the American taxpayer The main problem, apart from general distress, was to get exports moving again so that the country would be able to pay for the food and raw materials it needed, which in the immediate post-war period had been provided only through the Allied occupation forces, financed largely by the USA. The solution adopted was a reform of the currency, fixing the yen in 1948 at 360 to the dollar as part of the Dodge Line financial measures.[45] As post-war recovery set in, this left the cost base in Japan, measured by international standards, at an exceptionally low level, exactly as happened in Germany.

Japan's response was very similar to that of all the other developed countries which had been defeated at one stage or another of the war. All found themselves, in varying degrees, in the same competitive position, as the victorious Allies hugely underestimated the vanquished nations' capacity to recover. Talent poured into industry as opportunities to make fortunes on world markets appeared. Japanese sales abroad began to soar. By 1973 Japanese merchandise exports were 27 times higher in volume terms than they had been in 1950. Germany's by contrast were 15 times higher, the USA's 4 times and Britain's 2.4 times.[46] In 1950 Japan's share of world trade was 1.3 per cent. In 1973 it was 16.4 per cent.[47] Nothing shows more clearly than these figures that the world's history, especially since the post-1945 trade liberalisation, is largely written in export competitiveness and an alignment of exchange rates which makes astounding success possible if parity is favourable or inhibits it if it is not.

Initially Japan's post-war exports consisted mostly of comparatively simple goods, in all of which Japan had an enormous price advantage because production costs, measured internationally, were so low. Japan's long history of textile manufacturing and metalworking made establishing newer industries, such as those involving the use of plastics, where the technology was comparatively simple, quick and easy. As had happened in the nineteenth century, however, the Japanese were not content to see their role as solely producers of cheap goods. The economy rapidly developed a formidable capacity for moving upmarket and for making its own capital goods, as well as expanding heavy industries in steel, shipbuilding, oil refining and electricity-generating capacity. Crude steel production, which had been 557,000 tons in 1946, reached almost 120 million tons by 1973. By then Japan was generating over 20 times as much electricity as at the end of World War II. Perhaps the most outstanding success story of all was that of the motor vehicle industry. Starting from the 8,200 units of all kinds made in 1945, by 1973 Japanese manufacturers were producing over 7 million vehicles, and by 1983 more than 11 million.[48] Riding on the massive growth in exports, which averaged a cumulative increase over 15 per cent per annum from 1950 to 1973, the Japanese economy grew extremely rapidly. Having only exceeded its 1943 peak wartime output for the first time in 1953, by 1973 it was 7.6 times its size in 1950, after a cumulative average growth rate throughout these 23 years of 9.2 per cent.[49] The comparatively low increase in the population – just over 1.1 per cent per annum between 1950 and 1973[50] – avoided much dilution of the increase in GDP, so that GDP per head also rose strongly by 8.0 per cent per annum. By 1973 Japanese living standards were on a par with Britain's and not far behind most of western Europe's – a massive change from the position which had prevailed a quarter of a century earlier.[51]

There is a vast literature about the reasons for the remarkable achievements of the Japanese economy, especially during the period up to 1973, when its growth rate was at its highest. Undoubtedly, a number of factors played important roles. All the countries defeated in World War II had a resurgence once the war ended, as older leaders were discredited and new opportunities beckoned those, hungry for success, who replaced them. All had well-educated, well-trained, experienced labour forces. The disruption caused by the large-scale warfare of the first half of the twentieth century left a substantial legacy of inventions and technical possibilities, and the Japanese were exceptionally well placed to exploit them. Other characteristics more specifically orientated to Japan's institutions and culture have also been cited. The homogeneity, discipline and national pride of its people undoubtedly helped to generate a focused work ethic. Some argue that the consensual Confucian tradition may also have assisted. The heavily protected domestic market, generating massive savings, produced a large pool of investible funds available to the export sector. By far the strongest argument that none of these special factors was fundamental to Japanese success, however, lies in the fact that their alleged influence evaporated as soon as the Japanese economy lost the real reason for its rapid growth, which was its undervalued exchange rate which, until 1971 stayed at 360 yen to the US dollar.[52] Because the Japanese export drive was so successful and investment in production facilities available for the world market was so high, Japanese export prices rose during the 1950s and 1960s by barely 1 per cent a year,[53] despite relatively high levels of domestic inflation, which averaged 5.2 per cent per annum between 1950 and 1973.[54] The result was that Japanese exports became more and more competitive, thus fuelling expansion's next stage. Although, immediately after the 1971 move towards floating rates, the yen's nominal value strengthened against the dollar by some 20 per cent and then slowly further hardened, the competitiveness of Japanese exports continued to increase.[55]

The turning point came in the mid-1980s, when the yen suddenly strengthened and the exchange rate moved from 238 to the dollar in 1985 to 168 in 1986 and 145 in 1987. After staying roughly stable until 1990, the yen moved up again, peaking at just under 100 in 1995 before weakening to 131 in 1998.[56] The reason for the yen's hardening was the huge balance of payments surplus which the Japanese started to accumulate from the early 1980s onwards, after decades when their current account had been in rough balance. There was a massive surplus on merchandise account, which passed $44 billion in 1984 and averaged almost $90 billion per annum in the late 1980s, partly offset by a deficit on services but increased by a rising net income from investments abroad. Overall the current account surplus run up by the Japanese economy between 1984 and 1994 totalled a staggering $932 billion.[57]

The effect on the volume of Japanese exports of the strengthening yen at the beginning of the 1990s was immediate. The fall by about 20 per cent of the price in yen which Japanese exporters could charge the rest of the world put a severe strain on their previously buoyant profitability. The increase in export volume slowed to a crawl. Between 1973 and 1985 the cumulative annual rise had been 8.6 per cent. From 1985 to 1994 it was 2.0 per cent.[58] As the stimulus to the economy from exports wore off, so did the overall growth rate but only after a period of speculative boom in the 'bubble economy' of the late 1980s. This kept GDP rising between 1985 and 1991 at a 4.4 per cent per annum average but no longer on the sustainable basis which had applied when exports were growing faster than GDP. When the boom broke and Japanese banks were left holding massive uncovered debts, the economy stalled. In 2000, Japanese GDP was only 10.4 per cent higher than in 1991.[59] Expenditure on investment, once another major growth component, was the same in 1997 as six years earlier.[60] The twenty-first century's first decade was no better, with growth averaging just under 1 per cent.[61] All efforts made to reflate the economy and get it growing again found-ered on the yen's value, propped up by all the well-known difficulties of selling into the Japanese market, being far too high.

Japan's major mistake was to allow its huge balance of payments surplus to accumulate in the 1980s. Every country's surplus is matched by corresponding deficits somewhere else, and the rest of the world choked on the success of Japanese exporters, unrequited by sufficient imports to keep Japan's current account in reasonable balance. At the time MITI might have thought it wise to promote the myriad ways in which the Japanese discouraged imports, thus allowing their economy's surprisingly inefficient non-export-orientated part to stay protected, but the price eventually paid for this error was very heavy.

In the end, therefore, there is nothing that cannot be explained about the Japanese economy. It was only an extreme example of the impact which an exceptionally low cost basis can achieve, followed by this huge advantage being lost thanks to policy mistakes being made which caused the currency to appreciate massively. As has been true of so many other countries' leaders, however, Japan's appear never to have understood or appreciated the fundamental underlying reasons for the success over which they presided. If they had, they would hardly have allowed the conditions so important to the economy for which they were responsible to melt away as pointlessly and damagingly as they did.

The USSR and the command economies

By far the largest departure from the organic way in which most of the world's economy has grown was the deliberate attempt to get rid of the capitalist system undertaken by the successful revolutionaries in Russia in 1917, and their successors in subsequent regimes devoted to running their economies on non-market lines. While the writings of Karl Marx had been the basis on which communist beliefs were founded, Marx had little to say about running an economy when a revolution he advocated had taken place. Lenin (1870–1924) and his associates and successors therefore had to formulate policies as they went along, without much of a blueprint from which to work, other than the general objective of eliminating as much private ownership as they could, while getting the economy to grow as fast as possible with a crash programme of industrialisation.

The Russian economy they inherited had expanded substantially during the late nineteenth and early twentieth centuries, with a 2.0 per cent growth rate per annum between 1870 and 1900 and a more impressive 3.2 per cent between 1900 and 1913.[62] Mostly as a result of state initiatives, by the start of World War I there was a reasonably extensive railway system[63] and some heavy industry. Russia's standard of living was, however, well below that of most of the rest of Europe, although slightly above Japan's.[64] Russia suffered heavy loss of life in World War I, and its economy was severely disrupted. Another 10 million died in the course of the revolution, the civil war and the attacks on the new regime from Western powers fearful of what a successful replacement of capitalism might presage. As a result, it was 1930 before the Soviet economy regained the level of output it had enjoyed in 1913.[65] Its rulers had to build on a poor, backward and fractured economic base.

Although the Soviet regime started off relatively liberal during its New Economic Policy phase, it soon toughened its stance. Lenin died in 1924 and was succeeded by Joseph Stalin (1879–1953), who introduced the system of five-year plans, the first two of which covered the period 1928–39. Heavy and light industries were developed, and agriculture collectivised. The country began to be transformed as industrialisation proceeded, and the urban population quickly doubled.[66] The cost, however, was prodigious in human terms, as millions died in the Ukraine and Kazakhstan famines of 1932–4 and in political purges and liquidations, and also in economic terms, as state policies drove down the prevailing standard of living to mobilise more and more resources for investment in the future.

Even though the Soviet economy grew relatively quickly during the 1930s, because of high capital-to-output ratios growth was much slower than would have been achieved if Western standards of return on the use of capital had been attained. Between 1928 and 1940 Soviet output rose by an estimated 81 per cent. The average per annum growth rate was 5.1 per cent.[67] Until 1941 the USSR avoided being attacked during World War II thanks to its 1939 non-aggression pact with Germany, but once the German invasion began in August 1941, the USSR endured four traumatic years of carnage and physical damage. About 25 million Soviet citizens are believed to have died during the war years,[68] and the damage done to the area the Germans occupied was immense. Thus, in spite of huge investment in new production facilities, the output of the Soviet economy was over 20 per cent lower in 1946 than in 1940.[69]

The post-World War II period, however, saw a steady increase in output as it rose every year between 1947 and 1958 at an average rate estimated at 7.3 per cent, a pace considerably higher than what was being achieved anywhere except Japan and Germany.[70] This began to cause mounting concern in the West, particularly in USA, whose growth rate was barely half the Soviet economy's, prompting Nikita Khrushchev (1894–1971) to promise while in the USA in 1959 that the USSR would shortly overtake the US standard of living.[71] As time wore on, however it became increasingly clear that the threat was empty. Although the Soviet economy had responded reasonably well to large investments in basic industries, running a consumer-orientated economy was much more difficult to manage without a market framework.

Although valiant attempts were made to get the Soviet economy to produce more consumer goods of reasonable quality, once Stalin's influence had worn off and Khrushchev denounced his excesses in 1956, results were remarkably unsuccessful. The Soviet economy continued to have a high proportion of its GDP devoted to investment, but the growth rate in the economy slowed, and consumers remained dissatis-fied. Between 1959 and 1973 the economy grew at a more than respect-able estimated 4.9 per cent per annum, but thereafter, during the era presided over by Leonid Brezhnev (1906–82), annual growth slowed to 1.9 per cent.[72] During the whole of the period 1973–89, before the USSR began to disintegrate, GDP per head in the Soviet Union increased cumu-latively at less than 1 per cent per annum.[73] Allowing for the ongoing military build-up, the average Soviet citizen's disposable income stopped rising after 1973, stabilised of course at a far lower level than in the USA, where a remarkably similar stagnant real-income phenomenon was to be found among most of the population.

Unquestionably, part of the reason for the relatively poor performance in the USSR's later years was the exceptionally heavy military burden the economy had to bear, particularly from the mid-1960s onwards, when the Cold War intensified.[74] After all allowances are made, however, the system's root problem was the impossibility of running an increasingly complex economy on the basis of central plans that largely suppressed market signals. Not only did the rate of growth slow, but ever more serious problems of resource allocation, as appropriation became ever more complicated, reduced the real value to the final consumer of the goods and services which were produced.

The problems of the Soviet economy were mirrored in varying degrees of intensity by all the eastern European countries obliged to adopt command economies at the USSR's behest after communist regimes were installed following post-war Soviet occupation. A particularly interesting example is the German Democratic Republic, long regarded as being the most successful of the Soviet satellites. Prior to reunifica-tion, Western estimates of East German per capita GDP levels had put them at about three-quarters of the Federal Republic's and about two-thirds of the USA's. When in 1990 the Berlin Wall came down and East and West Germany were reunited, these estimates were found to be about 50 per cent too high. With the actual East German GDP per head only about two-thirds of what it was thought to be, it confirmed the deep-rooted inefficiency of even a comparatively well-run command economy and emphasised the economic weaknesses from which the erstwhile USSR had suffered.[75]

It is therefore hardly surprising that the process of reintegrating the two parts of Germany was far more difficult and expensive than envis-aged. Part of the problem was the well meaning but very damaging undertaking by Helmut Kohl (b. 1930) to provide parity between the

Ostmark and the Deutsche Mark which, at a stroke, made almost all of the former DDR's output grossly overpriced and uncompetitive. The condition of even those parts of the DDR's economy which were thought to be performing reasonably well, however, generated requirements for massive remedial expenditure. East Germany's concentration on production at all costs had left environmental considerations well down the order of priorities. The result was pollution over large areas on a scale which those used to Western-style regulation found hard to comprehend. With the goods produced having never been exposed to competitive pressures, their quality was far below world standards – apart from the fact that they were now also very expensive. The legacy of command economies – for those who lived in them and the states which succeeded them – has not been a happy one. The wrenching transitions required tended to be more pronounced for those longest exposed to communism. For example, from 1990 to 1992 alone, Russian GDP fell by over 30 per cent.[76] The weaknesses of the command economy approach lay exposed for all to see.

Yet a sense of balance is required. The Soviet economy and those of its satellites had some points in their favour. Although achieved at very high cost, growth rates were for long periods higher than those elsewhere. Much of the time they were also steadier. As the Western world plunged into depression post-1929, the Soviet economy grew every year from 1928 onwards, except for a minor 1 per cent fall in 1932. Also, command economies employ virtually everyone, although at a heavy cost in the efficiency of labour force use. These achievements, combined with the Soviet ability to expand without outside assistance, were sufficient to attract partial copying by many third world countries, once they had gained independence after World War II. Command economies had no problem maintaining a high demand level or – however expensively – achieving high investment levels. The difficulties which in the end overwhelmed them were scarce-resource allocation and quality of output.

The Third World

While the main emphasis so far has been on these countries which industrialised earliest and which therefore now have the highest standards of living, most of the world's population lives elsewhere. In 2010, out of a population of almost exactly 7 billion, just under 20 per cent of the world's inhabitants lived in its fully developed parts.[77] In 1992, two decades ago, the average income per head among the then remaining

76 per cent of humanity, measured in 1990 US dollars, was $2,173, compared with $19,175 for those in industrialised countries.[78]

The developing and undeveloped nations of the world are not, however, by any means homogeneous, either in their absolute standards of living or in their growth records during the previous decades. The broad picture, according to purchasing power parity (PPP) figures for 2010 compiled by the IMF, is that the standard of living in Latin America is a little above the world average of $10,922, with Argentina ($15,901), Chile ($15,040), Mexico ($14,406), Venezuela ($12,048) and Brazil ($11,723) above the world mean and Colombia ($9,593) and Peru ($9,358) below it. In Asian countries the spread is much wider. Of the larger countries, Taiwan ($35,604), Japan ($33,885) and South Korea ($29,997) had reached levels comparable to those in the EU ($30,455). Thailand ($9,221), China ($7,544) and Indonesia ($4,347), were much lower, with India ($3,408), Pakistan ($2,721), Bangladesh ($1,585) and Myanmar ($1,256) lower still. Africa's income levels were both lower than Asia's and even more skewed. South Africa ($10,518) had a relatively high average figure, masking very large income differentials within its boundaries, but all other major African countries had GDP per head at best little more than 10 per cent of Western levels, with Nigeria, at $2,437, shading down to desperate poverty in Liberia ($396) and Zaire ($329), where the average income for the whole population was less than $1 per day.[79]

As to the growth records leading to where they are now, the Latin American economies all started growing fairly early. By 1913 their average living standards were a little less than half those in the Western industrialised economies. By 1950, mainly because they were not involved to any significant degree in either of the world wars, they were at just over half the Western level. Thereafter, their growth rates continued to perform more or less on a par with those of the more advanced economies, helped by the boost given some of them by the discovery and exploitation of large oil deposits. Between 1950 and 1973 Latin America's combined cumulative average growth rate was 5.3 per cent per annum. Between 1973 and 1992 it was 2.8 per cent and since then to 2009 it has been 3.1 per cent.[80] With high growth rates in the population, however, the South American economies' expansion was not matched by corresponding increases in living standards, which grew much less than those in the Western world – cumulatively, over 1 per cent per annum more slowly.[81]

In Asia the growth record has been much more impressive, with an overall cumulative average growth rate of 6.0 per cent between 1950 and

1973, 5.1 per cent between 1973 and 1992 and 7.3 per cent[82] between 1992 and 2010, starting from a base position which in 1950 showed GDP per head to be, on average, not much more than one-tenth of the West's level. With a population growth rate markedly lower than South America's, living standards rose correspondingly more quickly – cumulatively by 3.8 per cent in the first period, 3.2 per cent in the second[83] and 5.9 per cent in the third.[84] A point of considerable significance, however, is that while Japanese per annum growth slowed dramatically from about 1990 onwards, most of the other major Asian economies did better in the third period than the first two. Improved performance included much better results between 1992 and 2009: 4.2 per cent growth per annum for Pakistan, 5.4 per cent for Bangladesh, 5.5 per cent for Malaysia, 6.8 per cent for India and 10.2 per cent for China. These figures illustrate all too graphically how rapidly economic power is moving from the West to the East. The average cumulative growth rate across the whole of the developed world between 1992 and 2010 was 2.1 per cent.[85]

In 1950 Africa's average standard of living was a little higher than Asia's,[86] and between 1950 and 1973 Africa's overall growth record, at a cumulative 4.4 per cent, was only a little below the world average (4.9%).[87] The period 1973–92, however, showed the growth rate slowing to 2.8 per cent a year. The major problem in Africa was less the slow increase in GDP than the very high birth rate, leading to population growth of 2.4 per cent a year in the first period and 2.9 per cent in the second.[88] The result was a 2.0 per cent per annum increase in living standards between 1950 and 1973, with a fall of 0.1 per cent a year between 1973 and 1992.[89] Between 1992 and 2010 the growth rate rose to 3.5 per cent, accelerating in the 2000s as exploitation of Africa's natural resources gathered pace. With the very high birth rate in Africa, however, the rise in living standards remains very low.[90]

The experiences of the last 50 years of the developing and less developed countries covered in this brief survey offer some important lessons. Unquestionably, some of the poor results achieved were the consequence of maladministration, corruption, warfare and instability, factors which no economic policies, however well conceived, are capable of overcoming. Leaving these factors aside, however, a number of patterns can be detected.

First, the Soviet model of forced industrialisation has been an extremely poor one. Not only did it lead to large-scale waste and misallocation of resources, but the bureaucratisation and industrial favouritism it encouraged militated against opening the economies adopting this approach to the stimulus of international competition. The results – high import tariffs, exchange controls and restrictions on capital movements – were designed to protect indigenous industries often owned by the state or by those associated with its political leaders. Economies adopting such policies tended to suffer from the need to service the costs of large-scale borrowing to finance investments, many of which achieved little or no financial return and failed to produce world-class goods and services. The inefficient, uncompetitive export sectors which were the consequence were unable to launch themselves successfully on to world markets. Most countries which once modelled themselves at least in part on the USSR long since ceased doing so. Their economic performance has improved accordingly.

Second, a number of social policies clearly favour fast growth and rising living standards. The more successful economies tend to be those with high literacy rates and good technical training, rather than those, such as India, which are inclined to concentrate resources on university education for a few at the expense of the wider population. In the mid-1990s, 38 per cent of men and 66 per cent of women in India were still illiterate, compared with 16 per cent and 38 per cent, respectively, in China and 9 per cent overall in Taiwan, with their much more difficult kanji-based writing to be learned.[91] It is also evident that countries with reliable legal systems, well-regulated financial sectors, successfully planned infrastructures and fair and impartial tax systems usually have an edge on those lacking them, though it is not difficult to find examples of countries which have prospered without these advantages. None of these requirements, desirable though they are, appear to be a sine qua non of economic success.

Third, rising populations have clearly been a major factor in increasing the size of many of the world's economies, but the dilution of GDP caused by a growing number of people among whom it has to be shared has held living standards down in many countries, especially in Africa, where the population rise is very rapid. Far the most effective way to slow population growth is to raise living standards, but this becomes a difficult chicken-and-egg problem. The time that the world's richer parts can go on ignoring the need to deal with this issue through direct and indirect assistance, however, may be shorter than is realised.

Fourth, the strongest link between those economies which have achieved high growth rates, as against those which have not, is exactly the same for poorer countries as it is for richer ones. The most important requirement is a competitive export sector which sucks in talent and investment to where they can be most productively employed, enables a cumulative increase in foreign sales to be accomplished and thence fuels sustainable high rates of growth in the economy as a whole. Growth in exports drives expansion generally, as can easily be seen from the statistics.[92] Countries whose exports, particularly whose merchandise sales abroad, grow faster than the world average are the ones whose economies expand most rapidly, and vice versa. From Chile to South Korea, from Turkey to China, the record is the same.

Using appropriate macroeconomic policies to achieve the desired end, therefore, the crucial policy variable is the cost base for internationally tradable goods and services. If it is set low enough to generate a buoyant export market, getting various complementary economic policy elements to work successfully is not difficult. If the cost base is too high, however, no supplementary mixture of policies will offset this major obstacle. Relative if not absolute stagnation will inevitably result, as scarce talent is concentrated ever more heavily in sectors of the economy which have comparatively little to contribute to competitiveness and growth.

9
The Monetarist Era

As the certainties of the Bretton Woods world crumbled away in the early 1970s, intellectual fashions in economics moved decisively away from the Keynesian orthodoxy of the previous quarter of a century. Monetarism became the theoretical and practical discipline to which the vast majority of those involved in economic affairs, in both the academic and policymaking worlds, began to subscribe. It is no coincidence, however, that monetarism's prevalence has been highly correlated with deteriorating economic performance. Monetarist doctrines are inclined to receive their most sympathetic hearing among political and intellectual leaders who are at the helm of the slowest growing economies. There are interlocking reasons why this is so. It is partly that monetarist prescriptions lead to slow growth and partly that the cultural attitudes which breed a proclivity for them flourish especially strongly in economies with poor growth and employment records.

This was particularly but by no means exclusively so in the Anglo-Saxon countries, the USA and Britain. The same ideas have also managed to get a grip on the whole of the European Union, leading to the determination, exemplified in the provisions of the 1991 Maastricht Treaty, to put monetary stability before prosperity. The loss of confidence in Keynesian policies after the inflation and international dislocation of the early 1970s caused policy shifts in a monetarist direction, particularly in Germany and France. This change in intellectual fashion, as much as anything else, is responsible for the EU switching from being one of the world's fastest growing regions to becoming an area of exceptionally slow increase in output accompanied by painfully high levels of unemployment. Countries which gave monetarist prescriptions less priority, on the other hand, in Europe and elsewhere, continued to grow apace. Norway, a prime example outside the EU, which achieved the highest rate of GDP per head within the OECD between 1973 and 1992, just ahead of Japan, increased its population's living standards by 71 per cent. The Norwegians succeeded in combining this achievement with one of the better OECD records on inflation, with an unemployment rate barely a third of what was then the EU average.[1] Over the same period Britain and the USA, both strongly influenced by monetarist ideas, achieved GDP per head increases of only 31 and 26 per cent, respectively. The EU as a whole achieved 41 per cent.[2]

Monetarist prescriptions, stripped of theorising and rhetoric, are familiar to anyone who has studied economic history. Their hallmarks – relatively tight money and high interest and exchange rates – slow productive enterprise and make it harder to sell abroad and easier to import. They discriminate against manufacturing investment and drain industry of talent. Monetarist ideas – and the devotion to balanced budgets and financial conservatism which preceded them, harking back to nineteenth-century classical economics – have never been far below the surface, especially in the USA and Britain. This is why, post-1973 and especially in the 1980s, macroeconomic conditions prevailed in both countries and subsequently in most of the rest of the Western world which were almost wholly responsible for the low growth and productivity increases of the subsequent quarter-century. They were also directly responsible for the huge widening of incomes seen over the last 25 years, with which the attenuation of manufacturing capacity, itself a direct result of monetarist policies, is heavily bound up.

These are familiar themes, and it is therefore worth exploring why a combination of self-interest and social attitudes produce an environment where monetarist ideas can take strong hold even though they lack intellectual coherence, are undermined by prescriptive inadequacies and have such damaging consequences. Why should mature, stable, slow-growing economies be particularly prone to producing a climate of opinion where such ideas can flourish?

The answer is that monetarist policies' implications are far from unattractive to large sections of the population, especially in slow-growing economies where the lenders' position tends to be strong and the borrowers' weak. Those who have achieved success in finance rather than manufacturing often move into positions of influence and political power. As they do so, monetarist doctrines, which appeal to people with financial backgrounds, become predominant. The attitudes of those whose business is lending money, who have an obvious stake in high interest rates and scarcity of the commodity they control, become politically significant, not least because their opinions have a self-fulfilling quality. If it is greatly feared that losing their confidence will lead to a run on the currency, those whose decisions keep the parity up are very powerfully positioned. Those whose incomes depend on high interest rates – pensioners and many others – are also inclined to support a policy which seems obviously in their favour. Bankers, financiers and wealth holders are the immediate beneficiaries of the deflationary policies which follow, buttressed by those who can see no further ahead than obtaining immediate benefits from low-cost imports and cheap holidays abroad. The losers are those engaged in manufacturing and selling internationally tradable goods and services.

When the economy grows slowly, finance's power and influence increase against industry's. This is partly a result of the process of accumulation of capital wealth, much of which tends to be invested abroad rather than at home, because slow growth in the domestic economy creates better opportunities overseas. This was the story of Britain in the nineteenth century, of the United States for a long period post–World War II, of Japan from the 1980s onwards. China may be starting to move in the same direction. This process has profound effects on social attitudes and political power, particularly if the conditions prevail for a long period of time, as they have in most of the slow-growing industrialised countries.

If the economy is run with relatively tight money and high interest and exchange rates, the inevitable consequence is to produce adverse trading conditions for all output exposed to international competition. Adequate returns on investment are much harder to achieve. It becomes ever harder to pay the going wage or salary rates for the calibre of employees required for success in world markets. Of course, there will always be exceptionally efficient companies or even industries, such as pharmaceuticals in Britain, which long buck the trend. They are not, however, critically important. The average is what counts, and here the results are impossible to dismiss. With the profitability of large sections of manufacturing in the Western world having fallen so much that for them to continue in business is no longer worthwhile, the proportion of GDP derived from manufacturing has fallen precipitously in most Western economies over the last four decades. This fact explains why in 2010 China produced 627 million tons of crude steel, compared with 173 million tons in the whole of the EU and 81 million in the USA.[3] In the same year China produced 18.3 million vehicles, Japan, once the world leader, 9.6 million, and the USA, the world leader before Japan took over, no more than 7.8 million.[4] The same trends affected swathes of other industries in many other developed economies. Meanwhile, in countries which give their industrial base a better deal, fortunes are made in manufacturing, and the rest of the economy struggles to keep up.

Western universities' most able graduates nowadays go decreasingly into industry. The easiest money and most glittering careers beckon in the professions, in finance and in the media. The academic world, politics and government service look ever more attractive, and for those bent on a career in mainstream business, distribution or retailing generally offers more security and better prospects than manufacturing. If the most able people choose not to go into industry but instead become lawyers or bankers or television personalities, the educational system responds accordingly. Subjects orientated towards making and selling are downgraded in favour of those required for other careers. Science falls in status compared with the arts. Commercial studies come to be seen as second-rate options compared with professional qualifications. Practical subjects, such as engineering, are perceived as less glamorous and attractive – and potentially less lucrative – than the humanities. In the USA, from the mid-1980s to the early 1990s, when an extreme example of monetarist policies was in full flight, freshman enrolments fell sharply in subjects where employment prospects had been adversely affected, particularly by the bloodletting which manufacturing suffered at the time. Those planning to pursue business studies fell from 21 per cent of the total in 1980 to 14 per cent by 2009, and the proportion choosing engineering fell from 11.2 to 9.7 per cent, while those studying arts and humanities rose from 10.5 to 13.3 per cent.[5]. These figures provide clear evidence as to how quickly and profoundly the educational system becomes part of cultural conditioning, with peer pressure, career prospects and the priority and prestige accorded different subjects determining where the nation's talent bends its energies.

A significant consequence of the social bias infecting the whole of this process is that it determines the background of people most likely to reach the peak of their careers running major companies, especially in manufacturing. An interesting contrast between economies such as the USA's and Britain's, which have grown slowly, and those which have grown fastest is that quite different people tend to become CEOs.

In slow-growing economies chief executives are often professional people such as lawyers and accountants. Where the economy is growing quickly, they tend to be engineers and salesmen. No doubt both cause and effect are operating here. If the most able people in the commercial field are in the professions, they will rise to the top of big companies, where their particular talents will be especially in demand to deal with powerful financial interests. In fast-growing economies, where financial interests are less immediately pressing and the most able people are not in the professions, engineers and salesmen tend to hold the top positions. It is hardly surprising that companies run by accountants and lawyers are particularly concerned with financial results, while those controlled by salesmen and engineers are more orientated to markets and products.

Nor is the low status of industry only a financial or social matter. It has a large impact on the political weight of manufacturing interests versus those of other parts of the economy. Exercising political power requires talent, takes time and costs money. With all these in increasingly short supply, particularly in American and British industry, the results are clear to see. Few members of Congress or Parliament have any significant hands-on manufacturing experience. The role models to whom the younger generation looks up are nowadays seldom those running manufacturing industries. Those in law, accountancy, the media and – at least until recently – investment banking look more impressive and secure. Thus, it is small wonder that economic ideas promoting finance over manufacturing tend to find favour. Yet it does not follow that these ideas are well founded. Still less is it true that they are in the best long-term interests of the economy as a whole or even of those in the financial community itself. In the end, those concerned with finance depend as much as anyone else on the underlying economy's performance and, in particular, on its capacity to hold its own in world markets.

Monetarist theory and practice

The appeal of hard money has a long history. Those with established wealth have always been keen that it should earn as substantial a return as possible. The desire for high rates of interest and low rates of inflation is almost invariably shared by those with a banking background and was therefore widely prevalent before monetarist orthodoxies became fashionable. They were underpinned by the thinking of a number of key figures, not least Professor Friedrich Hayek

(1899–1992) and his University of Chicago associates, all of whom had serious reservations about the Keynesian revolution. Monetarist ideas, in their standard form, would not have become accepted as widely as they were, however, without the theoretical and statistical foundation provided by Milton Friedman and his associate, Anna Jacobson Schwartz, in their seminal 1963 book *A Monetary History of the United States, 1867–1960*, in which they made three important claims which had a major impact on economic thinking all over the world. First, they made a clear association between the total amount of money in circulation and changes in money incomes and prices – but not economic activity, until approximately two years later. Changes in the money supply therefore affected the price level but, not except perhaps for a short period of time the level of output in the real economy. Second, these relationships had proved to be stable over a long period. Third, changes, particularly increases in the money supply, had generally resulted from events independent of the needs of the economy, in consequence they added to inflation without raising the level of economic activity.

The attractive simplicity of these propositions is easy to see. The essence of the monetarist case is that increases in prices and wages not mirrored by productivity increases can be held in check by nothing more complicated than the process of controlling the amount of money in circulation. Ideally, a condition of zero inflation is achieved when the increase in the money supply equals the rise in output in the economy. Since both wages and prices can go up only if extra money to finance them is made available, rises in either cannot occur unless more money is provided. Thus, as long as the government is seen to give sufficient priority to control of the money supply, everyone will realise that it is in his or her interest to exercise restraint, reducing the rate of inflation to whatever level is deemed desirable.

These prescriptions have attracted much support to the monetarist banner, although it has always been clear that its intellectual underpinning was severely deficient. To start with, the theory begs the fundamental question as to which way of measuring the money stock is appropriate when many different ways of determining it are available. It is also well known that the ratio between the stock of money, however defined, and the volume of transactions can vary widely as the so-called velocity of circulation alters. In addition, the widespread criticism of the methodology used by Friedman and Schwartz in their analysis of the relationship between money and prices in the USA indicates that the statistical basis from which their conclusions were drawn was not nearly as sound as they claimed it was.

As with much else in economics, a major feedback problem with the monetarist position makes distinguishing between cause and effect difficult. It may be true that over a long period the total amount of money in circulation is closely related to the total value of the economy's output. Yet it does not follow that the money supply determines the money value of the GNP and hence the rate of inflation. Instead, the total amount of money in circulation may well be a function of the need for sufficient finance to accommodate transactions. An increase in the money supply, simply to provide this accommodation, might then accompany an increase in inflation caused by some other event. It need not cause rising prices at all.

Common sense dictates that changes in the money supply are only one of a number of factors determining rises or falls in inflation. In rejecting this proposition, monetarists allege that all alterations in the rate of price increases are caused by changes in the money supply some two years previously. They also claim that inflation's future course can be guided within narrow limits by controlling the money stock. Empirical evidence demonstrates that this contention is far too precise and greatly overstates the predictive accuracy of monetarist theories.

For this amount of fine-tuning to be possible requires an unequivocal definition of money. It is one thing to recognise a situation where far too much money – or more accurately, too much credit – is being created. Monetarists are right in saying that if credit is so cheap and so readily available that speculation on asset inflation is easy or that the economy is overheating because of excess demand financed by credit creation, then the money supply is too large. This is a broad quantitative judgement. It is quite another matter to state that small alterations in the money supply generate correspondingly exact changes in the rate of inflation. Yet this is the claim which monetarists put forward.

The claim is implausible for a number of reasons. One is the difficulty in defining accurately what is and is not money. Notes and coins are clearly money, but where should the line be drawn thereafter? What kinds of bank facilities and money market instruments should be included or excluded? Many measures are available in every country, depending on what is put in and what left out. None has been found anywhere or for any length of time to have had a strikingly close correlation with subsequent changes in the inflation rate. Often, different measures of the money supply move in different directions. This is very damaging evidence against propositions which are supposed to be precise in their formulation and impact.

For monetarists another major problem, referred to above, is that there can be no constant ratio between the amount of money, however defined, in circulation and the aggregate value of transactions, because the rate at which money circulates can and does vary widely over time. The velocity of circulation – the ratio between the GDP and the money supply – is far from constant. In the USA the M3 velocity fell 17 per cent between 1970 and 1986, but by 1996, ten years later, it had risen 22 per cent. It has been exceptionally volatile in Britain, where it rose by 7 per cent between 1964 and 1970 and by a further 28 per cent between 1970 and 1974, only to fall by 26 per cent between 1974 and 1979.[6] Other countries, such as the Netherlands and Greece, have also had large changes in the velocity of circulation, particularly during the 1970s.[7] More recently the huge money supply increases in relation to GDP imply very substantial reductions in the velocity of circulation. In the USA, for example, M2 rose 79 per cent[8] between 2000 and 2010, while the economy grew by 49 per cent.[9]

Changes in monetary policy caused some of these movements, but a substantial proportion, especially recently, resulted from radical changes in the financial environment caused by deregulation's effects on credit creation and the growth of derivatives and other new financial instruments, not from government action. Such variations undercut belief in the rigid relationship that monetarism requires. Statistical records on the money supply and inflation everywhere show what one would expect if very little causation was at work. Except in circumstances of gross overcreation of money and credit, money supply changes have had little or no impact on the inflation rate. The need to provide enough money to finance all transactions has, over the long term, proved a much more important determinant of money supply than attempts to restrict it to control inflation, although some countries have certainly had tighter monetary policies than others. In the short term, there is no systematic evidence that changes in the money supply affect subsequent inflation rates with any precision at all.

It is not surprising, therefore, that the predictions of monetarists about future levels of inflation based on money supply trends have turned out to be no better, and often worse, than those of people who have used more eclectic, common-sense methods. Monetarists have not

confined their predictions, however, solely to the future rate of inflation. There are three other areas of economic policy – unemployment,
interest rates and exchange rates – where, over the last 40 years, their
ideas have had a decisive effect on practical policy.

The monetarist view of unemployment is that there is an unavoidable
'natural' rate, one set essentially by supply-side rigidities. An attempt
to reduce unemployment below this level by reflation will necessarily
increase wage rates and then the price level. The employed will be left
no better off than they were before, and with the increased demand
having been absorbed by higher prices, the numbers of the employed
will remain unchanged. Increasing demand pushes up only the inflation rate, not output or the number of people working.

At some point, as pressure on the available labour force increases
and the number of unemployed falls, a bidding-up process will no
doubt take place, and wages and salaries rise. This is a altogether
different matter, however, from postulating that unemployment levels
like those seen over much of the developed world since the 1980s are
required to keep inflation at bay. Nor is it plausible that supply-side
rigidities are the major constraint on getting unemployment down.
There is no evidence that these rigidities are significantly greater
now than they were in the 1950s and 1960s, and on balance they are
almost certainly less. If, during the whole of these two decades, it was
possible to combine high rates of economic growth with low levels of
unemployment and with inflation stabilised at an acceptable level,
why should one believe that it is impossible now for these conditions
to prevail again?

Monetarism also had a considerable influence on interest rates,
particularly during the 1980s. The tight control of the money supply
which monetarists advocated then could only be achieved if interest
rates were used to balance a relatively low supply of money against a
credit demand which has to be choked off by raising the price of money.
This requirement was made to seem less harsh by suggesting that a
positive rate of interest would always be required to enable lenders to
continue providing money to borrowers. It was alleged that any attempt
to lower interest rates to encourage expansion would fail, as lenders
withdraw from the market until the premium they require above the
inflation rate reappears.

There is yet another proposition more strongly based on assertion
than on evidence, especially in the light of recent experience. For
years on end in many countries, real interest rates paid to savers have
been negative, sometimes even before tax. Lenders, who never regard

negative interest rates as fair, frequently complain bitterly when they appear, though they can do little about them, since their ability to withdraw from the market is limited. High positive rates of interest, however, are undoubtedly a discouragement to investment, partly directly but much more importantly because of their influence on driving up the exchange rate.

This is particularly paradoxical in relation to exchange-rate policy, where monetarist ideas had their third major impact on practical issues. Monetarists have always argued that no policy for improving an economy's competitiveness by devaluation will work, because the inflationary effects of a depreciation will automatically raise the domestic price level to where it was in international terms. The devaluing country will be left with no more competitiveness than it had before but with a real extra inflationary problem with which it will have to contend. This proposition, still widely believed, is easy to test against historical experience. The large numbers of substantial exchange-rate changes over the last few decades provide plenty of empirical data against which to assess this monetarist assertion's validity. The evidence, amply displayed in Table 3.1 in Chapter 3, is overwhelmingly against it. Example after example of devaluations failing to produce sufficient excess inflation, if any, to erase the initial competitive advantage can be found. On the contrary, there is ample evidence indicating that exactly the opposite effect has been experienced in a wide variety of different economies. Those which devalue tend to perform progressively better, as manufacturing sectors expand and the internationally tradable goods and services they produce become cumulatively more competitive.

Countries which gain an initial price advantage therefore tend to forge ahead, with increasingly competitive import-saving and exporting sectors. Rapidly growing efficiency in the economic sectors involved in international trading gains them higher shares in world trade and provides platforms for further expansion. High-productivity growth generates conditions which may even allow them, with good management, to experience less domestic inflation than their more sluggish competitors. In practice, monetarist policies have had pronounced effects on exchange rates of countries where they have been most effectively imposed, but the impact is invariably to push them up. The economies concerned then suffer the undesirable yet all too familiar mix of sluggish growth, output increases too low to absorb wage and salary increases, and sometimes higher price inflation than their more favoured competitors.

Monetarist theories start by appearing simple and straightforward but end by being long on complication and assertion, and short on predictive and practical prescriptive qualities. They pander to the prejudices of those who would like to believe their conclusions. They lack convincing explanations about the transmission mechanisms between what they claim are the causes of economic events and the effects which they declare will necessarily follow. Where they can be tested against empirical results, the predictions their theories produce generally fail to achieve levels of accuracy high enough to be deemed worthwhile.

Monetarist theories have nevertheless reinforced all the prejudices widely held in favour of cautious financial conservatism, which monetarism accurately reflects. By allowing themselves to be persuaded by these misguided doctrines, those responsible for running a nation's affairs find it easy to acquiesce in accepting low growth and high unemployment levels which would never be tolerated if everyone realised how unnecessary they were. Thus, policies which should have been rejected continue to be accepted although they fail to work. Because expectations have been lowered, the deflationary consequences of high interest rates, restrictive monetary policies and overvalued exchange rates have not caused the outcry that might have been expected and which they deserved.

Slow growth in Europe

From the Common Market's establishment in 1958 until 1973, the average rate of growth among its countries was 5.1 per cent, the mean level of unemployment was little more than 2 per cent, and the average rate of inflation was 3.9 per cent. For the 20 years from 1973 to 1993, the growth rate averaged 2.1 per cent, and the inflation rate 7.0 per cent.[10] The rate of unemployment fluctuated over the period, but overall it was much higher than it had been previously. The registered unemployment level across the whole European Union during the 1980s and 1990s averaged close to 10 per cent, an almost fivefold increase.[11] Even then, the claimant count, which this figure represents, substantially underestimates the total number of those who would work if they had the opportunity to work at a reasonable wage.[12] What went wrong? Had the whole world plunged to a much lower growth rate after 1973, it would be plausible to argue that the Western world's experience was part of a universal trend. As Table 10.1 (see Chapter 10) shows, however, the fall elsewhere was much smaller than the West's. The growth rate in the whole of the rest of the world dropped from 5.1 per cent (1959–73) to 3.4 per cent (1973–92) and then picked up to 6.3 per cent (1992–2009).

Three major developments were responsible for the substantial sea change to the Community economies' fortunes in the 1970s. The first was the oil crisis, caused by OPEC's quadrupling of the price of crude oil, following the breakdown of the Bretton Woods system and the 1973 Yom Kippur War. The second was the change in intellectual fashion towards a harder-line version of economic theory and doctrine, as monetarist ideas replaced Keynesian thinking among large numbers of those responsible for economic policy in the Community countries. The third involved the political initiatives taken within the Community, intended to lead to closer integration by linking the currencies of the constituent economies, first in the currency Snake, then with the exchange-rate mechanism and finally with full monetary union.

The effect of the quadrupling of oil prices in 1974[13] on the economies of Europe, none of which then was producing a significant quantity of oil, was to shift about 2 per cent of their GDPs away from their own populations to those of the oil-exporting countries. With good management and a well coordinated response, this situation should not have been impossibly difficult to contain. The problem was that the oil shock came on top of other causes of instability, in some countries with a crisis in the banking system as the early 1970s boom broke. In all countries the main strain was felt in the balance of payments. Everyone reined in at once, trying to shift the trade balance problems elsewhere. Growth rates fell back sharply as deflationary policies were implemented everywhere. Indeed, the economies then comprising the Common Market collectively saw no growth in either 1974 or 1975 before resuming a much slower growth trajectory than had prevailed.[14]

If the oil price hike and the breaking boom were the immediate real-world causes of the deflationary policies which checked Community growth in the mid 1970s, the willingness of the authorities to persevere with them was greatly reinforced by the spread of monetarist doctrines. This second change in direction occurred largely in response to the pressing need to bring inflation down from the dangerous heights to which it had risen in some countries in the mid 1970s. Britain's year-on-year inflation peaked at 24 per cent, France's at 14 per cent, Italy's at 19 per cent and Germany's at a much more modest 7 per cent.[15]

Monetarist ideas had a particularly strong appeal in certain powerful quarters. The Bundesbank's strong anti-inflation tradition harked back to the German hyperinflation of 1923. Understandably, it welcomed ideas which reinforced its collective view of monetary priorities. Nearly all Europe's central bankers followed this highly respected bank's lead. As monetarist ideas also became very much the academic fashion, an endless succession of newspaper articles popularised them to a wider audience. Despite intellectual weaknesses apparent from the outset, monetarist ideas were implanted with extraordinary success right across Western Europe as the norm which few people were willing to challenge.

The third and most significant long-term influence on Community policies has been the drive to achieve further integration by locking Community currencies together and thus losing the flexibility which exchange-rate changes provide when competitiveness diverges. The first steps were taken just over ten years after the Common Market was established. In March 1970 the Council of Ministers set up a high-level group to prepare plans for, not just a customs union, but a full economic and monetary union among the original Six. The chairman was Pierre Werner (1913–2002), then Luxembourg's prime minister and minister of finance, who gave his name to the report produced within a few months. It concentrated on the two principal routes which might be chosen to achieve the convergence, involving an uneasy marriage of Keynesian and monetarist approaches, required to make monetary union a viable proposition. Nevertheless, in March 1971 the Council of Ministers, accepting the Werner Report's broad thrust, agreed, as a first step towards implementation, that exchange rates of the member currencies be maintained within 0.6 per cent of each other from 15 June 1971 onwards.

The start date for the Werner proposals came at an awkward time, though saying so is not to excuse their subsequent abandonment. In May 1971 the dollar crisis began; it led to the break-up of Bretton Woods at the Smithsonian Conference and abandonment of the existing IMF exchange-rate bands. With major fluctuations in the European rates, the new narrow bands for what came to be called the Snake were difficult to establish. A European Monetary Cooperation Fund was set up, operated by the central banks, to keep market rates within 1.125 per cent on either side of the central parities. In view of their impending

Community membership, Britain, Denmark and Eire, as well as the original Six, joined the new arrangements.

The life of the Snake, however, was relatively brief. Speculative fever in international money markets switched from the dollar, after its Smithsonian devaluation, to sterling. Within six weeks of joining, British authorities were forced to abandon attempts to maintain the agreed parity for the pound and it dropped out of the Snake, taking the Irish punt with it. Six months later in January 1973, the Italian government abandoned its commitment to keep the lira within the required limits and withdrew. A year afterwards in January 1974, the French followed suit. The franc rejoined the Snake in July 1975, but its second attempt to keep to the agreed parity lasted no longer than the first. In March 1976 it left permanently. Thus, in less than four years three of the four major Community currencies had abandoned efforts to keep up with the stability and low inflation rate of the Deutsche Mark. Reduced to a Deutsche Mark zone, the Snake embraced, apart from Germany, only the Benelux countries and Denmark. This first major attempt to bring together all the Community currencies had failed. Phase 2 of the Werner plan, the originally proposed move to monetary union, was quietly forgotten.[16]

Lessons should have been learnt from this experience to avoid similar problems in future. To ensure the Snake failure, because its introduction came at a difficult and turbulent time was an unconvincing explanation. If the Snake was worth having at all, it should have been more useful in stressful than in easier conditions. Political pressures for resuming attempts to lock Community currencies together, however, proved stronger than arguments from experience. Within three years, at the initiative of Roy (later Lord) Jenkins (1920–2003), the commission's president, at summit meetings in Copenhagen and Bremen, monetary union was back again at the top of the Community agenda.[17]

The main argument put forward for monetary union on this occasion was that the full benefits of the Community's customs union could not be achieved in an environment of exchange-rate instability and uncertainty. It was alleged that fluctuating rates were damaging to trade and steady economic growth. While an appealing argument, it lacked evidence that it was true. A number of studies, including a particularly extensive one carried out by the Bank of England, had shown that disruption caused by exchange-rate movements had little, if any, effect on growth rates, a finding reaffirmed by a recent WTO study.[18] That Common Market countries had been growing at unprecedented rates without their currencies being locked together was ignored. Also alleged was that floating exchange rates were inherently inflationary. Again, however, no concrete evidence was produced in support of this argument, and, as Chapter 3 shows, there is ample evidence that in most cases it is false. Nevertheless, in 1979 the Snake, reborn as the exchange-rate mechanism (ERM), became part of a new European monetary system (EMS).[19] When it began operations in March 1979, the new EMS had a substantially more potent battery of weapons to deploy against the markets than the Snake had in its time. Its first phase had two main objectives: The first was to achieve a high degree of stability in the participating currencies' exchange rates while the second was to secure convergence in the constituent economies' performance. Both proved difficult to achieve. In the decade following its inception, there were 12 realignments of one or more of the central rates, caused by widely differing experience with inflation and competitiveness. Over this period the central rate of the strongest currency, the Deutsche Mark, appreciated by 18 per cent; while the weakest, the lira, fell by 29 per cent. The combined impact of these changes was that the parity of the lira at the decade's end vis-à-vis the Deutsche Mark was 50 per cent of its value at its beginning. The ERM's effect was merely to delay exchange-rate changes, not to stop them. Nor was greater success achieved on convergence. Living standards across the Community did not grow significantly more equal, although the Irish economy, with a living standard well below the EEC average, grew considerably more rapidly than the rest. Nor did variables such as inflation rates come together. For example, in 1981 the consumer price index increased by 6 per cent in Germany, 13 per cent in France and 18 per cent in Italy.[20]

These inflation-rate variations highlighted the basic problem with the Snake and ERM. For nearly all the period of their operation, because of the Germans' low price rises and export competitiveness, other countries in the exchange-rate systems found it extremely difficult to compete with them. As their trade balances deteriorated, they faced the familiar choice of deflation or devaluation. With the latter ruled out, except in extreme circumstances, they had to deflate. As about half of all Germany's exports went to other Community countries during the ERM period,[21] its main export markets were depressed, pulling down the German growth rate. As a result, the whole of the Community's economy slowed (see Table 9.1). Against a long-term background of

Table 9.1 Growth in the EEC during the snake and exchange rate mechanism (ERM) periods

Year	Totals all Countries except Germany GDP in 1985 US$	Totals all Countries except Germany Annual % Growth	Germany Alone GDP in 1985 US$	Germany Alone Annual % Growth	Totals all Countries including Germany GDP in 1985 US	Totals all Countries including Germany Annual % Growth		Comments on Growth Rates
1966	664		377		1,041			1950–69
1967	700	5.4	376	–0.3	1,076	3.4		Average
1968	737	5.3	396	5.5	1,133	5.3		5.5%
1969	785	6.6	426	7.5	1,211	6.9	SNAKE	Snake
1970	827	5.4	447	5.0	1,274	5.3	SNAKE	Period
1971	856	3.5	461	3.1	1,317	3.3	SNAKE	Average
1972	888	3.7	481	4.3	1,368	3.9	SNAKE	3.7%
1973	940	5.8	504	4.8	1,443	5.5	SNAKE	Fall from
1974	974	3.7	505	0.2	1,479	2.5	SNAKE	6.9% to
1975	963	–1.1	498	–1.3	1,461	–1.2	SNAKE	–1.2%
1976	1,014	5.3	525	5.3	1,539	5.3		1976–1979
1977	1,046	3.1	540	2.8	1,586	3.0		Average
1978	1,070	2.4	556	3.0	1,626	2.6		3.6%
1979	1,123	4.9	579	4.2	1,703	4.7	ERM	
1980	1,041	–7.3	585	1.0	1,627	–4.5	ERM	
1981	1,157	11.1	586	0.1	1,743	7.1	ERM	ERM
1982	1,170	1.2	580	–0.9	1,751	0.5	ERM	Period
1983	1,182	1.0	590	1.8	1,772	1.2	REM	Average
1984	1,209	2.3	607	2.8	1,816	2.5	ERM	2.1%
1985	1,236	2.2	619	2.0	1,855	2.2	ERM	
1986	1,268	2.6	634	2.3	1,906	2.5	ERM	ERM
1987	1,298	2.3	643	1.5	1,941	2.1	ERM	Period
1988	1,349	3.9	667	3.7	2,016	3.9	ERM	Fall from
1989	1,395	3.5	691	3.6	2,087	3.5	ERM	4.7% to
1990	1,432	2.6	731	5.7	2,163	3.7	ERM	–1.0%
1991	1,449	1.2	764	4.5	2,213	2.3	ERM	
1992	1,467	1.3	776	1.6	2,243	1.4	ERM	
1993	1,459	–0.6	761	–1.9	2,220	–1.0	ERM	
1994	1,483	1.6	782	2.8	2,265	2.0		1993–1997
1995	1,522	2.6	792	1.2	2,313	2.1		Average
1996	1,546	1.6	802	1.3	2,348	1.5		2.0%
1997	1,584	2.4	820	2.2	2,403	2.4		

Sources: Table 7 on pages 120 and 121 in *National Accounts 1960–1992*. Paris, OECD, 1994 and Table 0101 in *Eurostatistics 11/95 and 4/00*. Luxembourg: The European Community, 1995 and 1999.

falling growth rates, each time the Community currencies were locked together, the performance of all the participating countries deteriorated – more quickly in the period of the Snake, more slowly under the ERM.[22]

Notwithstanding these problems, further moves were afoot to proceed to full monetary union. The drafters of the Single European Act had succeeded in making achievement of monetary union a specific commitment of the treaty, with a target date of 1992. In 1988 Jacques Delors (b. 1925), then the president of the Commission, persuaded the Council of Ministers to give him the task of 'studying and proposing concrete stages leading towards economic and monetary union'. While these proposals were being considered before been embodied in the 1991 Maastricht Treaty, which set out the programme for moves to a single European currency, the ERM ran into serious difficulties. During the summer of 1992, with market pressure attacking the weaker members of the ERM, the lira was devalued. In September 1992 a wave of speculation against sterling swept the pound out of the ERM. The franc's parity with the Deutsche Mark only just survived, thanks to massive intervention by the Bundesbank. Finally, the pressure against the whole ERM system reached a point where it was no longer possible to hold it together. In August 1993 the narrow bands were abandoned, and fluctuations up to 15 per cent on either side of the central rate against the ECU were allowed to take place while preparations went ahead for full monetary union.

Monetarist policies in the USA

The problems the USA faced were significantly different from those in most of Europe, although the intellectual background to the way they were tackled had much in common.

Compared with many other countries, the USA weathered the 1970s reasonably well. Small reductions in output in 1970, 1974 and 1975 were offset by substantial growth in other years, producing an erratic but still a tolerably satisfactory outcome in the circumstances of the time. Real GDP growth averaged 3.2 per cent per annum for the decade, a little below the 3.8 per cent average for all developed countries in the OECD.[23] The reduction in the dollar's post-Smithsonian parity, augmented by better than average US performance on inflation, gave those parts of the American economy exposed to international trade an increasing edge. Thus, exports of goods and services, net of inflation, rose

7.3 per cent per annum, compared with total imports, which increased only at 4.9 per cent.[24]

Unfortunately, this reasonably good performance was heavily undermined by adverse movements in relative costs. In particular, during the 1970s the price of oil rose hugely, with a major price increase in 1979 following the one in 1973.[25] By 1980 the USA was spending $79 billion a year on oil imports, compared with only $3 billion in 1970.[26] As a result, the balance of trade in goods and services began an alarming deterioration. In the late 1970s further rapid increases in the value of oil imports began to swamp the deteriorating surplus earned on manufactures. Since 1976 the USA has had a trade deficit every single year.[27]

To maintain a high rate of growth in the 1980s, the USA urgently needed a considerably more competitive exchange rate. An increase in the country's exports of manufactured goods might have offset the heavy burden across the exchanges occasioned by the extra cost of oil imports. Unfortunately, the opposite policy was put into operation. Under the incoming administration of President Ronald Reagan (1911–2004), heavily influenced by monetarist ideas, interests rates were raised sharply. The US Treasury Bills rate, which had fallen to just under 5 per cent during the boom years of the late 1970s, averaged over 14 per cent in 1981.[28] Inevitably the dollar soared on the foreign exchanges. With 1973 as the base and equalling 100 – thus already allowing for the 10 per cent post-Smithsonian devaluation – the trade-weighted value of the US dollar had fallen to 89 by 1979. This trend was then dramatically reversed – a classic example, incidentally, of the ability of policy decisions to change the exchange rate. By 1982 the index had reached 108, and by 1985 it was 123. In six years the dollar had sustained a real appreciation of 38 per cent.[29] As a result, the USA's growth in GDP during the 1980s fell to a cumulative 2.8 per cent per annum. Because the population was growing quickly, GDP per head grew at only 1.8 per cent a year.[30]

Predictably, the proportion of US GDP derived from manufacturing fell heavily. Between 1980 and 1993 it dropped from 21 per cent of GDP to 17 per cent, a relative reduction of just under a fifth.[31] People employed in manufacturing occupations also fell slightly in absolute numbers but much more steeply as a proportion of the total labour force. Of those in employment, the proportion working in manufacturing dropped from 22 to barely 16 per cent.[32] The problem was then a familiar one: productivity increases are much more difficult to secure across the board in the service sector than in manufacturing. This decline in industrial output as a proportion of GDP contributed directly and heavily to low growth in overall productivity, a key negative characteristic of this period in US economic history. Reflecting the decline in manufacturing and the impact of the policies pursued by the Reagan and Bush administrations on the growth rate, the US savings and investment ratios fell heavily, too, dropping from about 20 per cent in 1980 to under 15 per cent by 1993.[33]

Between 1980 and 1993, the first year of the Clinton presidency, the economy grew at a cumulative 2.7 per cent per annum and GDP per head rose on average 1.4 per cent a year,[34] yet none of these benefits found their way to the average worker as compensation per hour. On the contrary, across the board average earnings per hour fell. For the whole US economy in real terms, income per hour peaked in 1973, at $8.55 measured in constant 1982 dollars. By 1998 it was only $7.75. Thus, over the 25 years between 1973 and 1998, earnings per hour for the average American dropped in real terms a staggering 9 per cent.[35] Against the background of the steady rise in real earnings per hour in the US economy in the 1950s and 1960s of a little under 2 per cent per annum – about 18 per cent per decade[36] – who in 1973, predicting a fall for the next quarter of a century, have been given a hearing?

The decline in real hourly earnings, barely offset by a higher labour force participation rate and longer working hours and aggravated by a tougher line on social security payments, caused income distribution, even before taxes, to become much more uneven. Up to 1980 the proportion of aggregate income going to the bottom 40 per cent of income earners had been roughly stable at about 17 per cent. By 1993 it was 14 per cent. For the bottom quintile the drop was even more precipitate: from 5.3 to 4.1 per cent. Thus, the whole of this vast swathe of the American population – well over 50 million people – was about 8 per cent worse off on average in 1993 than in 1980.[37] At the other end of the spectrum, those in the top 5 per cent of income earners saw their share of total incomes rise between 1980 and 1993 from 15 to 20 per cent of the total.[38] As a result, their total income increased in real terms by about two-thirds.

Distribution of income became even more uneven post-tax, as tax rates on the rich were cut. The theory was that revenues ought to increase if rates were lowered, because there would be fewer incentives for avoidance and lower rates would stimulate enterprise and hence yield more revenue. This Laffer Curve approach to tax policy – one of the more egregious elements of the supply-side economic policies fashionable at the time – never came near to improving the overall federal collection rate, although it served a purpose in justifying lower tax rates on the rich. It was one reason why the US fiscal deficit began to widen.

The other major reason for deterioration in the federal government's finances was a vast increase on defence outlays. The result was that the overall government's fiscal stance, at both federal and state levels, which had been $346 billion in surplus in 1979 plunged in its deficit, reaching a negative $109 billion by 1983. An immediate repercussion from the fiscal deterioration was a large increase in the value of outstanding federal debt. In 1980 gross federal debt had been $906 billion, representing 33 per cent of GDP. By 1993 it was $4,409 billion, equivalent to 67 per cent of GDP and still rising in money terms, though stabilising as a percentage of GDP.[39]

A consequence of the heavily increased military spending of the Reagan years was that it drew a higher proportion of the relatively weakened US industrial base into defence work. This situation seriously exacerbated trade balance problems in the same period. By 1980 the total US foreign payments position was still in balance, as the surplus on investment income offset a $19 billion deficit on goods and services. From then on, the position went from bad to worse. By 1984 the trade deficit was $109 billion, and by 1987, $153 billion.[40] Most of this huge deterioration came from a catastrophic turnaround in trade in manufactured goods. As late as 1980 the USA had a reasonably healthy $12 billion surplus in trade in manufactured goods but by 1984 the surplus had turned into a deficit of $93 billion and $126 billion by 1988.[41]

An inexorable accounting identity applies to foreign trade. Deficits on current account have to be made up by exactly corresponding capital receipts. To pay for the accumulated multibillion-dollar deficits, the USA became a major net borrower from abroad and a major net seller of investment assets to foreigners. This was a drastic change. The USA, once by far the world's largest creditor, became much its biggest debtor. Its net international investment position at cost was a positive $392 billion in 1980; in 1993 it was a negative $503 billion.[42]

During the 1989–93 George H. W. Bush (b. 1924) presidency, the faltering economy grew by only 1.2 per cent in 1990 and contracted by almost 1 per cent in 1991.[43] No doubt this contributed to Bush's defeat in 1992, although by then the economy had started to pick up again. The economy inherited by the new president, Bill Clinton (b. 1946), therefore brought with it all the structural imbalances which the monetarist era had wrought, combined with considerable room for bouncing back from the 1990–1 shallow depression.

Between the spring of 1993, when the Clinton administration took over, and the end of 1998, there were some positive signs but not nearly enough to counteract the impact of the Reagan and Bush policies on the American economy. Between 1992 and 1998 the growth rate nevertheless averaged a compound 3.2 per cent per annum – a good deal better than the 2.6 per cent achieved between 1980 and 1992.[44] Clinton's record on the federal deficit was also much better than his two immediate predecessors'. A combination of contained expenditure and rising tax revenues reduced the deficit, which had peaked at $290 billion in 1992, to $22 billion in 1997, with a balanced budget projected for 1999 and subsequent years. The gross federal debt at the end of 1998 was $5,478.7 billion,[45] however, and interest charges on this large sum were an additional drain on the government's current resources.

By far the largest and most fundamental problem facing the Clinton administration as it neared its end was the foreign payments balance, for which a US currency strengthened vis-à-vis the rest of the world bore a heavy responsibility. The trade-weighted value of the dollar rose from an index of 87 in 1992 to 98 in 1998.[46] A combination of devaluations in the Far East and the weakening of most major currencies in Europe had left the dollar dangerously exposed. The US economy, despite its travails, may still have seemed immensely powerful, but the borrowing required to finance a deficit on this scale was beginning to look daunting. The net investment income which used to buttress the US foreign payments position turned negative for the first time in 1997.[47] The scene had been set for the intransigent problems to be faced by the US economy once the unsustainable boom of the early 2000s broke in 2008.

The tiger economies

A remarkable phenomenon in the second half of the twentieth century was the growth rates achieved by the so-called tiger economies – Hong Kong, Singapore, South Korea and Taiwan. Table 9.2 sets out the cumulative growth rates, increases in population and rises in GDP per head – a close proxy for living standards – which they managed to secure for their populations.

Table 9.2 Growth statistics for the tiger economies

	1913–1950	1950–1973	1973–1990	1990–2010
Cumulative Percentage Growth in Gross Domestic Product Per Annum				
Hong Kong	n/a	9.2	7.6	4.0
Singapore	n/a	7.8	7.4	6.8
South Korea	1.7	7.6	8.5	5.3
Taiwan	2.7	9.3	8.0	5.1
Cumulative Percentage Growth in Population per Annum				
Hong Kong	n/a	3.5	1.8	0.1
Singapore	n/a	2.8	2.0	2.3
South Korea	1.9	2.2	1.4	0.1
Taiwan	2.7	3.0	1.6	0.1
Cumulative Percentage Growth in GDP per Head of the Population				
Hong Kong	n/a	5.7	5.8	3.9
Singapore	n/a	5.0	5.4	4.5
South Korea	−0.2	5.4	7.1	5.2
Taiwan	0.0	6.3	6.4	5.0

Sources: Tables D-1e and F-4 in *Monitoring the World Economy 1820–1992* by Angus Maddison. Paris: OECD, 1995; Country Table Pages in *International Financial Statistics* Washington DC: IMF 2010 and 2011; and Tables 1-1a and 2-2 in *Taiwan Statistical Yearbook 2011.*

Several key points stand out from these statistics. First, the rapid growth all these economies achieved towards the end of the twentieth century was not a new development. All of them began growing fast once the disruption caused by World War II abated. Second, there is not much sign of a slowdown after 1973, roughly the time which clearly marked the sudden break from relatively fast to consistently much slower growth in the advanced industrialised economies – including Japan a little later. Whatever slowed growth in these major countries evidently did not have the same affect on the tiger economies. Third – a rather different point – the tiger economies gave little sign as they became very much better off that success would slow their growth rates very significantly. It is often alleged that economic growth becomes more difficult to achieve the higher the level of GDP per head. This was only partly true of the tigers. Since they largely avoided this pitfall, it is not clear why other economies should not be able to do the same.

The major reason why the tigers' performance was hardly noticed until the twentieth century's last quarter is that even as late as 1973, their combined GDPs represented only 1.2 per cent of world output.

By 1990 this ratio had more than doubled, to 2.7 per cent.[48] Even more impressive was their impact on world trade. Their total manufactured exports, including re-exports, which were 3.8 per cent of the world total in 1973, were 12.9 per cent in 1994.[49] Over one-eighth of world trade in manufactured products was being generated by four countries containing in total only 1.4 per cent of the world's population.[50]

Indeed, this astonishing export achievement provides the immediate explanation of the tigers' success. Between 1950 and 1992 South Korea's merchandise export volume rose cumulatively by 17 per cent per annum. Taiwan's rose by 16 per cent, compared with 8.5 per cent for the world as a whole.[51] The competitiveness of their exports made them extremely attractive to buyers all over the world. The opportunities thus created, as always happens in such circumstances, sucked talent and resources into sectors of the economy where they could be most productively employed. It is hardly surprising that all the tiger economies, with the huge investment opportunities opened up by fast growth, had high proportions of their national incomes devoted to investment, generally an average of 30 per cent or more.[52] As a result, industrial output soared, and with it productivity. In South Korea, for example, between 1968 and 1997, industrial output increased at a cumulative average of 13.4 per cent per annum, and productivity in these sectors of the South Korean economy rose by 8.3 per cent a year.[53] Nor was it just the tiger economies which followed this pattern. In 1970, 4 per cent of manufacturing output was in East Asia; by 1995 it was 11 per cent. Over the same period the figure in the industrialised countries fell from 88 to 80 per cent.[54] In 1994, 43 per cent of South Korea's GDP came from industry, and 38 per cent of GDP was used for gross domestic investment,[55] roughly twice the US ratios at the time.

The tiger economies were able to achieve very rapid growth rates because each of them, for a variety of reasons, found itself in the situation of the other fast-growing economies after the post-war recovery period. Each had a highly competitive export sector from which all else flowed. This is not to deny that hard work, discipline, access to world markets, good primary education, reasonably competent government and the other characteristics of the most successful economies were not important to the tiger economies, too. Yet the overwhelming significance of the export competitiveness factor was that it provided an environment where all the tiger economies' other characteristics could flourish and be used to best advantage.

In a number of key respects, their rapid growth also made it much easier for them to accomplish other social and political objectives which most people think desirable. Unemployment rates were very low throughout the period, with all the benefits they bring. Jobs were available for anyone who wanted to work. With the dependency ratio – the ratio between the number of people not working and thus reliant on the value added of others who were – relatively low, the need for government taxation and expenditure was kept low. Money spent on education and training was seldom wasted, as most people who took courses to improve their skills easily found jobs thereafter. Rapid growth's impact on the distribution of income was also not what is frequently supposed. It is often thought that fast growth leads to incomes becoming more dispersed, but the figures show otherwise. The fast-growing Asian economies have had more, not less, even distributions of income than is common in Western industrialised economies. With the pre-tax per capita income of the top decile taken as a ratio of that of the bottom two deciles, studies carried out around 1970 showed it to be 7.6 for South Korea, 7.5 for Japan, 10.5 for Germany and the Netherlands and 14.9 for the USA. Only Sweden at 8.1 and Britain at 9.1 got close to the Asian ratios, though Australia came in at 7.2.[56] The distribution of income has widened substantially in the West over the last four decades, especially post-tax, whereas it has stayed roughly constant in most of Asia.[57]

Reflected in the relatively even distribution of income in the tiger economies are other benefits. Almost everyone is literate. Life chances have been reasonably equal, thus helping to reduce social tensions and produce more cohesive societies. All of them have avoided the high crime rates, especially those involving various forms of theft, which have become an increasing problem in the West. They all have low infant-mortality rates, high standards of public health and long life expectancies, generally in the mid-seventies.[58]

Should the tiger economies therefore become models for the rest of the world? To some extent, the answer may be yes, they should, but in other respects, unfortunately, the figures do not stack up. As with Japan during a similar phase of post-war development and now China, the problem with the tiger economies is that they achieved their huge success by cornering more than their fair share of economic activities which generate high-productivity increases and, hence, fast rates of economic growth. Their high concentration on industrial output, where rapid increases in output per head are easiest to secure, have been bought at the expense of other economies. These particularly include

Britain, the USA and much of continental Europe. By letting cost bases become too high, these areas have laid themselves open to becoming net importers of manufactured goods.

The solution to this problem, however, is not to slow down the tigers' progress, at least as far as avoidable. Rather, it is to ensure that demand is generally sufficient, especially in the Western world, for industrial output to flourish as it has not only in the tiger economies but also round much of the rest of the Pacific Rim. To achieve this goal, however, some significant rebalancing of manufacturing's concentration will inevitably be required.

10
Twenty-First-Century Perspectives

In retrospect, 2000 to 2008 may very well turn out to be viewed as the last years during which Western economies did reasonably well before the storm to come. At least on the surface, in the USA and Europe economic performance seemed satisfactory and relatively stable, as the US economy, helped by rapid rises in the value of housing, recovered from the dot-com boom and bust of the late 1990s and several economies in Europe boomed on the strength of low Eurozone interest rates. Inflation everywhere was low, averaging 2.3 per cent in the USA and 2.1 per cent in Europe.[1] In many countries property values, thanks to historically low interest rates, increased markedly, making property owners feel richer. From 2002 to 2007 average UK house prices rose 90 per cent,[2] and over 200 per cent in Ireland between 1997 and 2007.[3] Stock exchanges recovered strongly. In the USA the Dow Jones Industrial Average almost doubled between 2002 and 2007,[4] with similar increases in Europe. The euro, established in 1998 as the constituent currencies were locked together and the currency in day-to-day use throughout the Eurozone since 2001, appeared to have got off to a good start. Living standards rose, too, although averages could be misleading. A very high proportion of increased GDP everywhere, particularly the USA, went to the already well off. Those not so fortunately placed on the income scales derived considerably less benefit from overall growth rates, which nevertheless remained positive throughout the Western world.[5] Between 2000 to 2007 US GDP grew by 17.8 per cent and the EU's by 19.8 per cent.[6] The West, therefore, did not appear to most people to be under serious threat.

This apparently benevolent state of affairs belied reality in two crucial and closely related developments, one internal and the other external. The internal problem was that the prosperity, thought by most people to be on a sustainable basis, was in fact largely founded on the creation of a huge amount of debt owed by people living within the Western world, many of whom were never creditworthy enough to assume liabilities on the scale with which they encumbered themselves. The external problem was that many Western countries, although not all, were running ever larger external payments deficits. Thus, both their citizens (internally) and their economies as a whole (externally) were living beyond their means while also getting cumulatively more in debt to those countries, particularly China, Taiwan, Germany, Holland and Switzerland, which were running large balance of payments surpluses.[7]

As long as those who are advancing credit are reasonably confident that individuals, companies and countries to which they lend money are going to be able to pay it back – or at the very least are going to be able to service the interest charges involved – mounting debt may appear to be sustainable. The root problem for the Western world was that from 2008 onwards, confidence that this requirement would be met began to evaporate. The first major breach came as it became clear that sub-prime housing debt in the USA was nothing like as secure an asset as had been assumed, notwithstanding the role of the credit rating agencies in claiming that, packaged up into consolidated units, it was. As it became obvious that a large number of financial institutions were unsure of the value of the assets they held, interbank transactions started to freeze up, culminating in the collapse of Lehman Brothers, a major US investment bank, on 15 September 2008.[8] The dangers of contagion spreading were averted, at least for the time being, by a concerted international effort to provide liquidity to the West's major banks but at the cost of creating more debt. Furthermore, as confidence in the future drained away, more threats to the banks' balance sheets emerged, not least in the form of property loans in, particularly, the USA, the UK, Ireland and Spain, which it was increasingly clear were no longer covered in value by the assets which secured them.

As Western economies began falteringly to recover from the big falls in GDP which many sustained in the 2008 crisis, new threats emerged. In Europe the Eurozone's major structural faults grew ever more evident. Although among the weaker economies the faults looked like liquidity or solvency problems, the root malaise they all suffered from was lack of competitiveness, a classic exchange-rate overvaluation problem of the same sort and over a similar time scale as the one that had sunk the Snake and the ERM. As happened with prior attempts to lock EU currencies together, Germany in particular succeeded in containing costs and developing increased export competitiveness far more effectively than less disciplined countries, including not only Greece, Ireland and Portugal but also much larger ones including Spain, Italy – and possibly even Belgium and France. As the weaker Eurozone members reined in their economies to reduce deficits and the rate of debt accumulation, Germany's exports faltered, as more than half went to other EU countries and over a third to other Eurozone economies.[9] Again, exactly as with the Snake and the ERM problems, the growth rate for the entire single currency area contracted, until by mid-2011 near stagnation was reached. Meanwhile the euro's strength on foreign exchanges, buoyed by Germany's stellar export performance, made effective competition in world markets almost impossible for Europe's struggling southern economies.

In the USA different problems materialised, though all were related to the fundamental competitiveness and debt disequilibria which had become the West's hallmark. Mirroring the US's huge payments deficit was a massive federal fiscal shortfall combined with falling house prices and high and rising unemployment. Something had to be done about the government deficit, but getting Democrats and Republicans to come to a reasonable agreement about the way ahead proved impossible. The Democrats sought to take measures to reflate the flagging economy and reduce unemployment, but the deficit's size – triggering the US loss of its AAA credit rating from Standard and Poor's (August 2011) – increased this option's danger.[10] The Republicans, encouraged by their intransigent Tea Party wing, refused to support tax increases, even those which involved closing loopholes in already agreed tax measures. Under the strain of an ever more uncertain future, markets on both sides of the Atlantic buckled.

The danger now is that the whole Western world will fail to grasp the fundamental reasons for the malaise which has overtaken it, so that the future, far from providing even modest growth, instead produces stagnation accompanied by rising unemployment and very possibly increased social tensions and political extremism. The remainder of this chapter looks at the West's current condition in more detail. The final chapter then suggests how the root problems of lack of competitiveness and accumulating debt can be resolved.

Trade imbalances

The fundamental problem with the world economy at present is that trade imbalances cannot be financed with any reasonable expectation that the debts involved are going to be repaid, at least at face value. This situation exists mainly because most global trade is in manufactured goods. Some countries, because they have very competitive exchange rates, have sequestered much more than their fair share of manufacturing capacity; others – including most of those in the West – have allowed the reverse conditions to develop. As a result, most economies with weak manufacturing sectors suffer in varying degrees from chronic balance of payments difficulties. Getting a grip on the problems scale requires looking at how large the imbalances are, at current trends, and at what is happening to the debts accumulating as a result of them.

Table 10.1 sets out the current-account balance of payments position of most of the world's major economies. It is made up of four components, these being the deficit or surplus on trade in goods, trade in services, investment income and transfers. A very clear picture emerges. Some countries have very large surpluses and others have equally substantial deficits. As an accounting identity – a recurrent theme – all current-account deficits have in aggregate to be matched by exactly equal and opposite capital movements. Some of these take the form of asset acquisitions in either individual or portfolio form. Most, however, are financed by debt which is why the enormous debt balances shown in Table 10.2 have been allowed to accumulate.

Since the numbers are so large, one may well ask how this situation was ever allowed to arise. At first sight it seems obvious that repaying such large sums of money or even servicing their interest charges would present great difficulties. There are several reasons why it was not so obvious that the problems were as serious as they now look like turning out to be.

First, the US dollar, the euro and, to a much lesser extent now, sterling are all reserve currencies. The dollar is used on a huge scale to finance globalised trade and to facilitate payments throughout the world. Being a reserve currency necessarily involves the holding of very large sums, on which little interest is paid, as working balances both within the banking system and elsewhere. As the world's economy expands and more and bigger balances are required, larger and larger volumes of funding are needed. This therefore provides a rational reason for the creation of debt which trade imbalances facilitate.

Second, although in theory almost all debts are at some stage due to be repaid, lenders seldom expect repayment in the reasonably near future. Nor do they particularly worry whether repayment will be possible at any time, at least in individual cases, provided a strong covenant and a solvent debtor seem to be involved. This is so because they are not concerned about any debts owed to them provided they can rely on finding someone else to assume their debt if asked to do so. As long

Table 10.1 Current account balances – selected countries – 2010 ranked in order of overall current account balances, all financial figures are in billions of US dollars unless otherwise indicated

	Trade Balance	Services Balance	Income Balance	Transfer Balance	Overall Current Account Balance	Total GDP in Local Currency	Exchange Rate	Total GDP	Pop-Ulation in Millions	Current Account Surplus/ Deficit (-) as % GDP	Current Account Balance per Head in US$	Growth in GDP % 2000/ 2010	Growth in GDP % per Head 2000/2010
China	254.2	-22.1	30.4	42.9	305.4	39,798	7.775	5,119	1,354.1	6.0	226	190	177
Japan	91.0	-16.1	133.3	-12.4	195.8	479,215	81.450	5,884	127.0	3.3	1,541	10	10
Germany	204.7	-25.2	59.7	-50.8	188.4	2,494	0.748	3,332	82.1	5.7	2,296	13	13
Russia	151.4	-27.8	-48.4	-4.1	71.1	46,083	46.935	982	140.4	7.2	507	80	84
Switzerland	15.9	41.5	25.1	-12.1	70.4	546	1.447	377	7.6	18.6	9,258	22	20
Singapore*	30.2	8.5	-3.1	-3.0	32.6	304	1.288	236	4.8	13.8	6,741	88	71
South Korea	41.9	-11.2	0.8	-3.2	28.2	1,172,803	1.135	1,033	48.5	2.7	582	63	60
Saudi Arabia*	105.2	-65.2	8.6	-27.7	21.0	1,630	3.750	435	26.3	4.8	798	45	35
Ireland	49.2	-11.3	-37.8	-1.9	-1.9	154	0.748	206	4.6	-0.9	-407	40	33
Greece	-37.5	17.3	-12.2	0.1	-32.3	230	0.748	308	11.2	-10.5	-2,892	34	33
France	-71.2	12.8	48.9	-35.0	-44.5	1,931	0.748	2,581	62.6	-1.7	-711	16	15
Brazil	20.2	-30.8	-39.6	2.8	-47.4	3,675	1.686	2,180	195.4	-2.2	-242	49	43
India	-97.9	6.9	-12.9	52.2	-51.8	78,756	44.810	1,758	1,214.5	-2.9	-43	120	101
United Kingdom	-151.3	69.4	56.3	-30.5	-56.2	1,454	0.639	2,276	61.9	-2.5	-908	20	19
Spain	-62.3	36.7	-28.7	-9.4	-63.6	1,063	0.748	1,420	45.3	-4.5	-1,404	29	25
Italy	-24.7	-12.0	-10.3	-20.9	-67.9	1,548	0.748	2,068	60.1	-3.3	-1,130	7	6
United States	-643.6	147.8	163.0	-137.5	-470.3	14,660	1.000	14,660	317.6	-3.2	-1,480	23	21

Source: IMF *International Financial Statistics Yearbook 2011* Country Tables & GDP Volume Measures.
*Singapore and Saudi Arabia Account Balance Figures are for 2009.

Table 10.2 Figures showing government and consumer debt trends in the USA and UK (all at current prices)

	Currency		2006	2007	2008	2009	2010
US Individuals	US$bn	Consumer Credit	2,385	2,522	2,561	2,449	2,403
		Mortgages	13,462	14,524	14,619	14,326	13,947
		Total	15,847	17,046	17,180	16,775	16,350
US Government			8,860	9,229	10,700	12,311	14,025
UK Individuals	£bn	Consumer Credit	198	201	208	205	197
		Mortgages	1,082	1,190	1,227	1,224	1,228
		Total	1,280	1,391	1,435	1,429	1,425
UK Government			648	696	862	1,050	1,238
Debt as a percentage of Gross Domestic Product:							
US GDP	US$bn		13,399	14,062	14,369	14,119	14,660
US Individuals as a percentage of GDP			118	121	120	119	115
US Government as a percentage of GDP			66	66	74	87	96
Total as percentage of GDP			184	187	194	206	211
UK GDP	£bn		1,328	1,405	1,446	1,395	1,454
UK Individuals as a percentage of GDP			98	99	99	102	98
UK Government as a percentage of GDP			49	50	60	75	85
Total as percentage of GDP			147	149	159	177	183

Sources: USA: Tables B-1, B-76, B77 and B-87 in *Economic Report to the President*. Washington DC: US government Printing Office, 2011. UK: Bank of England and *Credit Action* Internet Tables and pages 744 and 745 in *International Financial Statistics*. Washington DC: IMF, 2011.

as markets are deep, liquid and confident in debtors' capacity generally to meet their obligations, which has long been the case in the West, the risks for each individual creditor, even large ones, are low enough for confidence to be maintained. Only when the realisation dawns that a significant number of major debtors are getting past the point where their liabilities are manageable does the systemic danger of debt accumulation become apparent. This situation starts to be reached once markets see that the rate at which debt and total interest payments due on it are accumulating is beyond the capacity of debtors to pay. A big part of the reason why this situation has been slow to materialise is that, as long as economies are growing, their capacity to service increasing amounts of debt keeps rising. Only when economies stop growing while their debts are increasing – as is happening now – does the line between solvency and insolvency suddenly hove much more sharply into view.

Third, at least until very recently it looked as though at least Western sovereign debt – debt owed by governments – was so solidly reliable that virtually no risk was involved in holding it. There was always some danger that currencies would depreciate – providing an exchange-rate risk that the debt denominated in a devaluing currency would be worth less than it had been in other currencies – but no apparent risk that any developed Western sovereign nation would default. As long as any currency had a central bank which, if need be, could create unlimited amounts of money, a sovereign nation could meet its obligations. Furthermore, if most governments' policy was to avoid depreciating their currencies if they could possibly avoid doing so, the exchange-rate risk appeared also to be kept within bounds. Within the eurozone, however, the situation is different. Because the single currency is managed by the European Central Bank, not by individual countries, the weaker economies no longer have the ability to create whatever funds might be required to meet their obligations. This is one of the major reasons why the Eurozone is currently in such difficulties and faces a risk of sovereign defaults.

Fourth, if all balance of payments surpluses necessarily involve capital transfers of one sort or another to deficit countries, the huge sums of money involved as the surpluses develop have to go somewhere, and it was not obvious where else much of it could go unless into buying deficit countries' debt. Furthermore, if the result, for example, of Chinese purchases of US Treasuries is also to keep China's currency and hence its exports highly competitive by soaking up funds from its export surplus, the policy clearly has a certain rationale. Even with the risk that funds spent on US Treasuries might never be repaid except in heavily depreciated dollars, the short-term gain to the Chinese in the huge boost to its economy from its success as an exporter, based on maintaining its undervalued currency to keep its manufactured output competitive in world markets, is evidently a major offsetting factor.

Thus, a significant number of factors has persuaded the herd instincts of the markets that the accumulation of debt on the scale which has materialised was sustainable. The danger is that, as market sentiment turns and becomes pessimistic, precisely the recessionary conditions which make the world's major debt problems less and less manageable will be precipitated, bringing just the sort of major financial crisis it is in everyone's interest to avoid. The way in which a major crisis may envelop us all will be different in the USA and the UK than in the Eurozone countries, mainly because the existence of the EU's single currency makes the adjustments required more difficult to accomplish than they would otherwise be. The danger – building up fast at the moment – on both sides of the Atlantic is, however, broadly similar. Debt is growing more rapidly than the capacity of many governments and countries, as well as some individuals and companies, to service and repay it. This trend is unsustainable. It cannot and will not last indefinitely. This is why fundamental review of economic policy objectives in the West is becoming so pressingly urgent.

Fiscal crises

The reason why many of the western world's economies are in such difficulties at present is attributable to a combination of both problems inherited from the past and difficult choices for the present and future. The former has left legacies of excessive debt accumulated during recent years by countries, governments, individuals and some types of companies, such as property developers, leading to an overhang of borrowing, at least a fair proportion of which is never going to be repaid. The problem looking ahead is that governments still spend too much in relation to the revenues they can reasonably expect to garner from taxation, fees, charges and other sources of income, while consumers struggle to pay off previous borrowings. The remedies proposed are to encourage the corporate and consumer sectors to pay down debt while requiring governments to cut expenditure to reduce their outgoings to a figure closer to their revenues, the aim being to reduce fiscal deficits and the need to borrow more money.

Statistics on the growth particularly of consumer debt in many countries and the widening of government fiscal deficits plainly show where the pressures for the policy directions described above come from. Table 10.1 shows the trends which have materialised in the USA and the UK which are mirrored in many other Western countries.

Clearly, neither the rate of accumulation of private debt nor the scale of recent government deficits is sustainable. Whether the policies being adopted in many Western countries to deal with this situation have realistic chances of success is, however, very far from clear.

The significant retrenchment by consumers, government and those sectors of the commercial world which allowed themselves to become overextended is heavily deflationary. If consumers reduce their propensity to buy goods and services on credit while paying down debt wherever they reasonably can, overall consumer demand has to drop. If governments cut back on expenditures while trying to raise revenue through increased taxation, higher fees and charges, again, public sector net demand on the economy will fall. If the corporate sector believes that the future is not likely to be one where demand is rising, it is unlikely to increase investment, even if finding the cash to finance it is not a problem, as it quite widely is now the case. This leaves the only major element of demand on the economy left to fill the gap as an increase in net exports. At the best of times, this is not an objective most Western economies – with some exceptions – have found easy to secure. If developed Western countries' major export markets tend to be other Western economies – as they are – and nearly all these economies are in encountering similar difficult economic conditions, their capacity for absorbing more imports is correspondingly poor. There may be scope for increasing exports to China, India and other parts of the world still expanding strongly, but there is stiff competition for their import markets and, on present trends, much too little which most Western economies can sell to them to plug the gap. If all Western economies try to reduce borrowing and fiscal deficits at the same time, therefore, the likely consequence is, at best, a period of little if any growth. At worst – even discounting other potential major destabilising threats, particularly those associated with the Eurozone – there could be a further significant decline in GDP across the whole of the Western world.

The pressure for reflationary policies to reduce unemployment and to get the West's economies growing again will then be very substantial. The risks in adopting such policies, however, are also significant. If, say, the USA and the UK, both with very high government deficits, have to keep borrowing large sums to finance revenue shortfalls in relation to expenditures, retaining their creditworthiness will be crucially important. The USA has already faltered. The UK has so far retained its AAA rating only because of the government's determination to cut expenditure on a scale which may prove very difficult to sustain if the economic outlook worsens. The Continent has already

seen downgrades and more are threatened. Thus, reflationary policies of any size may simply not be feasible given the difficulties in
presenting them credibly to markets fearing that increased borrowing
is likely to be involved.

It is not clear, however, that deflationary policies favoured by the
markets will be much, if any, better at reducing the need to finance
deficits than action taken to reflate the West's economies, which at
least might reduce unemployment and increase government revenues.
The problem is that reflation entails more borrowing, at least in the
short term, with all the risks of credit-rating downgrades. The outcome
on government borrowing, if driven mainly by cuts in outgoings, will
depend on whether reductions in expenditures can be achieved on a
sufficiently wide scale to offset additional calls on government spending
as recessionary conditions bite. If unemployment then rises, with all
the attendant cost pressures on government resources, combined with
falling revenues as the economy contracts, there may be little if any
reduction in deficits as a result of cuts in public expenditure.

The reality, therefore, is that all Western governments faced with high
deficits have little room for manoeuvre. To continue borrowing without
seeing interest rates on their indebtedness rise, they must show the
markets that they are trying to get deficits under control. They cannot
pursue reflationary policies to any significant extent because these will
inevitably involve increased borrowing, at least initially, which the
markets will not accept. The consequence, however, is that they are being
forced into deflationary policies which may well not produce the results
the markets hope to see and may well be increasingly difficult to get electorates to accept. The West's economies are therefore faced with problems
to which there are no obvious solutions within the policy frameworks
within which they are used to operating. Their difficulties have, however,
been made considerably worse by other policy errors, particularly those
associated with the establishment of the EU's single currency, which now
severely exacerbate an already poor economic outlook.

Europe's single currency

The EU's project to have a single currency – the euro – operating across
as much of the EU as possible, preferably all member states, has, as
was earlier described, roots going back to at least the 1970s. Always a
political rather than an economic endeavour, the establishment of the
single currency, it was hoped, would cause the performance of all the
countries concerned to converge, although it was never clear why this

should happen. The reality was that the countries which were to make up the Eurozone were too diverse to make up a stable area, all using the same currency. Experience with the Snake and the ERM had shown that Germany, in particular, had highly entrenched capacities for holding down costs and increasing export competitiveness in relation to most other EU nations, especially those in southern Europe. Whereas the USA has a relatively highly mobile labour force, speaking a common language and capable of moving to exploit economic advantage, the EU, with its many languages and other home country ties, has found mobility much less easy to achieve. Furthermore, though in the USA a considerably lower proportion of GDP passes through government hands than is the average in Europe, federal disbursements still account for about 20 per cent of GDP.[11] This permits very substantial transfers to be made from the more to the less prosperous areas of the country. In the EU no such mechanism exists. The total budget is capped at no more than 1.23 per cent[12] of EU GDP, and much of this, involved with the Common Agricultural Policy, does little if anything to redistribute income from richer to poorer countries.

Locking the currencies of the disparate countries making up the Eurozone in 1998 – supposedly irrevocably – and replacing them with euro notes and coins in 2001 was always therefore a high-risk strategy. As has happened with most earlier currency unions, however, the project got off to quite a good start. From a technical standpoint the euro's introduction was managed with commendable smoothness. In the relatively benign conditions of the twenty-first century's early years, the Eurozone did reasonably well. Yet as with all prior currency unions which did not morph into unitary states, problems of disparate performance and compatibility gradually and then rapidly increased. When the single currency was established, the Germans, having foreseen some of the problems which might ensue, had insisted in 1997 on a Growth and Stability Pact being implemented. It was designed to limit Eurozone country budget deficits to 3 per cent of GDP and total borrowing to 60 per cent of GDP.[13] The situation was not helped by the fact that with both Germany and France ignored these restrictions early on when it suited them to do so, making it more difficult to establish any serious commitment to fiscal discipline later in among the more vulnerable single currency members.

Some of the problems stemmed from long-established features of the constituent economies. Greece, Italy and Spain, for example, had long histories of higher levels of inflation than Germany and other Nordic economies. Greece clearly joined the single currency on the basis of wildly optimistic statistics and by all accounts widely known to be so at the time. Portugal and others were uncompetitive from the beginning. These mismatches were then exacerbated by features intrinsic to the single currency concept. With only one currency, there could be only one interest rate. It tended to be too high in countries with low inflation rates and much too low in countries where prices were rising strongly. Unsustainable property booms, particularly in Spain and Ireland, financed by low interest rates were the result, with the feel-good impact of rising property values helping to push up the price level generally.

As always happens, the relatively rapidly rising price levels in the less disciplined countries increasingly bit into their capacity to pay their way in the world. All of them began to experience deteriorating balance of payments conditions. The initial increase in indebtedness which was entailed was relatively easily absorbed by the markets, which felt confident that the single currency was such a solid project that Greek debt, for example, was as good – or almost as good – as German debt. Even in early 2008 almost no interest premium was paid on non-German euro bonds.[14] By early 2011, however, the situation had completely changed. Greece was paying a 12 per cent premium and Ireland 10 per cent. Later in the year Italy was paying close to 7 per cent and even France began having to pay significantly more than Germany.[15] These spreads were a harsh but realistic indicator of market sentiment about the relative decline in creditworthiness of these different countries over the period concerned.

Initially with Greece, then with Ireland and Portugal, it became apparent that without much more assistance from other single currency members – and others – than had been envisaged, all these countries would not be able to meet their debt obligations. Contagion then began to spread to the much larger economies of Spain and Italy with Belgium and even France being viewed as economies which might not be able to continue within the single currency without receiving very large bailouts. The first bailout – for Greece in May 2010 – was followed by a further one for Ireland in November 2010 and one for Portugal in April 2011.[16]

The dilemma faced by EU political leaders, particularly Germany's Chancellor Angela Merkel (b. 1954), became acute. It was increasingly clear that the Eurozone could not survive without massive transfers from the stronger economies to the weaker. As Germany was much the largest and strongest, it was obvious that there was no alternative but for the Germans to be the major paymasters. Germany, however, was hugely reluctant to undertake this open-ended commitment. If major subventions from Germany were to be forthcoming, there would have to be much tighter oversight of the budgets and economic management of the economies receiving the assistance. This was evidently going to involve the imposition of drastic economic retrenchment, combined with insistence on wholesale reforms of labour markets, pension entitlement and institutional arrangements, changes for which there was no democratic mandate and to which there was certain to be strong resistance from entrenched interests. Furthermore, these changes were to be implemented in heavily deflationary employment and economic conditions, which were bound to increase hostility to any such programmes' being generally accepted.

At the time of writing, it was not certain how this situation might get resolved, though there seems to be sufficient determination among EU leaders to keep the Eurozone in being in substantially its present form for some time. Even with further attacks on the weaker members by nervous markets, they may be able to do enough to stop defaults taking place and the single currency breaking up, at least for the time being. Whether they will be able to achieve the objective indefinitely, however, remains to be seen. A major component of the single currency's problems is that, when the Eurozone was established, cross-border bank lending was positively encouraged by the EU Commission, as a way of promoting growth in those economies with relatively low GDP per head. This lending did increase living standards short-term in the countries such as Spain and Ireland but only by creating unsustainable property booms. The legacy of encouraging banks in one country to lend in others is very large cross-country bank indebtedness, compounded by existing bad debts caused by unwise large-scale property loans and speculation in sub-prime obligations, which have already put a major strain on EU banks' balance sheets. An EU break-up would leave many European banks insolvent. A series of major bank liquidations would plunge the EU economy – and much of the rest of the world's – into crisis. Thus, refinancing banks to avoid bankruptcies is likely to be preferred to collapse. The problem, then, is whether even the EU's sovereign states, with all their other debt commitments, would have enough borrowing power to do this.

While it is easy to understand the extreme reluctance of EU leaders to allow the single currency to break up, pursuit of the policy they seem to favour – keeping the single currency substantially as it is – holds two major dangers. The first is that this policy does nothing to overcome the Eurozone's weaker members' root problem. This is not just one of solvency or liquidity. It is fundamentally one of competitiveness. It is therefore, an exchange-rate and cost-base issue. If these economies were able to devalue substantially, there would be very serious short-term problems to overcome, but the longer-term outlook would be much more favourable as happened in the case of Argentina in 2002, for example.

While Argentina retained its own currency, the peso, it was tied, supposedly irrevocably, to the dollar in 1991 with the intention of stabilising and disciplining the Argentine economy. Because costs in Argentina still rose much more quickly than in the USA, economic conditions gradually worsened to an intolerable point, leading to Argentina defaulting in its creditor in 2002. The pezo then fell in value by 70 per cent in four months causing great temporary hardship as GDP fell by 11 per cent. Argentina then rapidly recovered, however growing cumulatively by 9 per cent per annum between 2003 and 2007. By 2010 manufacturing output had doubled from its 2002 level[17] – a portent of what may happen in Europe if the single currency does break up.

The second fundamental problem faced by the EU leaders is that, far from the single currency remaining bad but getting no worse, they are deteriorating all the time, partly because every month which goes by, the total amount of debt which one way or another has to be financed goes up to as balance of payments and government deficits continues to accumulate. At the goes up same time, if economic performance within the Eurozone continues to deteriorate and to produce little or no economic growth, the capacity of all the deficit economies to meet their debt obligations gets steadily worse, making eventual defaults inevitable.

If this is the situation, there must then be a strong argument for coming to grips with the fundamental problem now rather than later, when the total amount of debt to be managed may be too great for the Eurozone countries to handle. Allowing the single currency to break up in an orderly way, while there is still time to do so, is preferable to the uncontrollable disorder of having the markets completely lose confidence in Eurozone member states and a significant number of EU governments are no longer able to borrow. This is likely to happen once it becomes more and more certain that the eventual outcome can only be defaults. With money being withdrawn from potentially defaulting countries faster and faster, an intolerable strain will be put on the solvency of these countries' banks, potentially involving bailout costs so high as to be unmanageable. Problems of competitiveness within single currency areas eventually materialise as banking crises whereas with countries with their own currencies, once parities get too far out of line, they take the form of currency crises. The basic problem and solution, however, are the same.[18]

Of course, the problem of dealing with single currency defaults is made hugely more complicated and difficult by the fact that the same currency exists in all Eurozone countries. While most euro-denominated debt and contracts could be dealt with by a defaulting country passing a law making all euros within its jurisdiction worth a fraction of those in Germany but leaving the depreciated euro as legal tender until a new currency could be introduced, there would inevitably be cases where which euro value applied was unclear. Sooner or later these problems will have to be confronted and solutions found. Currency unions have broken up in the past, and the problems involved in dissolving what were thought to be permanent arrangements have been somehow overcome, generally after a relatively short period of turmoil. It seems very probable that, sooner or later, this will happen in the Eurozone.

US and UK travails

The situation in both the USA and the UK ought to be more manageable than in the Eurozone's. Both the USA and UK are major economies, with their own currencies and thus without the constraints facing Eurozone members. Although what happens in the Eurozone is bound to have a major impact on them neither the USA nor the UK has completely unmanageable commitments, through the IMF or otherwise, towards underwriting the continuation of the single currency. If major changes in exchange-rate policies are required, both are much better positioned to implement them than the single currency economies are. There are, however, different reasons why the sorts of policies which are fundamentally required to stabilise and improve the positions of both the USA and the UK in the world economy may be exceptionally difficult to implement.

Perhaps the most important reason of all stems from the fact that the USA and the UK have been relatively unsuccessful in achieving reasonable rates of growth for longer than any other major economies. This has allowed attitudes to both harden and permeate public opinion more broadly than elsewhere in favour of the hard money, high-exchange-rate policies which have been the fundamental reason for their undoing.

First, though both economies have very strong finance sectors and exceptionally successful and powerful importing companies, they have relatively weak and discredited manufacturing sectors. Thus, large sections of the apparently more successful business communities are left in a much stronger position to work for policies which most immediately suit them well, including keeping the exchange rate as high as possible.

Second, the two countries' academic climate, no doubt influenced by those who call the shots in the commercial world, has been orientated towards the hard money, monetarist school, much more so than elsewhere. Although enthusiasm for the more extreme versions of monetarist theorising has become much less common than it was a few decades ago, there is still a legacy left from those days, which colours how economics is taught, current affairs are discussed and policies formulated. As long as fighting inflation is regarded as economic policy's major role, with a competitive exchange rate and similar objectives largely ignored or regarded as unobtainable because the exchange rate is thought almost entirely impossible to influence and at the market forces' mercy, there will be no powerful forces at work to get the cost base down so that export markets can be recaptured.

Third, decades of poor growth performance relative to that of many other places in the world seem to have inured everyone to regarding slow growth as inevitable. With widening income dispersion leaving most influential commentators relatively well off, there is less pressure than there might be to embrace radical change to improve economic performance and correspondingly less willingness to search for solutions which go against the grain of conventional thinking. There is little doubt that the markedly widening gaps in income, wealth and life chances have had a major impact in this respect. On both sides of the Atlantic, a small elite segment of the population enjoying a very high standard of living has become ever more powerful in controlling events and manipulating public opinion to its advantage. These people have no great interest in altering the status quo thinking on economic policy and show little inclination to do so.

This situation may change, as the deficit problems of the USA and the UK become more acute. In October 2011 the USA already had government debt amounting to almost $15 trillion, almost exactly 100 per cent of GDP.[19] Comparable figures for the UK were £970 billion and 63 per cent of GDP.[20] These figures, however, exclude large potential liabilities. For example, the British net government debt, with all financial sector intervention included, is nearly £2.3 billion – almost 150 per cent of GDP.[21] Both countries also had exceptionally high fiscal deficits, running in 2011 at $1.3 trillion (8.7% of GDP) in the USA[22] and £143 billion (11.7%) in the UK.[23] Though these figures are clearly much too high to be sustainable, it is far from clear that either country has workable and achievable policies to get them down to a manageable level, at least without severe deflationary implications.

In the USA it has so far proved impossible to get bipartisan agreement on any policies which might reduce the deficit to manageable proportions. The Democrats refuse to cut expenditure, and the Republicans to raise taxes. The UK government is much clearer about what it wants to achieve in terms of deficit reduction, but it is not at all certain that its targets will be achieved. In the end it may well turn out that the outcome of the current US policy stance is not much different from what happens in the UK, since in practice the constraints under which both governments have to operate force them towards similar outcomes. Whatever the different starting points, both are probably going to finish up with deficits which remain stubbornly high while growth falters, unemployment stays relentlessly high, government services deteriorate and living standards stagnate.

Reasons for these projected outcomes are not hard to find. They stem from the same source, which is that both countries have chronically underperforming export sectors, the product of years of having exchange rates set much too high. Manufacturing in both countries has thus been deeply undermined. Table 10.1 shows how substantial both countries' trade and payments deficits are. The consequences are all too familiar. It is impossible to run the economy at full throttle because of balance of payments constraints. As unemployment increases, so do the many claims on public expenditure resulting from dependency on state support. Without the productivity increases which are so much easier to achieve in manufacturing than elsewhere in the economy, the growth rate falters, and government revenues lack buoyancy. As public sector borrowing increases, so does the proportion of government revenues that must be used to service debt. Slowly and then more quickly, the US and the UK economies are teetering towards the point when both their sovereign and government debt positions will start to look unsustainable to the markets. Without major policy changes, both governments will then be faced with stark choices. With borrowing costs rising as creditworthiness falters, they can fight off major exchange-rate changes with higher interest rates, but doing so will depress their economies even further. On current form, nevertheless, both may well choose this course, at least as long as they can sustain it as a policy stance. Alternatively, even at this late stage both could take steps, before the markets turn against them, to make their economies more competitive in international terms, to secure a stable long-term future, to get their debts and borrowing back under control and to provide a much better future for all their citizens.

11
Policies for the Future

The evidence presented in this book so far indicates that the West does not have a viable set of economic policies capable of guiding it to a sustainable economic future, which is generally accepted by policymakers, a majority of the informed public and by most academic commentators. Instead, in the absence of a viable consensus, there appears to be a major risk that – at best – the Western world is headed for a long period of slow or non-existent growth. At worst the picture could be much gloomier. If many Western countries' policies to reduce fiscal deficits depress not only their economies but their export markets for the other Western economies in the same condition, a major depression could result. If the authorities in these countries then continue to pursue the same policies as they have up to now, they will be left with no weapons to fight the falling living standards, rising unemployment and political dissatisfaction which will result.

If this is what happens, there will be momentous consequences for the world as a whole but particularly for the West. It is clear for all to see that for the past few decades the centre of gravity of the world's economy has been shifting eastwards. If the countries on the Pacific Rim continue to grow much more rapidly than those in the West, not only will the West's relative economic stature decline but so will its political, intellectual and military influence. The pull of western ways of organising its countries' affairs, with all that liberal democracy brings with it, is also all too likely to suffer a reduction in its appeal as other more authoritarian ways of governance appear to deliver better economic results.

If the West is in a constant state of economic crisis, it is also much less likely than if it was prosperous and confident to be willing to contribute to the urgent tasks which the world will need to see being tackled in future. It is much more likely to adopt new protectionist policies and to be unwilling to unwind those which already exist, thus worsening the prospect for the Third World, which urgently needs trade opportunities to increase its living standards. Lessened, too, will be its willingness to respond to climate change threats which are likely to require expensive action. If the USA loses credibility as the world's hegemonic state, economically, politically and militarily, who will take its place?

If the West allows itself to drift into the state of economic paralysis, which now seems more than possible many living in Western countries will pay a terrible price. The upper echelons socially and economically may not suffer much, because they will still have interesting and rewarding jobs and their standards of living in world terms will remain very high. For the less advantaged, however, the outlook is much more gloomy and insecure. High levels of unemployment – among those actively seeking work and those who have effectively dropped out – are very damaging socially and a tragedy personally for those who cannot find decent jobs. Constant problems with public expenditure levels – caused both by the perceived need to cut deficits and rising interest charges as debts to be serviced increase – are likely to have the greatest impact on the most disadvantaged. As confidence fades in the political centre, whose stock in trade has unfortunately been the very policy mix which has allowed present problems to become so acute, moderation risks being replaced by extremism as the electorate's focus turns inwards. The stakes are getting very high. The West has a huge amount to lose if it cannot get its economic house in order.

Unsustainable trends

The apparently insoluble problems Western economies face may have manageable solutions, but there is a complex skein of arguments and conclusions as to what these might be and why the West is in its current predicament. Summarising the case presented so far may therefore help set the scene for considering how the West might negotiate a different world economic order.

The starting point is to realise the critical importance for a well-developed and diversified economy of a manufacturing base of sufficient size to both cope with domestic requirements and to enable it to hold its own in world markets. From a home market point of view, strongly rising exports allow an economy to run at full throttle, unconstrained by balance of payments problems. In addition, securing productivity increases is much easier in manufacturing than in most other parts of an economy. A small manufacturing base is thus strongly associated with slowly growing living standards and a large one with much more rapidly growing prosperity. A weak manufacturing economy limits the number of high-quality blue-collar jobs, while a strong one offers more and better employment opportunities. Furthermore, industrial decline is very likely to produce regions which, because of poor economic condition, generate insufficient value added to keep up with the more prosperous areas of the country.

From a foreign trade perspective, unless the picture is distorted by very large exports of raw materials, it is still normal for Western advanced economies to have manufactured exports representing around 60 per cent of export earnings. The buoyancy of these exports, relative to their competitors', is absolutely critical to their performance. An economy's growth rate is almost wholly determined by whether it gains or loses shares of world trade. If the share is going down, the growth rate tends to be lower than the world average. If it is increasing, it will almost certainly be higher.

The key requirement for export success is a competitive exchange rate because this has a bigger influence on a country's relative competitiveness than anything else. There are no supply-side substitutes for the competitive benefits a relatively low parity can provide. The prices charged to the rest of the world for the whole of whatever an economy can sell abroad determines whether its exports are competitive or not, and the exchange rate is far the most important determinant of whether this condition is fulfilled. Since whether a country's share grows faster or slower than the world average determines its overall economic growth rate and since whether the share rises or falls is wholly a function of export competitiveness, the exchange rate in turn is the crucial variable in fixing what a diversified economy's growth rate will be.

If the exchange rate is fixed at a level enabling an economy to grow faster than the world average, there is no reason it cannot do so more or less indefinitely, as China has done for the last 40 years. For a wide variety of reasons affecting everything from career choices of the most able to the education system's bias towards providing training geared to successful exporting companies' needs and from who holds political power to the climate of public and academic opinion, export success reinforces itself and export failure does the reverse.

Countries which have overvalued exchange rates have weak balance of payments positions which in turn make it more difficult for their governments to maintain a level of demand which keeps all the factors of production at full stretch. As a result, unemployment becomes an ever greater problem, often partly masked by the fact that a larger and larger proportion of the potential labour force has dropped out of the labour market altogether as hope of finding employment fades. As prospects for growth worsen, investment falls. As uncompetitive exchange rates make manufacturing and exporting unprofitable, talent drains from these activities, exacerbating their relative decline, further reducing export prospects and increasing import penetration. Lack of international competitiveness tends thus to feed on itself, making the condition of anywhere suffering from these problems steadily more acute.

There are no insuperable problems about changing the exchange rate of any economy which is determined to do so, although there will always be large numbers of people who think they will suffer if this happens. In particular, the widely believed argument that devaluations always produce increases in inflation is wrong both in fact in the light of the many cases where depreciations have taken place while inflation has not gone up, and for good theoretical reasons if all the countervailing disinflationary factors association with currency depreciation are taken into account. Higher growth rates are associated with greater inflation rates than the 2 per cent or so which is the target for most western economies, caused by leading sector inflation with these price increases being caused by uneven growth within each economy. External shocks, such as big increases in commodity prices, may also push up inflation and may cause unwanted price rises, but these impacts will be felt on all economies, whether they are growing fast or slowly. Some level of inflation is generally beneficial and there is no general evidence in reasonably well run economies of either price increases getting cumulatively larger or moderate rates of inflation adversely affecting overall economic performance.

Nearly all economies in the Western world are losing share of world trade, indicating that their exchange rates are too high for them to keep up with the growth in the world economy as a whole and to keep all their domestic factors of production at full stretch. The problems that Western economies have in failing to achieve as much export success as they would like washes over in several different directions, not least because it presents their governments with very awkward political choices. Because of balance of payments constraints, they cannot expand domestic demand as much as they and their electorates would like. As has already been seen, a good deal of this shortfall in demand manifests itself as increased unemployment, which in turn adds to the expenditure pressures on all democratically elected governments to increase public spending to offset the lack of sufficient effective demand elsewhere and to keep the economy growing at sufficient speed to avoid more and more resources falling idle.

Because weak export performance tends strongly to lead to balance of payments deficits, which must be financed by equivalent capital receipts, countries with overvalued exchange rates necessarily have increasingly acute debt problems. With faltering growth rates and increased borrowing, the total net debt position of the economy deteriorates. This trend is then replicated in what happens to the balance between government income and expenditure and the reasons for thus happening are not difficult to identify. They are the direct result of interactions between the four major components of demand on the economy. If imports exceed exports, the trade balance is a net drain on GDP. Investment tends to flag in uncertain conditions and it therefore tends to widen the gap in demand caused by an external payments deficit if in these conditions, corporate saving tends to exceed corporate investment. Consumer expenditure can only help to fill the gap which is left if average consumers, by borrowing, spend more than they earn. Government expenditure is thus left as the last available significant demand source. In deflationary conditions it is hardly surprising that there are strong political pressures to reflate the economy, to be achieved by the government deliberately both spending more than its revenues and tolerating the creation of more consumer debt.

The balance of payments still acts however, as a major constraint on the extent to which reflationary policies can be pursued. No government can afford to see this balance widen indefinitely. If the economy then falters, it is all too easy for government's fiscal position to decline rapidly as economic conditions deteriorate. Tax receipts drop as expenditures on unemployment and all its related costs go up. If the temptation to provide a further reflationary boost then materialises, on top of others that had already taken place – as happened in both the USA and the UK during the last decade, for example – it is not surprising that government deficits reached 10 per cent of GDP or more. By 2009 one in every four pounds the UK government spent was borrowed.[1] The US and UK governments – and many others in the West – have found themselves hemmed in by a vicious combination of balance of payments and fiscal deficits which make any reasonable rates of economic growth impossible to achieve.

A further key consequence has been a mounting sea of debt involving Western countries, their governments and their consumers, all of whom have had to borrow to cover the fact that they were spending more than their incomes or their revenues. Up to a point borrowing and accumulating debt tends to be sustainable, as long as creditors are reasonably content that those who owe them money will eventually be able to pay it back or at least to service their debts by meeting the interest charges on them as they fall due. The problem with Western world is that confidence that these conditions will continue to be fulfilled is fading. One reason for this happening is that slow growth makes it much more difficult for those with debts to pay them off than if resources available for debt servicing are growing. Another is that as debts mount year by year, they become progressively more difficult to sustain.

Within the existing policy constraints which most people in the western world accept, it is then extremely difficult to see what realistically can be done to remedy the situation in which so much of the West finds itself. To maintain the creditworthiness required to enable borrowing to continue, the pressures to cut expenditure are very strong. If many countries do this at the same time, however, the general deflationary impact is all too likely to lead to increasingly depressed economies but to little or no reduction in their economies' or their governments' – and quite possible their consumers' – need for borrowing. This is because revenues are likely to fall as fast if not faster than expenditures can be cut, leaving no net improvement in the borrowing and debt position, which indeed it then more likely steadily to get worse.

The main reason why the West has allowed so many of its economies to drift into their current precarious state goes back to major academic and policy misjudgements made in the 1970s as the post World War II Keynesian consensus broke down, the US devalued the dollar, and prices started rising very rapidly. Getting inflation down was then seen as the overwhelming priority and the main weapons used to overcome it were very high interest rates and monetary contraction. It is debatable whether the reductions in inflation which then materialised were caused as much as was thought at the time by these monetarist policies. In fact, the rate at which prices were increasing fell everywhere, including in countries which did not adopt monetarist policies. Where there cannot be any doubt, however, was that the result of the policies which were adopted to fight inflation pushed up most western countries' exchange rates just at the time when Pacific Rim countries, particularly China, were getting fully into their stride. The consequence is that the West allowed itself to become de-industrialised on a huge scale while manufacturing leapt ahead in the Far East. The resulting payments imbalances in the West then led straight to its present sovereign, government and consumer debt crises.

If correct, this chain of argument leads directly to the only way in which the state of Western economies' finances can be radically improved: by tackling the root cause of all the difficulties these economies face – the weakness of their manufacturing bases and consequently their current account payment balances. If these problems could be overcome, debt problems would become far more manageable and sustainable. This can be done by getting the exchange rates of all the countries in debt difficulties to whatever levels may be required to enable them to put their foreign trade and their governments' and consumers' incomes and expenditures in balance. But is this a proposition which can either be sold to or forced onto the rest of the world? A devaluation implies an equal and opposite revaluation. Are there persuasive arguments to put to those whose currencies have to rise in value that it is in their interests to see this happening? If not, is there action which the West can take unilaterally to make the necessary currency realignments occur?

How much devaluation?

Clearly a crucial issue is to estimate how large the parity changes for most Western countries would have to be to enable them both to extricate themselves from their debt traps with which so many of then are falling and then to resume an acceptable rate of economic growth. The calculations – which are not difficult to do, at least to estimate the scale of the devaluations needed to meet different objectives –are set out below. Essentially, there are two separate stages to be reached, although in practice they are likely to merge into each other. The first is to eliminate the current account deficit, and the second is to create conditions which will allow the economy to be run at full stretch. It is also worth reviewing what might be done to reach the same growth rates that the fastest-growing economies have reached. This is done later in this chapter.

Large numbers of studies have been conducted into the sensitivity of the imports and exports of developed – and underdeveloped – countries to price changes. While fluctuations in exchange rates not expected to be permanent do not have a very clear impact,[2] those which are intended as a matter of policy to be long lasting evidently do. Numerous studies, whether done by academic researchers or by the IMF and other organisations, show that, given exchange-rate changes which are regarded by all concerned as likely to be permanent, both imports and exports have elasticity values (ignoring their signs) of about 1. Tables 11.1 and 11.2 provide the figures. Export and import elasticities with values of one mean that if any economy, with these elasticities, devalues its currency, the volume of exports will rise by about 1 per cent, while the volume of imports will fall by 1 per cent. If import prices are set by world prices and export prices in the domestic economy, a 1 per cent devaluation will have the following effects:

- The total value of imports, measured in the domestic currency, will remain the same because they will rise in price by 1 per cent but fall in volume by 1 per cent, with these two changes cancelling each other out.

Table 11.1 The elasticity of demand for exports and imports of sixteen industrial and eight developing countries (summary of numerous late 20th century academic studies)

	Elasticity of Demand for Exports	Elasticity of Demand for Imports	Sum
Industrial Countries			
Austria	1.02	1.23	2.25
Belgium	1.12	1.27	2.39
Canada	0.68	1.28	1.96
Denmark	1.04	0.91	1.95
France	1.28	0.93	2.21
Germany	1.02	0.79	1.81
Iceland	0.83	0.87	1.70
Italy	1.26	0.78	2.04
Japan	1.40	0.95	2.35
Korea	2.50	0.80	3.30
Netherlands	1.46	0.74	2.20
Norway	0.92	1.19	2.11
Sweden	1.58	0.88	2.46
Switzerland	1.03	1.13	2.16
United Kingdom	0.86	0.65	1.51
United States	1.19	1.24	2.43
Average	1.11	0.99	2.10
Developing Countries			
Argentina	0.60	0.90	1.50
Brazil	0.40	1.70	2.10
India	0.50	2.20	2.70
Kenya	1.00	0.80	1.80
Morocco	0.70	1.00	1.70
Pakistan	1.80	0.80	2.60
Philippines	0.90	2.70	3.60
Turkey	1.40	2.70	4.10
Average	1.10	1.50	2.60

Notes: The estimates above refer to elasticities over a two to three year period. The figures are based upon the result of a number of different studies. Individual studies give differing estimates depending on the time periods involved, the econometric methodology employed and the particular data sets used.

Source: *Does Exchange Rate Policy Matter?* European Economic Review vol 30 (1987), p 377, reproduced on page 63 of *International Finance* by Keith Pilbeam, Basingstoke, UK: Macmillan, 1994.

- The total value of exports, measured in the domestic currency, however, will increase by 1 per cent because their price, measured in domestic currency, stays the same, but their volume increases by 1 per cent.

Table 11.2   Elasticity of demand for exports and imports, 2001–2004 (estimates produced by the IMF and published in 2010)

	Export Long Run	**Import Long Run**	**Total**
Australia	0.70	1.61	2.31
Austria	1.20	0.88	2.08
Belgium	2.10	0.56	2.66
Canada	1.32	0.83	2.15
Czech Republic	0.82	1.20	2.02
Denmark	1.27	0.78	2.05
Finland	1.23	0.01	1.24
France	1.14	1.03	2.17
Germany	2.51	0.10	2.61
Greece	1.13	1.11	2.24
Hungary	0.88	0.83	1.71
Iceland	0.91	1.46	2.37
Ireland	0.84	0.34	1.18
Italy	0.99	0.97	1.96
Japan	1.72	0.75	2.47
Korea	1.02	0.21	1.23
Luxembourg	2.65	2.63	5.28
Netherlands	1.04	0.73	1.77
New Zealand	1.01	0.94	1.95
Norway	0.33	1.61	1.94
Portugal	1.65	1.46	3.11
Slovakia	0.84	0.83	1.67
Spain	1.08	1.33	2.41
Sweden	1.84	0.04	1.88
Switzerland	1.27	0.78	2.05
United States	1.77	1.52	3.29
United Kingdom	1.37	1.68	3.05
Mean	1.28	0.97	2.25
Median	1.14	0.88	2.02

Sources: Export Supply Elasticities Table 2, page 21, and Import Demand Elasticities Table 1, page 15 in *A Method for Calculating Export Supply and Import Demand Elasticities* by Stephen Tokarick. Washington DC: IMF Working Paper WP/10/180, published 2010. NB Signs have been reversed for Imports in the table above for the sake of consisterncy

The overall effect of these impacts on imports and exports is that a 1 per cent depreciation will improve the trade balance of the devaluing economy by 1 per cent. In the real world, however, some of a devaluation's impact will fall on consequential price changing within the domestic economy. Not all the increased costs of imports will be passed on to the consumer, and exporters will take some of the benefit of a lower exchange rate in raising prices. A reasonable estimate is that these price effects will reduce the balance of payments impact on the trade balance by a third.

How much, then, would a country like the UK, with an average current account deficit of about 2.5 per cent of GDP and with about 30 per cent[3] of the economy involved in exports, have to devalue to eliminate the payments balance, other things being equal? The answer is 2.5 per cent divided by 30 per cent times 3/2, or 12.5 per cent.

Turning now to the second requirement – to run the economy at full stretch – the clearest and most readily available measure of the extent to which resources are underutilised is the level of unemployment. How much extra demand would be needed to bring this down to an acceptable level – say, 3 per cent – and how would this effect the exchange rate? If the potential output per head from those out of work was the same as those in employment, the answer would be easy to calculate. The increase in effective demand would be proportional to the needed increase in employment. For example, reducing, say, 8 per cent unemployment – close to the UK figure for autumn 2011 – to 3 per cent would require an increase in demand sufficient to lift the proportion of those in work from 92 to 97 per cent of the potential labour force, an increase of 5 divided by 92, or a little over 5 per cent.

It is clear, however, that this calculation is too simple, even if one looks only for broad approximations rather than exact figures. Three significant adjustments need to be taken into account to produce more reliable results.

First, there is substantial evidence that to reduce the registered unemployment rate by, say, 100,000 people, much more than 100,000 new jobs need to be created. The reason is that with increased employment opportunities, people who would not otherwise register as out of work are drawn back into the labour force. The converse tends to apply when unemployment increases. The ratio fluctuates and is difficult to pin down because changes in the size of the labour force are affected by many other factors than the unemployment level. Table 4.1 (in Chapter 4) shows examples of the ratios thrown up on both sides of the Atlantic during periods when there have been marked changes in the percentage of the workforce which was unemployed. These figures, strongly supported by International Labour Office reports,[4] suggest that a reasonable approximation is that for every 100,000 people taken off the unemployment register, roughly 150,000 new jobs need to be created, particularly when the impact of a tighter labour market on likely immigration trends is taken into account.

Second, increasing demand is bound to lead to higher remuneration for existing employees as the labour market tightens, even without hourly wage rises. More shift work will be needed, increasing overtime and payments for working during unsocial hours. People now counted as employed but involuntarily working part-time may take on full-time jobs. As a result, the average remuneration for all the existing labour force is likely to go up. Clearly the larger the rise in demand, the more pronounced this tendency will be.

Third, it is unlikely that the output per head of those currently unemployed will be as high as the average if they are reabsorbed into the active labour force. It will almost certainly be lower by a significant margin. Furthermore, the higher the level of unemployment from which we start, the larger this discrepancy is likely to be and the more unemployment is reduced, the more pronounced this factor is bound to become.

We are not dealing with exact figures here but within reasonably narrow limits the evidence suggests that these last two adjustments are likely to cancel each other out. Making this assumption then provides a relatively simple formula for calculating in a reasonably accurate way the approximate rise in effective demand needed to increase employment by any given percentage. If registered unemployment is 8 per cent and the target is 3 per cent, effective demand has to be increased by the 5 per cent or so already calculated, multiplied by an estimated additional 50 per cent, to take account of the extra people drawn into the labour force. The total rise needed, then, will be roughly 5 per cent times 1.5, which comes to about 7.5 per cent not allowing for pricing effects, and 7.5 per cent times 3/2 including them, which comes to about 11 per cent.

Adding 11 per cent to get the economy to full stretch to the 12.5 per cent needed to eliminate the existing deficit indications that the devaluation required to get the British economy back on to a growth rate of 3 to 4 per cent per annum would be of the order of 20 to 25 per cent – assuming everything else remains equal. In the present world economic climate this is a major assumption, one made more acute by the fact that any UK devaluation would have to be on a trade-weighted basis. If other major Western currencies attempted to devalue at the same time, the impact of a UK parity reduction would be blunted. If, however, the whole of the West started to grow faster, UK exports would be lifted correspondingly.

The large exchange-rate change needed by the UK simply reflects what needs to be done across much of the Western world, including many of the EU countries. Much of Europe has huge competitiveness problems, in several cases even more severe than those of the UK and the USA. Infact that many of these countries are locked into the single currency hugely complicates the adjustments which need to be made. The Eurozone as a whole has a current account surplus,[5] buoyed largely by Germany's export performance, which makes the euro relatively strong. Unless this changes, which seems unlikely, the choice will be between the single currency breaking up to allow for large-scale devaluations in the weaker Eurozone economies or severe deflation and austerity in the weaker countries as far ahead as anyone can see.

Especially if the single currency collapses, however, allowing parity changes on a more extensive scale than would otherwise be possible, the problems of adjustment the world economy faces will become even greater. If the older industrialised economies have to lower their cost bases vis-à-vis the rest of the world to enable them to get back to full employment and reasonable growth rates, a very substantial relative rise elsewhere, particularly in the Pacific Rim, will be required. If the Asian economies are not to be slowed down, however, world demand will have to increase rather more rapidly than it has in the past. Before turning to what needs to be negotiated by the West, it is worth considering what the world would look like if manufacturing and international trading and foreign payment balances were in much better balance than they are. If, as a result, the world economy could then grow both more rapidly and more steadily, almost everyone would be better off.

Wider perspectives

All the evidence presented in this book indicates that the Western world would be much more secure, stable and prosperous if there were substantial downward exchange-rate movement for most Western countries. We need now to explore in more detail the conditions required not only to achieve an increase in output while the labour force is used more effectively and under-used resources are brought back into commission, but also to maintain an optimum growth rate for the foreseeable future.

Bringing exchange rates in Europe and the USA down to a level which gets productivity to rise at around 3.5 per cent per head each year while providing a growth ratio of around 4 per cent per annum if the population is increasing, as is true in both the UK and the USA,[6] is a very important first step. Accomplishing this objective is not, however, sufficient for ensuring that the West's economies will grow with the vigour still exhibited in many Far Eastern countries or in Japan and most of Europe in the 1950s and 1960s. Other steps will have to be taken if the objective was to achieve these conditions and to understand what needs to be done if this goal is to be attained we need to revert back to some of the issues discussed in Chapter 1.

A major move in the right direction would have been taken if western economies could be made to grow at around 4 per cent on average each year. They would then come close to holding their own with the current world average growth rate which averaged 3.3 per cent in the 2000s, including a relatively poor performance throughout the period by western countries and the downturn post 2008.[7] Western living standards would then cease growing more slowly than the world average, as they have done over recent decades. To do this, the western economies would have to obtain and keep a sufficient share of the investment and production which has the falling cost curves and large returns characteristic of international trade. This means that the costs of output in the West, allowing for appropriate productivity levels, would have to be as low as the world average. If this does not happen in future, footloose investment and production of both goods and services – primarily in light industrial manufacturing – will continue to migrate to other parts of the world where overall costs, measured internationally, are lower.

Even a consistent growth rate of about 4 per cent per annum, close to the world average, is still quite low by Pacific Rim standards or by comparison with many European economies' achievements in the 1950s and 1960s. Would it is possible, for the Western economies to move up to growth rates of 6 or 8 per cent or more, rates regularly achieved in the Far East, if they wanted to? It might be, but still greater downward movements in the exchange rate would be required, to enable the major economies in the West to achieve the super-competitive status that would be needed to promote them to the same growth league as Singapore, South Korea and China. For a number of reasons, as we shall see, this might not be possible, as important constraints started to bite at a world level which might not apply to individual countries. Nevertheless, if only to show how 8% or more rates of growth could be achieved, it is worth exploring the structural changes which would be required to bring the western economies up to the Pacific Rim level of performance, to see how such high growth in output could be obtained.

To reach such a level, Table 1.2 (Chapter 1) suggests that Western exchange rates might have to drop another 20 per cent vis-à-vis the Far East's, in addition to any devaluations needed to deal with current account payment balances and underused domestic factors of production. How would returns on investment produce the very high growth rates the Far East economies achieve? Consider again the total returns achieved by different types of investment projects, encompassing all the income increases that investment brings to everyone in the economy.

These – the social rate of return – include higher wages, better products, larger tax receipts and higher profits, as well as returns to those who put up the money for the required investments. Recall the important point that returns on investment projects vary enormously. In part of the private sector and much of the public realm, they are little more than the interest rate and sometimes lower. This is typically the total rate of return obtained on investments, for example, in housing or roads or public buildings. At the other end of the spectrum, in some light manufacturing areas and parts of the service sector, the total rate of return is often far larger. It can be as great as 100 per cent per annum in favourable cases. In the middle are investments in heavy industry, which typically produce total rates of return around 20 or 25 per cent. Investment projects with exceptionally high total returns are characteristically those involved in international trade in goods and services, which tend to be heavily concentrated in countries with low exchange rates and competitive cost bases and are strongly discouraged by overstrong currency values. Furthermore, the high total returns on these investments produce large resources for reinvestment and ample opportunities for new profitable projects. The result is that a much greater proportion of the national income goes into investment than in slow growing economies. Now consider two examples:

- Country A has total gross investment of 15 per cent of GDP. Two-thirds of this – 10 per cent of GDP – produces an average total return of 10 per cent, and one-third – 5 per cent of GDP – produces an average total return of 20 per cent. This economy will have a growth rate of $(10\% \times 10\%) + (5\% \times 20\%)$, or 2 per cent per annum.
- Country B has total gross investment of 35 per cent of GDP. In terms of GDP share, 15 per cent produces an average 10 per cent total return, 10 per cent produces a 20 per cent total return and 10 per cent, in the highly competitive internationally traded sector, produces a 50 per cent total return. This economy will have a growth rate of $(15\% \times 10\%) + (10\% \times 20\%) + (10\% \times 50\%)$, or 8.5 per cent per annum.

Of course this is an oversimplified model, but this does not prevent it from demonstrating an important insight into how economies produce different growth rates, and how their structures adapt to, and reinforce the opportunities which their foreign trade relations open up for them. With an 8.5 per cent growth rate and gross investment at 35 per cent of GDP, productivity rises rapidly. The competitiveness of the internationally tradable sectors grows fast. Education and skill levels increase exponentially. The problem which these economies have is to avoid the growth of export surpluses, and the appreciation of their currencies, eroding away the competitiveness which makes such high increases in output possible.

Should the West aim for so high a growth rate? Almost certainly not. The size of the Western economies, taken together, would make it hard for them to secure a sufficient proportion of the world's high return investment for a growth rate as ambitious as 8 per cent or more to be sustainable, even if they captured much more than their fair share of the world's output where productivity gains are easiest to secure. Table 11.3 provides estimates of a more reasonable balance, showing how a 3.5 per cent per annum sustained growth rate in GDP per head could be spread round the whole of the developed world. For this to be achieved, manufacturing industry, where productivity increases are most easy to attain, would have to be given much higher priority by adjusting exchange rates to get the cost base right. Table 1.3 (Chapter 1) shows how in the USA, for example, over the 20 years from 1977 to 1997, 60 per cent of the increase in GDP per head came from manufacturing, which made up less than 20 per cent of the economy's output. Almost all the remaining sources of increased living standards were in agriculture, mining, wholesale trade, utilities and transport, which together constituted less than another 20 per cent of GDP. The remaining 60 per cent and more of the US economy made no net contribution at all to increasing real incomes over the whole of the period.

With faster-growing economies would go a corresponding ability for the West at least to retain, and probably to enhance, its international power and influence, rather than to see it slowly whittled away as other parts of the world grow much faster. The point to grasp is that making at least some of these kinds of choices is possible. It is not inevitable that Western economies should be left to languish near the bottom of the growth league, while other countries take advantage of opportunities they could seize. If the West's leaders want to see their economies grow at a rate of at least 3.5 per cent per annum, they could achieve this objective.

Negotiations

If there was a consensus among western policy makers that the current account imbalances between the West and major surplus countries had to be eliminated, to enable western countries to avoid the debt trap and stagnation which they currently face, there are broadly two ways in which this could be done. One would be for the surplus countries to eliminate their surpluses by a combination of increasing domestic demand and allowing their exchange rates to appreciate. The other

Table 11.3 Sources of growth in the world economy: GDP per head – now and perhaps in the future

	USA 1979–2009 Actual			Western Economies Est			Tiger Economies Est			in Balance – Projected		
	% of US Economy in 1997	Annual % Productivity Growth	Contribution to GDP/Head Growth	Estimated % of Current Economies	Annual % Productivity Growth	Contribution to GDP/Head Growth	Estimated % of Current Economies	Annual % Productivity Growth	Contribution to GDP/Head Growth	Possible % of Future Economies	Annual % Productivity Growth	Contribution to GDP/Head Growth
High Productivity Growth Sectors												
Manufacturing	19	3.0	0.6	18	3.0	0.5	30	15.0	4.5	23	10.0	2.3
Mining	2	1.6	0.0	2	3.0	0.1	1	3.0	0.0	2	3.0	0.1
Agriculture	2	4.4	0.1	2	4.0	0.1	9	4.0	0.4	6	6.0	0.4
Wholesale Trade	7	3.0	0.2	6	3.0	0.2	6	3.0	0.2	6	3.0	0.2
Medium Productivity Growth Sector												
Transport and Utilities	9	1.6	0.1	8	2.0	0.2	10	2.0	0.2	10	2.0	0.2
Low Productivity Growth Sectors												
Construction	4	-1.0	0.0	4	0.0	0.0	5	1.0	0.1	6	1.0	0.1
Retail Trade	10	0.3	0.0	10	0.3	0.0	8	1.0	0.1	9	1.0	0.1
Financial Services	18	0.1	0.0	17	0.0	0.0	10	1.0	0.1	14	1.0	0.1
Other Services	19	-1.0	-0.2	18	-1.0	-0.2	13	1.0	0.1	15	1.0	0.2
Government	12	0.0	0.0	15	0.0	0.0	8	0.0	0.0	9	0.0	0.0
Totals	100		0.8	100		0.9	100		5.6	100		3.5

Note: For each group of countries, the first column represents estimated proportions of total output derived from each activity, the second column provides an estimate of average productivity growth per annum, and the third column is a calculation, based on the first two, of the contribution in the total average growth in GDP made by each activity.

Sources: Tables B.13, B46 and B.100 in Economic Report to the President 1999 Washington DC: US Government Printing Office, 1999. Table 3, pages 221 et seq in World Employment Report. Geneva: International Labour Office, 1998, supplemented with estimates from a number of other sources.

would be for the deficit countries to force their exchange rates down to stabilise their current account balances. There are then, in principle, two ways in which these changes could take place. Either they could be achieved by consensus or by the West taking unilateral action which countries such as China could not resist. In the end, if the major adjustments which are needed are to be made, it is very likely that a combination of these approaches will be required.

Looking first at persuasion, while countries such as China are clearly doing extremely well in some ways out of the way exchange rates are currently aligned, it is important to separate out two related but separate issues. Taking China as a prime example, the Chinese economy is growing much faster than everywhere in the West because it has an undervalued currency, a rapidly growing share of world trade and far more than its fair share of manufacturing capacity. It is not doing so because it has a large current account surplus. Of itself, however, China's fast growth need not generate major financial difficulties for the rest of the world. What does cause major problems for everyone else is the fact that China's huge current account surplus has to be matched by deficits elsewhere in the world – mostly, in practice, in the West. There is no compelling reason, however, why China needs to combine fast growth with a payments surplus. If China's imports were liberalised and Chinese domestic demand was enhanced sufficiently, the surplus could be made to disappear, even if the Chinese economy kept on growing just as fast as it was previously.

Furthermore, China – or any other country with a chronic payments surplus – has good reason to avoid this condition. The notion that surpluses are beneficial is no more than a throwback to eighteenth-century mercantilist fallacies, whose futility was comprehensively exposed by Adam Smith.[8] It makes very little sense to have in 2010 in China's case 6.0 per cent of its national income in the form of a payments surplus which had to be lent to other countries who are very unlikely ever to be able to pay back all or even perhaps more than a small proportion of it. Table 10.1 (Chapter 10) shows that several other countries have surpluses as large or even larger proportionately – Germany, 5.7 per cent; Russia, 7.2 per cent; Singapore, 13.8 per cent; Switzerland, a staggering 18.6 per cent – which are equally likely to be lent elsewhere and never fully repaid. Furthermore, accumulating huge current account surpluses, which are unsustainable for the rest of the world, is an unstable and ultimately self-defeating policy. Sooner or later market forces will force the exchange rates of the surplus countries up – exactly as happened to Japan in the late 1980s, crippling the export competitiveness which had benefited it for the previous four decades and leaving its economy stagnating. In addition, if surpluses are so large that they destabilise the world economy – clearly now a real danger – the resulting depression is very unlikely to leave the Pacific Rim countries unscathed, even if they continue to do better than the West. Of course, there may be some nationalists in China and elsewhere who would be happy to see some set backs for their own economy if their gain was to see the West in serious disarray. Everyone will be better off, however including the Chinese, if their economy continues to advance relative to the West, with conditions in the West remaining reasonably stable. The Indian economy is a good example of what can be done with a rapidly growing share of world trade and a small but manageable current account deficit.

While the way the world economy is organised at the moment means that the immediate pressures on surplus countries to reduce their surpluses are nothing like as strong as the corresponding pressures on deficit countries to reduce their deficits, there is, therefore, a strong case that ever increasing surpluses are a thoroughly irrational use of resources. There thus does seem to be a reasonably good chance of persuading surplus countries that it is in their interests, as well as those of the rest of the world, to reduce them, especially if the alternative is a world depression. Even if surpluses were completely eliminated, however, this would not necessarily even up to any significant extent the shares of world trade and distribution of manufacturing capacity. It would, nevertheless, be a big step forward, relieving the West of much of the pressure which comes from its payments deficits. It would still, however, leave western economies with falling shares of world trade and lower growth rates and the problems of very unequal distribution of incomes, wealth and life chances which tend to be associated with economies with weak manufacturing sectors.

It therefore seems less likely that it will be easy to persuade enough of the surplus countries to have western parities reduced at their expense, especially if they very substantially reduce or even eliminate their current account surpluses. It may well also be the case that – in terms of equity across the world – that there is a strong argument for allowing the countries such as those on the Pacific Rim to grow more rapidly than those in the West, because their living standards are still, on average, a long way below those in western countries. Even getting rid of surpluses, however, is unlikely to happen without a great deal of pressure being applied and it may well still be the case that at the end of all negotiations, the West is still left with intransigent countries who will not co-operate.

If this happens, can the West force the issue to achieve some manageable combination of surplus reduction and exchange-rate realignment, enough at least to let Western countries to avoid the debt traps they face?

There is much they can do unilaterally if the will was there and then options will be considered in the next section, which deals with attitudes to be overcome in countries needing much lower parities. Meanwhile, developments likely to take place can also push matters in the direction they need to go, however much policymakers want to avoid them.

In the first place, the surplus countries which are owed vast sums of money by the West have good reasons for avoiding a situation where western countries are unable to pay their debts. It would make more sense for them to allow the West sufficient leeway to generate the capacity at least to keep servicing the existing debt and then hopefully to start reducing it. If this is not done, sooner or later, as is happening now in the Eurozone, defaults will loom. The probable process is that the Western economies' credit rating will weaken to a point where they can no longer borrow the money they need to finance their increasing debt. Once this happens, the outcome will be a forced and chaotic fall in exchange rates, producing financial chaos, bankrupt banks and a world depression – at the same time forcing exactly the exchange-rate realignments the Pacific Rim countries are trying to avoid.

It is also likely that the approach to this kind of environment is going to be extremely disruptive to the export markets in the West on which much of the prosperity in the rest of the world depends. If western markets contract substantially as a result of a depression, even if this is worse in the West than the East, this is not going to benefit countries such as China. Furthermore, if the economic condition of the West declines sharply, there are likely to be strong protectionist pressures which are likely to be even more damaging to Far East exporters. There is a very real danger that the outcome could be a beggar thy neighbour round of trade restrictions which could plunge the world economy into the same sort of depression which disfigured the 1930s.

There are thus likely to be strong pressures developing over the coming period which will force upon both the West and the East changes which none of their policy makers would very probably have wanted if they had been able to continue as before. There is, however, no reason why policy makers in the West should not use the opportunities presented to them to make the parity changes which are then increasingly obviously going to be required, by reinforcing and taking advantage of the trends which are taking place anyway. The question then is whether they will have the wisdom to do so. The really depressing potential outcome is that the West fails to see what needs to be done. Far from taking advantage of the way that the situation is developing, it may steadfastly resist the parity changes which are so urgently needed, thus compounding all the policy mistakes which have led the West into its current condition. How likely is it that this will happen and what would the consequences for the West then be?

The cost of inaction

As noted earlier, the evidence in this book indicates that the Western world would be more secure, stable and prosperous if it made major changes in its economic policy priorities. For at least 40 years – since the 1970s – the economic policy holy grail for the vast majority of the West's policymakers, supported by both the academic world and public opinion, has been to keep inflation at bay, with a target of about 2 per cent having been adopted by the USA, the UK and the European Central Bank. For most of the 1990s and the first decade of the twenty-first century, this goal was largely achieved. Since then, prices have risen rather faster, mostly as a result of commodity price rises which are likely to drop out of the year-on-year figures fairly soon with little impact on the underlying rate of inflation.

The fight against inflation has, however, been waged with scant regard either to the cost of pursuing this objective or to whether, in the absence of all the weapons which have been brought to bear, the outcome would have been that much different. The presumption has been that inflation is a major threat which justifies very heavy costs being incurred to keep it at bay. It has been assumed that if vigorous action is not taken to keep price rises in check that almost as a matter of course they will spiral upwards. There is, however, remarkably little evidence for this outcome. Price levels have been quite stable for most of the world's economic history, although of course there have been exceptions. Both world wars generated heavy inflationary upsurges. So did the collapse of the Bretton Woods system and the subsequent surge in the monetary base in the 1970s. Germany had two hyperinflations, one in 1923 and another as World War II ended. Russia saw inflation soar as communism collapsed and big policy mistakes were made while the economy was transformed to the current Russian version of capitalism. A number of poorly run developing countries have seen their currencies' value erode because of bad economic management. Nearly all the rest of the world, however, has done reasonably well at containing inflation. Prices may have risen by more than 2 per cent per annum, particularly where fast growth caused leading sector inflation, but with little sign of hyperinflation looming up. Nor did relatively moderate rates of price increase have a perceptibly negative impact on the performance of the economy in other respects.

The mindset which regards any sign of inflation rising above about 2 per cent per annum as a danger signal warranting action at the expense of other economic objectives is, however, deeply ingrained in Western policymakers. They have been willing to sacrifice growth, investment, and full employment to keep the 2 per cent target in sight, by pursuing deflationary policies and ignoring their impact on keeping the exchange rate much too high, thus promoting deindustrialisation in its Western countries, with all its consequent depressing impacts on the growth rate, unemployment levels and social conditions. When weakening foreign payment conditions materialised as the inevitable consequence of the trade imbalances caused by lack of sufficient manufactured exports, they were happy to keep on turning the deflationary screw, fearful of the supposed impact of any devaluation on inflation.

It is not, however, just fear of inflation which has been a potent source of political pressure to keep exchange rates high. There is plenty of support for this policy stance from many quarters, however misguided the effect for the economy as a whole. Powerful financial interests have always tended to support a high parity. So have importers. So have pensioners and others on incomes which rely on interest rates staying relatively high, as they have been for most of the last 40 years, although not recently. Everyone now habituated to having holidays abroad complains if costs go up. The way any currency's parity is described is suffused with value judgements. It is 'weak' if it is low, 'strong' if it is high. Devaluations are strongly associated in the public mind with rising inflation and lowered living standards, although there is no evidence that either historical experience or economic theory warrants this view.

Thanks to all these pressures and the perceptions which follow from them, all the steps needed to be taken to get the currency's value down will sound like anathema to large sections of the population. Instead of telling the world how determined they are to keep the value of the currency up, policymakers need to declare that they want it substantially reduced. Instead of deflating the economy to keep the current account payment balance and the government's fiscal balance from deteriorating, a deliberately reflationary policy needs to be pursued to weaken the payment balance and increase the deficit temporarily until the currency's value has fallen. The central bank needs to be instructed to sell the domestic currency and purchase foreign ones. Portfolio foreign direct investment needs to be discouraged. A really determined effort should be made to get banks to lend to small and medium-sized businesses, probably with the risk of additional provisions for bad debt somehow underwritten by the government. If implementing these policies causes the rating agencies to notch the country's credit rating downwards, the drop should be ignored – even, encouraged. A temporary creditworthiness reduction will help lower the currency's value. Once the elasticities of demand for exports and imports kick in, the net current account balance will right itself, and the creditworthiness of the country will automatically be re-established. These are the actions which need to be put in place.

If policies along these lines are implemented, there will certainly be a transitional period where resources shift towards manufacturing and exports and the saving rate rises. Inevitably, there will be some losers, but not many even in the short term. Long-term prospects will look a lot brighter as manufacturing revives, as the pressure of demand on the economy increases, as unemployment falls and as the economy grows strongly, perhaps at 3 or 4 per cent per annum – even faster if the devaluation is deep enough. These changes and developments have been witnessed time after time in economic history in widely different, relatively advanced and diversified economies and in a large number of relatively underdeveloped ones, too.

Achieving such a change in policy orientation, however, involves a massive change in perspective from a large number of people. Will this happen? For the foreseeable future, inertia may well ensure that it does not, in which case the economic climate in the UK and most of the rest of the West will continue in decline. If this happens, what will the future hold in store? The sequence of events might unfold along something like the following lines.

The Eurozone may stagger along from one crisis to the next for a while, as Europe's political leadership does all it can to avoid a Eurozone break-up. Even if collapse of the single currency is staved off, defaults, in the form of sovereign debts being written down, though virtually certain, will do nothing to solve the underlying problem which is the inability of all but the northern tier of Eurozone countries to compete with Germany. Eventually the situation, very probably in Greece first, will become intolerable, and Greece will drop out of the euro. Once this happens, contagion could easily spread not only to Ireland and Portugal but to the much larger economies of Spain and Italy – probably Belgium and France, too. There is then unlikely to be anything like sufficient creditworthiness or borrowing capacity either among banks or sovereign states or the International Monetary Fund to stop most of these countries falling out of the euro as well, accompanied by devaluations of the magnitude to which previous sections of this book have alluded. There will be a tumultuous period while these events take place, very probably accompanied by a deep but temporary depression. Once all the countries that are forced to leave the euro have done so, they can revert back to having their own central banks, who can then create sufficient money to recapitalise their clearing banks. Provided that by this stage moderate and rational political leadership is still the norm, so that the reaction to the unfolding crisis leads in the right direction, there will then be a sharp recovery. There may well continue to be a northern tier of euro countries, whose exchange rates will then appreciate sharply unless countervailing action is taken. Time will tell whether this is the outcome.

For those vulnerable countries, including the USA and the UK, outside the Eurozone, a large-scale European downturn is likely to trigger a major recession in the world economy, one to which they will be exceptionally vulnerable. As their export markets contract, current accounts and the government's fiscal balance are both likely to deteriorate sharply. Will the rest of the world continue lending them huge sums of money to finance debt they manifestly are going to have major problems repaying? It seems unlikely. Much more probable is that any battle to hold up the value of the dollar and the pound will be lost, and there will be a disorderly further large devaluation of both currencies against those of the Pacific Rim.

If this analysis is correct, the choice for the West is not whether the parity of most of its currencies will fall substantially in the reasonably near future. This will happen anyway. The choice is whether it happens in an orderly way, so that the damage in lost output, bankruptcies and much-increased unemployment can be minimised, or whether, after fighting against reality to the bitter end, a disorderly rout ensues. If the latter choice is made, the transition to an inevitable new world currency order looks to be much more damaging and to last much longer. This outcome will generate much more than just economic damage and put enormous strain on the West's political institutions. Liberal democracy itself may be under severe threat.

The fundamental problem with choosing to keep inflation down rather than get the exchange rate right as the most important economic policy objective is that for many years the vast majority of the West's political class, academic world and public opinion have made the wrong choice. The consequence of the resulting conditions is that its leadership is being discredited, and its power and influence in the world is being eclipsed. There are huge dangers here, but the opportunities to reverse these conditions are still available. There may well not be much time left, however, before events spin out of control. The stakes are very high.

Notes

Prelims

1. *Booknotes* interview with Brian Lamb, 1994.

1   Economic Growth

1. Table G-2 in *Monitoring the World Economy 1820–1992*, by Angus Maddison. Paris: OECD, 1995.
2. GDP volume measure tables in *International Financial Statistics*. Washington, DC: IMF.
3. Ibid.
4. Tables 11.13 and 11.14 in *Trends and Statistics in International Trade*. Geneva: WTO, 1995.
5. In *International Financial Statistics Yearbook 2011*, 67. Washington, DC: IMF, 2011.
6. Tables B-13, B-46 NS B-100 in *Economic Report of the President*. Washington, DC: US GPO, 1999.
7. Calculated from the figures in Table 131.
8. Tables B-46 and B-13 in *Economic Report of the President*. Washington, DC: US GPO, 2011.
9. GDP volume measures in *International Financial Statistics*. Washington, DC: IMF.
10. Gross capital formant as percentage of GDP tables in *International Financial Statistics*. Washington, DC: IMF.

2   The Exchange Rate

1. Table D, p. 19, in *Historical Statistics 1960–1986*. Paris: OECD, 1998.
2. Ibid.
3. Table B-110 in *Economic Report of the President*. Washington, DC: GPO, 1999.
4. Exchange Rate table on p. 3 in *International Financial Statistics*. Washington, DC: OMF, 2011.
5. P. 182 in *International Financial Statistics Yearbook*. Washington, DC: IMF, 1979.
6. Ibid., pp. 182–3.
7. Table 693 in *Statistical Abstract of the United States*. Washington, DC: US Department of Commerce, 2011.
8. Pp. 261–2 in *Peddling Prosperity*, by Paul R. Krugman. New York and London: Norton, 1994.
9. Table 687 in *Statistical Abstract of the United States*. Washington, DC: US Department of Commerce, 1998.

10. This paragraph draws heavily on an article in the *Political Quarterly* 82, no 2 (April–June 2011), by Maurice Mullard, entitled *Explanations of the Financial Meltdown and the Present Recession*.
11. *The Rise and Decline of Nations*, by Mancur Olson. New Haven and London: Yale University Press, 1982.

3   Inflation

1. Pp. 159–61 in *International Financial Statistics*. Washington, DC: IMF, 1998.
2. Pp. 58–9 in *International Financial Statistics*. Washington, DC: IMF 1979.
3. P. 31 in *Debt and Delusion* by Peter Warburton. London: Allen Lane / Penguin Press, 1999.
4. Country by country tables in *International Financial Statistics Yearbook*. Washington, DC: IMF, 2011
5. Answer to a parliamentary question.
6. Pp. 168–9 in *International Financial Statistic*. Washington, DC: IMF, 2000.
7. Pp. 122–3 in *International Financial Statistics*. Washington, DC: IMF, 1998.
8. Ibid.
9. Ibid., pp. 100–1.
10. Tables B-1 and B-69 in *Economic Report of the President*. Washington, DC: US GPO, 1999.
11. Calculations by Shaun Stewart.
12. Tables B-69 and B-1 in *Economic Report of the President*. Washington, DC: US GPO, 1999.
13. Bloomberg Internet report, 2005, on research done by Duke University.
14. Information obtained from the German Embassy in London.
15. Information obtained from the Japanese Embassy in London.
16. Table 5.8 in the *Annual Abstract of Statistics*. London: Central Statistical Office, 1995.
17. BBC report, September 2011.
18. ILO labour force surveys.
19. Table B-28 for US figures in *Economic Report of the President*. Washington, DC: US GPO, 2011.
20. P. 169 in *International Monetary Statistics*, 2000; p. 79 in *International Monetary Statistics*, 2011; country tables in both publications. Washington, DC: IMF.

4   Unemployment

1. Europa.eu website.
2. US Bureau of Labour Statistics website.
3. Tables B-1 and B-35 in *Economic Report of the President*. Washington, DC: US GPO, 2011.
4. Wikipedia for GDP and *Eurostat* Internet site for labour force data.
5. P. 154 et seq. in *Trade and Development Report, 1997*. Geneva: United Nations, 1997.
6. ILO labour force surveys.
7. Ibid.

8. Table C-16 in *Monitoring the World Economy 1820–1992*, by Angus Maddison. Paris: OECD, 1995. Tables for all EU countries in *International Financial Statistics*. Washington, DC: IMF, 1998.
9. Various tables in *Labour Force Statistics 1970–1990*. Paris: OECD, 1992. Table 0203 in *Eurostatistics*. Luxembourg: European Union, 1999.
10. Table 2.15 in *Historical Statistics 1960–1986*. Paris: OECD, 1992.
11. Table 0601 in *Eurostatistics*. Luxembourg: European Union, 1999.
12. Table B-35 in *Economic Report of the President*. Washington, DC: US GPO, 1999.
13. Various tables in *Labour Force Statistics 1970–1990*. Paris: OECD, 1992. Table 0203 in *Eurostatistics*. Luxembourg: European Union, 1999.
14. Table B-34 in *Economic Report of the President*. Washington, DC: US GPO, 1999.
15. Population figures by country in *International Financial Statistics Yearbook*. Washington, DC: IMF, 1998.
16. Table B-35 in *Economic Report of the President*. Washington, DC: GPO, 1999.
17. Various tables in *Labour Force Statistics 1970–1990*. Paris: OECD, 1992. Table 0203 in *Eurostatistics*. Luxembourg: European Union, 1999.
18. Calculated from Tables B-2 and B-35 in *Economic Report of the President*. Washington, DC: US GPO, 1999.
19. *Eurostat* Internet statistics.
20. Table 584 in *Statistical Abstract of the United States*. Washington, DC: US Department of Commerce, 2011.
21. *Eurostat* Internet statistics.
22. Table B-2 in *Economic Report of the President*. Washington, DC: US GPO, 2011.
23. *Eurostat* Internet statistics.
24. Table B-42 in *Economic Report of the President*. Washington, DC: US GPO, 2011.
25. UK Office for National Statistics, November 2011.
26. US Bureau of Labour Statistics, September 2011.
27. BBC report, October 2011.
28. IMF statistics quoted by Wikipedia.
29. Wikipedia entry 'List of Countries by real GDP Growth Rate for 2010 based on IMF statistics'.
30. P. 76 in *International Financial Statistics*. Washington, DC: IMF 2000, 2001. Table 3a in *Taiwan Statistical Data Book, 2011*.
31. Successive *Economic Reports of the President*. Washington, DC: US GPO, various years. E.g., pp. 69 et seq in the 2011 report.
32. *Employment Policy Institute Economic Report* 9, no. 9 (November 1995).
33. The subject of a number of best-selling books, as well as official reports.

5   Sustainability

1. *Happiness: Lessons from a New Science*, by Richard Layard. London: Allen Lane/Penguin Press, 2005.
2. Ibid., table, p. 64.
3. Ibid., table, p. 64.

4. Wikipedia entry 'World Population'.
5. P. 14 in *The Skeptical Environmentalist*, by Bjørn Lomborg. Cambridge: Cambridge University Press, 2001.
6. Wikipedia entry 'World Population'.
7. Wikipedia entry 'Longevity'.
8. Table 1-4, p. 29, in *The World Economy: A Millennial Perspective*, by Angus Maddison. Paris: OECD, 2001.
9. P. 141 in *Population: An Introduction to Concepts and Issues*, by John R Weeks. Belmont, CA: Wadsworth, 2002.
10. P. 50 in *The Skeptical Environmentalist*.
11. Ibid., p. 51.
12. P. 163 in *Population: An Introduction to Concepts and Issues*.
13. Wikipedia entry 'Fertility Rate'.
14. P. 146 in *Population: An Introduction to Concepts and Issues*.
15. Ibid., p. 104 et seq.
16. P. 328 in *Population: An Introduction to Concepts and Issues*.
17. Table on p. 51 of *World Population Prospects: The 2000 Revision*. New York: United Nations, 2001.
18. Nationmaster.com website.
19. P. 41 of *World Population Prospects: The 2000 Revision*.Nationmaster.com website.
20. United Nations website on Population Trends.
21. Ibid.
22. Ibid.
23. Ibid.
24. P. 294 in *Population: An Introduction to Concepts and Issues*.
25. Ibid., p. 357.
26. Wikipedia, reproduced with kind permission.
27. Table C4, pp. 325–7 in *The World Economy: A Millennial Perspective*.
28. Wikipedia 'Growth in GDP' figures show Zambia growing by 7.6% and Sierra Leone by 5.0% in 2010.
29. See Club of Rome website.
30. This section draws very heavily on *The Skeptical Environmentalist*.
31. Ibid., table 2, p. 139.
32. Ibid.; the 16 raw materials are gemstones, nickel, crushed stone, sand & gravel, sheet mica, phosphate rock, silver, sulphur, cobalt, tin, chromium, asbestos, lime, molybdenum, boron and talc & pyrophite.
33. Ibid., p. 137.
34. Ibid., p. 150 et seq.
35. Ibid., p. 156.
36. Ibid., p. 119 et seq.
37. Ibid., p. 126.
38. Ibid., p. 133.
39. Ibid., p. 136, updated to 2011.
40. Ibid., p. 135.
41. Ibid., pp. 176–7.
42. Ibid., p. 189.
43. P. 259 in *The Skeptical Environmentalist*.

44. Wikipedia.
45. P. 263 in *The Skeptical Environmentalist*.
46. Ibid., p. 266.
47. Ibid., p. 276.
48. Ibid., p. 278.
49. Ibid., p. 264.
50. Ibid., p. 302.
51. *A Question of Balance*, by William Nordhaus. New Haven and London: Yale University Press, 2008.
52. P. 317 in *The Skeptical Environmentalist*.
53. Ibid., p. 323.
54. Ibid., p. 282.
55. Ibid., p. 286.
56. Ibid., p. 288.
57. Leading article in the *Economist*, 19 November 2011.
58. P. 247 in *Population: An Introduction to Concepts and Issues*.
59. Ibid., p. 19.
60. Leading article in the *Economist*, 19 November 2011.
61. P.255 in *Population: An Introduction to Concepts and Issues*.
62. Ibid., p. 275.
63. Ibid., pp. 265–87.
64. Ibid., p. 280.
65. Leading article in the *Economist*, 19 November 2011.

6   The Industrial Revolution

1. Table 5.1, p. 100 et seq. in *Guns, Germs and Steel,*, by Jared Diamond. London: Jonathan Cape, 1997.
2. The description of the development of credit and money in this section draws heavily on an as-yet-unpublished work by Christopher Meakin and Geoffrey Gardiner.
3. Pp. 242 and 276 in *Hutchinson's Encyclopedia*. Oxford: Helicon, 1998.
4. Wikipedia.
5. Wikipedia.
6. P. 1009 in *Hutchinson's Encyclopedia*.
7. Ibid., p. 390.
8. P. 29 in *Frozen Desire*, by James Buchan. London: Picador, 1997.
9. P. 96 in *Hutchinson's Encyclopedia*.
10. Correspondence with Professor John Black.
11. P. 96 in *the Wealth and Poverty of Nations*, by David Landes. London: Little, Brown, 1998.
12. Pp. 283–5 in *Economic History of Europe*, by Herbert Heaton. New York and London: Harper Brothers, 1935.
13. Wikipedia entry 'Atlantic Slave Trade'.
14. Table B-21, p. 264, in *The World Economy: A Millennial Perspective*, by Angus Maddison. Paris: OECD, 2001.
15. P. 310 in *A History of Europe*, by J. M. Roberts. Oxford: Helicon, 1996.

16. P. 168 in *The Death of Inflation*, by Roger Bootle. London: Nicholas Brealey, 1996.
17. Calculation from Shaun Stewart.
18. Wikipedia entry 'Six Acts'.
19. Table B-10a in *Monitoring the World Economy 1820–1992*, by Angus Maddison. Paris: OECD, 1995.
20. P. 673 in *Economic History of Europe*.
21. P. 390 in *Economic Development in Europe*, by Clive Day. New York: Macmillan, 1946.
22. Statistics provided by Shaun Stewart.
23. Figures calculated from Table B-10a in *Monitoring the World Economy 1820–1992*.
24. Ibid., Table D-1a.
25. Tables UK.3 and G.2 in *Economic Statistics 1900–1983*, by Thelma Liesner. London; *Economist*, 1985.
26. Ibid., Tables UK.3 and G.2.
27. Table A-2 in *Monitoring the World Economy 1820–1992*.
28. Pp. 12 and 13 in *American Economic History*, by John O'Sullivan and Edward K. Keuchel. Princeton and New York: Markus Wiener, 1989.
29. Ibid., p. 49.
30. Table C88–114 in *Historical Statistics of the United States*. Washington DC: US Department of Commerce, 1960.
31. Table B-16a in *Monitoring the World Economy 1820–1992*.
32. Ibid., Tables B-10a and D-1a.
33. Ibid., Table A-3a.
34. Ibid., Table C-16a.
35. Figure 3.2, p. 76, in *Monitoring the World Economy 1820–1992*.
36. Ibid., Table D-1a.
37. Ibid., Table C-16a.
38. Various tables in *Historical Statistics of the United States*.
39. Table K-1 in *Monitoring the World Economy 1820–1992*.
40. Ibid., pp. 40–2.
41. Table B-12 in *Economic Report of the President*. Washington DC: US GPO, 2011.
42. Pp. 67 and 68 in *American Economic History*.
43. Ibid., pp. 59, 70.
44. P. 320 in *A History of the American People*, by Paul Johnson. London: Weidenfeld and Nicolson, 1997.
45. Tables E1–12 and E13–24 in *Historical Statistics of the United States*.
46. P. 57 in *American Economic History*.
47. Ibid., p. 345.
48. Table U1–14 in *Historical Statistics of the United States*.
49. Table B-1 in *Economic Report of the President*.
50. P. 464 in *A History of the American People*.
51. Table 1–2 in *Monitoring the World Economy 1820–1992*.
52. Ibid., Table K-1.
53. A series of tables in part 1 of *The Productivity Race*, by S. N. Broadberry. Cambridge: Cambridge University Press, 1997.
54. Table E-2 in *Monitoring the World Economy 1820–1992*.

7   International Turmoil: 1914–45

1. P. 1156 in *Hutchinson's Encyclopedia*. Oxford: Helicon, 1998.
2. P. 331 in *The End of History and the Last Man*, by Francis Fukuyama. London: Penguin, 1992.
3. Calculated for figures in Table UK.1 in *Economic Statistics 1900–1983*, by Thelma Liesner. London: *Economist*, 1985.
4. Ibid., Table US.1.
5. Ibid., Table US.7, UK.7, F.3 and G.7.
6. P. 1155 in *Hutchinson's Encyclopedia*.
7. Table F.2 in *Economic Statistics 1900–1983*.
8. Ibid., Table G.2.
9. Ibid., Table UK.2.
10. For a full account, see *The Great Inflation*, by William Guttmann and Patricia Meehan. Farnborough: Saxon House, 1975.
11. Table G.3 in *Economic Statistics 1900–1983*.
12. Ibid., Table F.2.
13. Ibid., Tables G.1 and G.2.
14. Ibid., Tables G.1 and G.2.
15. Ibid., Table G.6.
16. Ibid., Tables UK.1, UK.2 and UK.10.
17. P. 73 in *The European Economy 1914–1990*, by Derek H. Aldcroft. London: Croom Helm, 1993.
18. Table G.6 in *Economic Statistics 1900–1983*.
19. Ibid., Table G.1.
20. P. 85 in *The European Economy 1914–1990*.
21. Table G.1 in *Economic Statistics 1900–1983*.
22. Ibid., Table G.3.
23. Ibid., Table G.1.
24. Ibid., Table UK.15.
25. Calculations by Shaun Stewart.
26. Table UK.15 in *Economic Statistics 1900–1983*.
27. Correspondence with Geoffrey Gardiner.
28. Study by the Manchester Statistical Society; correspondence with Geoffrey Gardiner.
29. Table UK.2 in *Economic Statistics 1900–1983*.
30. Ibid., Table UK.9.
31. Ibid., Table UK.7.
32. Ibid., Table UK.2.
33. Ibid., Table UK.15.
34. Note from Shaun Stewart.
35. Tables F.1, F.2 and F.6 in *Economic Statistics 1900–1983*.
36. Ibid., Tables F.2, G.2 and UK.3.
37. Table US.1 in *Economic Statistics 1900–1983*.
38. Ibid., Table US.1.
39. Ibid., Tables US.1, US.2 and US.9.
40. P. 163 in *American Economic History*, by John O'Sullivan and Edward F. Keuchel. Princeton and New York: Markus Wiener, 1989.
41. Tables US.1, US.6 and US.7 in *Economic Statistics 1900–1983*.

42. P. 165 in *American Economic History*.
43. Ibid., p. 167.
44. Tables US.1, US.2 and US.10 in *Economic Statistics 1900–1983*.
45. Chapter 10 in *American Economic History*.
46. Table US.15 in *Economic Statistics 1900–1983*.
47. Ibid., Tables US.1, US.2 and US.10.
48. P. 187 in *American Economic History*.
49. Table US.7 in *Economic Statistics 1900–1983*.
50. P. 187 in *American Economic History*.
51. Tables US.1 and US.2 in *Economic Statistics 1900–1983*.
52. Ibid., Tables US.1, US.2, US.7 and US.9.
53. Table B-10a in *Monitoring the World Economy 1820–1992*, by Angus Madison. Paris: OECD, 1995.
54. P. 169 in *Towards True Monetarism*, by Geoffrey Gardiner. London: Dulwich Press, 1993.
55. Pp. 233–235 in *A History of Economics*, by John Kenneth Galbraith. London: Penguin, 1987.
56. *The Economic Consequences of Mr Churchill*, by John Maynard Keynes. London: Hogarth Press, 1925.
57. Wikipedia entry, 'John Maynard Keynes'.
58. House of Lords Record of Debates.
59. P. 239 in *A History of the World Economy*, by James Foreman-Peck. Hemel Hempstead: Harvester Wheatsheaf, 1995.
60. Ibid., p. 239 et seq.
61. Table G-2 in *Monitoring the World Economy1820–1992*.
62. Ibid., Table C-16a.
63. GDP volume measure tables in *International Monetary Statistics*. Washington, DC: IMF, 2000.
64. GDP volume measure tables in *International Monetary Statistics*. Washington, DC: IMF 2000, 2011.

8   Post-World War II

1. Table G.2 in *Economic Statistics 1900–1983*, by Thelma Liesner. London: *Economist*, 1985.
2. Ibid., Tables UK.2 and F.2.
3. Ibid., Tables G.1, G.2 and G.7.
4. Ibid., Tables F.1, F.2 and F.7.
5. Ibid., Table UK.1.
6. Ibid., Table UK.15.
7. Ibid., Tables UK.1, F.1. F2, G.1, G.2. It.1 and It.2.
8. P. 173 in *Treaties Establishing the European Communities*. Luxembourg: Office for Official Publications of the European Communities, 1973.
9. P. 23 in *The New European Economy*, by Loukas Tsoulakis. Oxford: Oxford University Press, 1993.
10. Table UK.1 in *Economic Statistics 1900–1983*.
11. EC and UK tables in *National Accounts 1960–1992*. Paris: OECD, 1994.
12. P. 450 in *National Accounts of OECD Countries 1953–1969*. Paris: OECD, 1960.

13. Table US.1 in *Economic Statistics 1900–1983*.
14. Table I-2 in *Monitoring the World Economy 1820–1992*, by Angus Maddison. Paris: OECD, 1995.
15. Tables B-79 and B-80 in *Economic Report of the President*. Washington, DC: US GPO, 1999.
16. Ibid., Tables B-1 and B-29.
17. Ibid., Table B-79.
18. Ibid., Table B-80.
19. Ibid., Table B-2.
20. P. 345 in *American Economic History*, by John O'Sullivan and Edward F. Keuchel. Princeton and New York: Markus Weiner, 1989.
21. Table B-63 in *Economic Report of the President*.
22. Ibid., Table B-103.
23. Table US.11 in *Economic Statistics 1900–1983*.
24. Table B-63 in *Economic Report of the President*.
25. Ibid., Table B-35.
26. Ibid., Table B-103.
27. P. 154 in *National Accounts 1960–1992*.
28. Table G-2 in *Monitoring the World Economy 1820–1992*.
29. P. 172 in *International Financial Statistics Yearbook*. Washington, DC: IMF, 1998.
30. Table B-4 in *Economic Report of the President*.
31. Ibid., Table B-35.
32. Ibid., Table B-63.
33. P. 52 et seq. in *Monitoring the World Economy 1820–1992*.
34. Ibid., Tables D-1a and D-1e.
35. P. 569, *Hutchinson's Encyclopedia*. Oxford: Helicon, 1998.
36. Chap. 23 in *The Wealth and Poverty of Nations*, by David Landes. London: Little, Brown, 1998.
37. P. 53 in *Monitoring the World Economy 1820–1992*.
38. Ibid., Table C-16a.
39. Ibid., Table B-16a.
40. Ibid., Table D-1a.
41. Table J.5 in *Economic Statistics 1900–1983*.
42. Table D-1a in *Monitoring the World Economy 1820–1992*.
43. P. 245 in *A History of the World Economy*, by James Foreman-Peck. Hemel Hempstead: Harvester Wheatsheaf, 1995.
44. Table J.2 in *Economic Statistics 1900–1983*.
45. Correspondence with Jim Bourlet.
46. Table I-2 in *Monitoring the World Economy 1820–1992*.
47. Ibid., Tables I-2 and I-4.
48. Table J.2 in *Economic Statistics 1900–1983*.
49. Table C-16a in *Monitoring the World Economy 1820–1992*.
50. Ibid., Table A-3a.
51. Ibid., Table D-1a.
52. P. 154 in *National Accounts 1960–1992*.
53. Answer to a parliamentary question.
54. Table 3.19 in *Monitoring the World Economy 1820–1992*.
55. Table 8.15, *Historical Statistics*. Paris: OECD, 1988.

56. Table B-110 in *Economic Report of the President*.
57. P. 525, *International Financial Statistics Yearbook*.
58. Ibid., pp. 522–3.
59. P. 113 in *International Monetary Statistics*. Washington, DC: IMF, 2004.
60. Ibid., pp. 524–5.
61. P. 76 in *International Financial Statistics Yearbook 2011*. Washington, DC: IMF, 2011.
62. Table C-16c in *Monitoring the World Economy 1820–1992*.
63. Ibid., Table 3-4.
64. Ibid. Tables D-1a and D-1c.
65. Ibid., Table B-10c.
66. P. 1088 in *Hutchinson's Encyclopedia*.
67. Table C-16 in *Monitoring the World Economy 1820–1992*.
68. P. 1088 in *Hutchinson's Encyclopedia*.
69. Table C-16c in *Monitoring the World Economy 1820–1992*.
70. Ibid., Table C-16c.
71. P. 28 in *The End of History and the Last Man*, by Francis Fukuyama. London: Penguin, 1992.
72. Table C-16c in *Monitoring the World Economy 1820–1992*.
73. Ibid., Table D-1c.
74. P. 1088 in *Hutchinson's Encyclopedia*.
75. P. 133 in *Monitoring the World Economy 1820–1992*.
76. Ibid., Table 10c.
77. UN website statistics on world population.
78. Table 1–2 in *Monitoring the World Economy 1820–1992*.
79. Wikipedia entry, 'List of Countries by GDP (PPP) per Capita'.
80. GDP volume measure tables in *International Financial Statistics*. Washington, DC: IMF, 2000, 2011.
81. Table 3–1 in *Monitoring the World Economy 1820–1992*.
82. GDP Volume Measure tables in *International Financial Statistics*.
83. Table 1–3 in *Monitoring the World Economy 1820–1992*.
84. GDP volume measure tables in *International Financial Statistics* and UN population statistics.
85. GDP year-on-year growth tables in *International Financial Statistics*.
86. Table 1–3 in *Monitoring the World Economy 1820–1992*.
87. Ibid., Table 3–1.
88. Ibid., Table G-1.
89. Ibid., Table G-3.
90. GDP volume measure tables in *International Financial Statistics* and UN population statistics.
91. Pp. 220, 534 and 1033 in *Hutchinson's Encyclopedia*.
92. Tables D-1b, D-1d, I-1 and I-2 in *Monitoring the World Economy 1820–1992*.

9   The Monetarist Era

1. Pp. 174–7 in *Main Economic Indicators*. Paris: OECD, 1999.
2. Table 20, pp. 128–9, in *National Accounts 1960–1992*. Paris: OECD, 1994.
3. Wikipedia entry, 'List of Countries by Steel Production'.

4. Wikipedia entry, 'List of Countries by Motor Vehicle Production'.
5. Table 281 in *Statistical Abstract of the United States*. Washington, DC: US Department of Commerce, 2011.
6. Table 5.2, p. 228, in *Economic Trends 1996/97 Annual Supplement*. London: Office for National Statistics, 1997.
7. Pp. 88 and 89 in *International Financial Statistics Yearbook*. Washington, DC: IMF, 1998.
8. Table B-69 in *Economic Report of the President*. Washington, DC. US GPO, 2011.
9. Ibid., Table B-1.
10. Various tables in *National Accounts 1953–1969* and *National Accounts 1960–1992*. Paris: OECD 1971, 1994.
11. Table 0601, *Eurostatistics 03/90*. Luxembourg: European Community, 1999.
12. ILO labour force survey reports.
13. P. 176 in *International Financial Statistics Yearbook*. Washington, DC: IMF, 1998.
14. Pp. 20–1 in *National Accounts 1960–1992*.
15. P. 122 in *International Financial Statistics Yearbook*.
16. *The Economics of Europe*, by Edward Nevin. London: Macmillan, 1994.
17. Ibid., pp. 273–4.
18. *The Relationship between Exchange Rates and International Trade: A Review of Economic Literature*. Geneva: World Trade Organization, 2011. Paper WT/WGTDF/W/57.
19. P. 275 in *The Economics of Europe*.
20. P. 122 in *International Financial Statistics Yearbook*.
21. Tables 0943 and 0955 in *Eurostatistics 5/88*. Luxembourg: European Community, 1998.
22. Table C-16a in *Monitoring the World Economy 1820–1992*, by Angus Maddison. Paris: OECD, 1995. Table 0101 in *Eurostatistics 4/99*. Luxembourg: European Community, 1999.
23. Table D-1a in *Monitoring the World Economy 1820–1992*.
24. P. 123 in *National Accounts 1960–1992*.
25. P. 172 in *International Financial Statistics Yearbook*.
26. Table US.1 in *Economic Statistics 1900–1983*, by Thelma Liesner. London: *Economist*, 1985.
27. Table B-103 in *Economic Report of the President*, Washington, DC: US GPO, 1999.
28. Ibid., Table B-73.
29. Ibid., Broad Index in Table B-110.
30. Table D-1a in *Monitoring the World Economy 1820–1992*.
31. Ibid., Table B-12. *Economic Report of the President* (1999).
32. Ibid., Table B-46.
33. Ibid., Tables B-1 and B-32.
34. Tables C-16a and D-1a in *Monitoring the World Economy 1820–1992*.
35. Table B-47 in *Economic Report of the President* (1999).
36. Ibid., Table B-47.
37. Table 747 in *Statistical Abstract of the United States*.
38. Ibid., Table 747.
39. Tables B-1 and B-87 in *Economic Report of the President* (1999).

40. Ibid., Table B-103.
41. Ibid., Table B-104.
42. Table 1295, p. 791, in *Statistical Abstract of the United States*.
43. Table B-2 in *Economic Report of the President* (1999).
44. Ibid., Table B-63.
45. Ibid., Table B-78.
46. Ibid., Table B-110.
47. Ibid., Table 103.
48. Based on Table G-2 in *Monitoring the World Economy 1829–1992*.
49. Table 11.13 in *Trends and Statistics – International Trade*. Geneva: World Trade Organization, 1995.
50. Tables A-3e, F-4 and G-1 in *Monitoring the World Economy 1829–1992*.
51. Ibid., Table I-2.
52. Pp. 162–3 in *International Financial Statistics Yearbook*.
53. Ibid., pp. 542–3.
54. Table 28 in *Trade and Development Report*. Geneva: United Nations, 1997.
55. Table 2–9 in *Monitoring the World Economy 1829–1992*.
56. Table 25, p. 200, in *Human Development Report 1997*. New York and Oxford: Oxford University Press, for the UN Development Programme, 1997.
57. Table 33 in *Trade and Development Report*.
58. Various entries in *Hutchinson's Encyclopedia*. Oxford: Helicon, 1998.

10   Twenty-First-Century Perspectives

1. P. 63 in *International Financial Statistics Yearbook*, Washington, DC: IMF, 2011.
2. Wikipedia entry, 'Affordability of Housing in the UK'.
3. Irish global property guide Internet entry.
4. Wikipedia entry, 'Dow Jones Industrial Average'.
5. Table 693 in *Statistical Abstract of the United States*, Washington, DC: US Department of Commerce, 2011.
6. P. 75 in *International Financial Statistics Yearbook*.
7. Figures from *International Financial Statistics Yearbook*.
8. Wikipedia entry, 'Bankruptcy of Lehman Brothers'.
9. Xinhuanet.com, global edition, entry on German exports.
10. www.reuters.com entry on the USA losing its AAA rating.
11. Table B-1 in *Economic Report of the President*, Washington, DC: GPO, 2011.
12. Data from www.europa.eu.
13. Wikipedia entry, 'Growth and Stability Pact'.
14. Details provided by Goldman Sachs.
15. Figures form www.economicshelp.org.
16. Wikipedia entries on the economies of Greece, Ireland and Portugal.
17. Wikipedia entry, 'Economic History of Argentina'.
18. Quote from a newspaper article by Roger Bootle.
19. Wikipedia entry, 'US Public Debt'.
20. Figures from www.economicshelp.org.
21. Ibid.
22. Bloomberg Internet report.
23. Figures from www.economicshelp.org.

11 Policies for the Future

1. P. 744 in *International Financial Statistics*. Washington, DC: IMF, 2011.
2. *The Relationship between Exchange Rates and International Trade: A Review of Economic Literature*. Geneva: WTO, 2011.
3. P. 748 in *International Financial Statistics*.
4. See ILO website for tables by country showing the ratios between those actively seeking employment and those who could be but are not economically active.
5. P. 317 in *International Financial Statistics*.
6. Population figures in national tables in *International Financial Statistics*.
7. P. 75 in *International Financial Statistics*.
8. Book IV: *Of Systems of Political Economy*, in *An Inquiry into the Nature and Causes of the Wealth of Nations*, by Adam Smith (1776).

Bibliography

Aldcroft, Derek H. *The European Economy 1914–90*, London: Routledge, 1993.

Aldcroft, Derek H. and Ville, Simon P. *The European Economy 1750–1914*, Manchester: Manchester University Press, 1994.

Ayres, Robert U. *Technological Forecasting and Long Range Planning*, New York et al.: McGraw Hill Book Company, 1969.

Bainbridge, Timothy and Teasdale, Anthony *The Penguin Companion to the European Union*, London: Penguin, 1996

Bairoch, Paul *Economics and World History – Myths and Paradoxes*, Chicago: Chicago University Press, 1993.

Barro, Robert J. *Determinants of Economic Growth*, Boston: Massachusetts Institute of Technology, 1999.

Beckerman, Wilfrid *In Defence of Economic Growth*, London: Jonathan Cape, 1974.

Beckerman, Wilfrid *Small is Stupid: Blowing the Whistle on the Greens*, London: Duckworth, 1995.

Beloff, Lord *Britain and the European Union: Dialogue of the Deaf*, London: Macmillan 1996.

Bernstein, Peter L. *Against the Gods – The Remarkable Story of Risk* New York: John Wiley & Sons, 1996.

Blaug, Mark *Economic History and the History of Economics*, New York et al.: Harvester Wheatsheaf, 1986.

Blaug, Mark *Economic Theory in Retrospect*, Cambridge: Cambridge University Press, 1996.

Blinder, Alan S. *Hard Hearts Soft Heads*, Reading, Mass: Addison-Wesley, 1987.

Block, Fred L. *The Origins of International Economic Disorder*, Berkeley, Los Angeles and London: University of California Press, 1977.

Booker, Christopher and North, Richard *The Castle of Lies*, London: Duckworth, 1996.

Boorstin, Daniel J. *The Discoverers*, New York and London: Penguin, 1983.

Bootle, Roger *The Death of Inflation*, London: Nicholas Brealey, 1996.

Bootle, Roger *The Trouble with Markets* London: Nicholas Brealey, 2009

Bragg, Melvyn *On Giants' Shoulders: Great Scientists and Their Discoveries*, London: Hodder and Stoughton, 1998.

Brandt Commission *North-South Co-operation for World Recovery*, London and Sydney: Pan Books, 1983.

Brazelton, W. Robert *Designing US Economic Policy*, London and New York: Palgrave 2001.

Brittan, Samuel *The Price of Economic Freedom*, London: Macmillan, 1970.

Brittan, Samuel *Is There an Economic Consensus?*, London: Macmillan, 1973.

Brittan, Samuel *A Restatement of Economic Liberalism*, London: Macmillan, 1988.

Brittan, Samuel *Capitalism with a Human Face* London: Fontana Press, 1995.

Broadberry, S.N. *The Productivity Race*, Cambridge: Cambridge University Press, 1997.

Buchan, James *Frozen Desire – An Inquiry into the Meaning of Money*, London: Picador, 1997.

Burkitt, Brian and Baimbridge, Mark *What 1992 Really Means* London: British Anti-Common Market Campaign, 1989

Burkitt, Brian, Baimbridge, Mark and Whyman, Philip *There is an Alternative*, London: Campaign for an Independent Britain, 1996.

Cassidy, John *How Markets Fail* London: Penguin Books, 2009.

Caves, Richard E. *Britain's Economic Prospects*, Washington: The Brookings Institution, 1968.

Chafe, William H. *The Unfinished Journey: America Since World War II*, New York and Oxford: Oxford University Press, 1995.

Chang, Ha-Joon *23 Things They don't Tell You about Capitalism*, London: Allen Lane, 2010.

Chowdhury, Anis and Islam, Iyanatul *The Newly Industrialising Economies of East Asia*, London and New York: Routledge, 1995.

Collier, Paul *The Plundered Planet* London: Penguin Books, 2011.

Connolly, Bernard *The Rotten Heart of Europe*, London: Faber and Faber, 1995.

Crosland, C.A.R. *The Future of Socialism*, London: Jonathan Cape, 1956.

Davies, Norman *Europe – A History* Oxford: Oxford University Press, 1996.

Denison, Edward F. *Why Growth Rates Differ*, Washington DC: The Brookings Institution, 1969.

Denison, Edward F. *Accounting for United States Growth 1929–1969*, Washington DC: The Brookings Institution, 1974.

Denison, Edward F. *Accounting for Slower Economic Growth*. Washington DC: The Brookings Institution, 1979.

Denman, Roy *Missed Chances: Britain and Europe in the Twentieth Century*, London: Cassell, 1996.

Diamond, Jared *Guns, Germs and Steel*, London: Jonathan Cape, 1997.

Eatwell, John, Milgate, Murray and Newman, Pete *The New Palgrave: A Dictionary of Economics* London: Macmillan Reference Ltd, 1998.

Edwards, Paul N. *A Vast Machine: Computer Models, Climate Data and the Politics of Global Warming* Cambridge, Mass: The MIT Press, 2010.

Eichengreen, Barry *Globalizing Capital – A History of the International Monetary System*, Princeton: Princeton University Press, 1996.

Einzig, Paul *The Case Against Joining the Common Market*, London: Macmillan, 1971.

Elliott, Larry and Atkinson, Dan *The Age of Insecurity* London: Verso, 1998.

Eltis, Walter *Growth and Distribution*, London: Macmillan, 1973.

Feldstein, Martin *The Risk of Economic Crisis*, Chicago and London: The University of Chicago Press, 1991.

Ferris, Paul *Men and Money: Financial Europe Today*, London: Hutchinson, 1968.

Foreman-Peck, James *A History of the World Economy since 1850*, New York et al.: Harvester Wheatsheaf, 1995.

Friedman, Irving S. *Inflation: A World-wide Disaster*, London: Hamish Hamilton, 1973.

Friedman, Irving S. and Schwartz, Anna Jacobson *A Monetary History of the United States, 1867–1960*, New York: National Bureau of Economic Research, 1963, reprinted 1993.

Fukuyama, Francis *The End of History and the Last Man,* London: Penguin, 1992.

Galbraith, James *The Predator State* New York: Free Press, 2008.

Galbraith, J.K. *The Affluent Society,* London: Hamish Hamilton, 1960.

Galbraith, J.K. *American Capitalism,* London: Hamish Hamilton, 1961.

Galbraith, J.K. *The New Industrial State,* London: Hamish Hamilton, 1968.

Galbraith, J.K. *Economics and the Public Purpose,* London: Andre Deutsche, 1974.

Galbraith, J.K. *Money – Whence It Came, Where It Went.* London: André Deutsch, 1975.

Galbraith, J.K. *A History of Economics – The Past as the Present,* London: Penguin Books, 1987.

Galbraith, J.K. *The Culture of Contentment,* London: Sinclair-Stevenson Ltd, 1992.

Galbraith, J.K. *The Good Society: The Humane Agenda,* London: Sinclair-Stevenson Ltd, 1996

Gardiner, Geoffrey *Towards True Monetarism,* London: The Dulwich Press, 1993

Giddens, Anthony *The Third Way* Cambridge: Polity Press, 1998.

Goldsmith, James *The Trap,* London: Macmillan, 1994.

Gordon, David and Townsend, Peter *Breadline Europe: The Measurement of Poverty.* Bristol: The Policy Press, 2000.

Gray, John *False Dawn* London: Granta Books, 1998.

Grieve Smith, John *Full Employment: A Pledge Betrayed,* London: Macmillan, 1997.

Gunther, John *Inside Europe Today,* London: Hamish Hamilton, 1961.

Guttmann, William and Meehan, Patricia *The Great Inflation,* Farnborough: Saxon House, 1975.

Hallett, Graham *The Social Economy of West Germany,* London: Macmillan, 1973.

Hama, Noriko *Disintegrating Europe,* London: Adamantine Press, 1996.

Harvey-Jones, John *Getting it Together* London: Heinemann, 1991.

Hayek, F.A. *The Road to Serfdom,* London and Henley: Routledge & Kegan Paul, 1944.

Heaton, Herbert *Economic History of Europe.* New York and London: Harper and brothers, 1936.

Henderson, Callum *Asia Falling* New York: McGraw-Hill, 1998.

Henig, Stanley *Political Parties in the European Community,* London: George Allen & Unwin, 1979.

Hicks, John *Capital and Growth,* Oxford: Clarendon Press, 1965.

Hicks, John *A Theory of Economic History* Oxford: Clarendon Press, 1969.

Hirsch, Fred *Money International,* London: Allen Lane, 1967.

Hirsch, Fred *Social Limits to Growth,* Cambridge, Mass: Harvard University Press, 1976.

Holland, Stuart *Out of Crisis: A Project for European Recovery,* Nottingham: Spokesman Books, 1983.

Howarth, Catherine et al. *Monitoring Poverty and Social Exclusion 1999.* York: The Rowntree Trust, 1999.

Hutchinson's *Encyclopedia,* London: Helicon Press, 1998.

Hutton, Will *The State We're In,* London: Jonathan Cape, 1995.

Isard, Peter *Exchange Rate Economics,* Cambridge: Cambridge University Press, 1995.

Ito, Takatoshi *The Japanese Economy*, Cambridge, Mass and London, England: The MIT Press, 1996.

Jamieson, Bill *Britain beyond Europe*, London: Duckworth, 1994.

Jay, Douglas *Sterling: A Plea for Moderation*, London: Sidgwick & Jackson, 1985.

Jay, Peter *Employment, Regions and Currencies*, London: Eurofacts, 1996.

Jay, Peter *Road to Riches or the Wealth of Man*, London: Weidenfeld and Nicolson, 2000.

Johnson, Christopher *In with the Euro, Out with the Pound*, London: Penguin, 1996.

Johnson, Paul *A History of the American People*, London: Weidenfeld and Nicolson, 1997.

Jones, E.L. *The European Miracle*, Cambridge: Cambridge University Press, 1993.

Kaletsky, Anatole *Capitalism 4.0* London: Bloomsbury Publishing, 2010.

Keen, Steve *Debunking Economics*, London and New York: Zed Books, 2001.

Kemp, Tom *Industrialization in Nineteenth Century Europe*, London: Longman, 1994.

Keynes, John Maynard *The Economic Consequences of Mr Churchill* London: Hogarth Press, 1925.

Keynes, John Maynard *The General Theory of Employment, Interest and Money*, London: Macmillan 1957 edition. First published 1936.

Kindleberger, Charles P. *World Economic Primacy 1500 to 1990*, New York and Oxford: Oxford University Press, 1996.

Krugman, Paul R. *The Age of Diminished Expectations*, Cambridge, Mass and London, England: The MIT Press, 1990.

Krugman, Paul R. *Peddling Prosperity*, New York and London: Norton, 1994.

Krugman, Paul R. *Rethinking International Trade*, Cambridge Mass & London: The MIT Press, 1994.

Krugman, Paul R. *Strategic Trade Policy and the New International Economics*, Cambridge, Mass and London, England: The MIT Press, 1995.

Krugman, Paul R. *The Self-Organizing Economy*, Malden, Mass and Oxford: Blackwell, 1996.

Krugman, Paul R. *Pop Internationalism*, Cambridge Mass and London, England: The MIT Press, 1997.

Krugman, Paul R *The Return of Depression Economics* London: Allen Lane, The Penguin Press, 1999.

Krugman, Paul R *End This Depression Now* New York: W.W. Norton & Co, 2012.

Kuznets, Simon *Modern Economic Growth* London: Yale University Press, 1965.

Lamont, Norman *Sovereign Britain*, London: Duckworth, 1995.

Landes, David *The Wealth and Poverty of Nations*, London: Little Brown, 1998.

Lang, Tim and Hines, Colin *The New Protectionism*, London: Earthscan, 1993,

Layard, Richard *How to Beat Unemployment*, Oxford: Oxford University Press, 1986.

Leach, Rodney *Monetary Union – A Perilous Gamble*, London: Eurofacts, 1996.

Liesner, Thelma *Economic Statistics 1900–1983*, London: *The Economist*, 1985.

Lingle, Christopher *The Rise & Decline of the Asian Century*, Hong Kong: Asia 2000, 1997.

Lipton, Michael *Assessing Economic Performance*, London: Staples Press, 1968.

Little, I.M.D. *A Critique of Welfare Economics* Oxford: Oxford University Press, 1957.

Lomborg, Bjørn *The Skeptical Environmentalist* Cambridge: Cambridge University Press, 2001.

Lomborg, Bjørn *Cool It: The Skeptical Environmentalist's Guide to Global Warming,* London, Marshall Cavendish, 2007.

Maddison, Angus *Economic Growth in the West,* London: George Allen & Unwin, 1964.

Maddison, Angus *Economic Growth in Japan and the USSR,* London: George Allen & Unwin Ltd, 1969.

Maddison, Angus *Dynamic Forces in Capitalist Development,* Oxford: Oxford University Press, 1991.

Maddison, Angus *Monitoring the World Economy 1820–1992,* Paris: OECD, 1995

Mai, Chao-Cheng and Shih, Chien-Sheng *Taiwan's Economic Success Since 1980,* New York and Cheltenham: Edward Elgar, 2001.

Marris, Robin *How to Save the Underclass,* London: Macmillan, 1996.

Marsh, David *Reculer pour Mieux Sauter,* London: Prospect, 1997.

Mayhew, Nicholas *Sterling – The History of a Currency,* London: Penguin Group, 1999.

Maynard, Geoffrey and van Ryckeghem, W. *A World of Inflation,* London: Batsford, 1976.

Mayne, Richard *The Recovery of Europe,* London: Weidenfeld & Nicolson, 1970

Meade, James E. *The Intelligent Radical's Guide to Economic Policy,* London: George Allen & Unwin Ltd, 1975.

Michie, Jonathan and Grieve Smith, John *Unemployment in Europe,* London: Harcourt Brace, 1994.

Minford, Patrick *Markets not Stakes,* London: Orion Business Books, 1998.

Mishan, E.J. *21 Popular Economic Fallacies,* London: Allen Lane, 1969.

Mishel, Lawrence, Bernstein, Jared and Schmitt, John *The State of Working America 2000/2001.* New York: Cornell University Press, 2001.

Moggridge, D.E. *Maynard Keynes – An Economist's Biography,* London: Routledge, 1995.

Monti, Mario *The Single Market and Tomorrow's Europe,* London: Kogan Page, 1996.

Nevin, Edward *The Economics of Europe,* London: Macmillan, 1994.

North, Douglass C. *The Economic Growth of the United States 1790–1860,* New York and London: W.W. Norton & Co, 1966.

Nove, Alec *The Soviet Economy* London: George Allen & Unwin, 1961.

OECD *The Residual Factor and Economic Growth* Paris: OECD, 1971.

Okita, Saburo *The Developing Economies and Japan,* Tokyo: University of Tokyo Press, 1980.

O'Leary, James J. *Stagnation or Healthy Growth? The Economic Challenge to the United States in the Nineties,* Lanham, New York, London: University Press of America, 1992.

Olson, Mancur *The Rise and Decline of Nations,* New Haven and London: Yale University Press, 1982.

Ormerod, Paul *The Death of Economics,* London: Faber and Faber, 1995.

Ormerod, Paul *Butterfly Economics,* London: Faber and Faber, 1998.

O'Sullivan, John and Keuchel, Edward F. *American Economic History: From Abundance to Constraint,* Princeton, N.J.: Markus Wiener Publishing Inc, 1989.

Patten, Chris *East and West* London: Macmillan, 1998.

P.E.P. *Economic Planning and Policies in Britain, France and Germany,* London: George Allen & Unwin, 1968.

Pilbeam, Keith *International Finance,* London: Macmillan, 1994.

Pinder, John *The Economics of Europe,* London: Charles Knight, 1971.

Plimer, Ian *Heaven and Earth: Global Warming: The Missing Science,* London: Quartet Books Ltd, 2009.

Porter, Michael E. et al. *Can Japan Compete?* London: Macmillan Press Ltd, 2000.

Postan, M.M. *An Economic History of Western Europe 1945–1964,* London: Methuen, 1967.

Reader, John *Africa: A Biography of the Continent,* London, Penguin Books, 1998.

Robbins, Lord *Money, Trade and International Relations,* London: Macmillan, 1971.

Ridley, Matt *The Rational Optimist* London: Fourth Estate, 2010.

Roberts, J.M. *The Hutchinson History of the World,* London: Hutchinson, 1976.

Roberts, J.M. *A History of Europe,* Oxford: Helicon, 1996.

Rohwer, Jim *Asia Arising,* London: Nicholas Brealey Publishing, 1996.

Roll, Eric *A History of Economic Thought* London: Faber and Faber, 1973.

Rome, Club of *The Limits to Growth,* London: Potomac Associates, 1972.

Rostow, W.W. *Why the Poor Get Richer and the Rich Slow Down,* London: Macmillan, 1980.

Rostow, W.W. *The Stages of Economic Growth,* Cambridge: Cambridge University Press, 1960.

Salter, W.E.G. *Productivity and Technical Change,* Cambridge: Cambridge University Press, 1969

Sampson, Anthony *The New Europeans,* London: Hodder and Stoughton, 1968.

Schonfield, Andrew *In Defence of the Mixed Economy,* Oxford: Oxford University Press, 1984.

Schumpeter, Joseph A. *Capital, Socialism and Democracy,* London: George Allen & Unwin, 1943.

Schumpeter, Joseph A. *History of Economic Analysis,* London: Routledge, 1997 reprint.

Schumpeter, Joseph A. *Ten Great Economists,* London: Routledge, 1997 reprint.

Sen, Amartya *On Ethics & Economics* Oxford: Blackwell, 1995.

Sen, Amartya *Development as Freedom,* Oxford: Oxford University Press, 1999.

Shonfield, Andrew *In Defence of the Mixed Economy,* Oxford: Oxford University Press, 1984.

Singh, Jyoti Shankar *A New International Economic Order,* New York and London: Praeger Publishers, 1935.

Skidelsky, Robert *Keynes: The Return of the Master* London: Allen Lane, 2009.

Skousen, Mark *The Making of Modern Economics,* Armonk, New York and London, England: M.E. Sharpe, 2001.

Slichter, Sumner H. *Economic Growth in the United States,* Westport, Connecticut: Greenwood Press, 1961.

Smith, Adam *The Wealth of Nations Books I–III,* London: Penguin Books, republished 1997; original published in 1776.

Soros, George *The Crisis of Global Capitalism* London: Little, Brown and Company, 1998.

Spence, Jonathan *The Chan's Great Continent* London: Allen Lane The Penguin Press, 1998.

Spiegel, Henry William *The Growth of Economic Thought*, Durham and London: Duke University Press, 1996.

Stein, Herbert *The Fiscal Revolution in America*, Chicago and London: University of Chicago Press, 1969.

Stewart, Michael *Keynes in the 1990s: A Return to Economic Sanity*, London: Penguin, 1993.

Stiglitz, Joseph *Making Globalization Work* London: Allen Lane, 2006.

Stiglitz, Joseph *Freefall* London: Allen Lane, 2010.

Stone, P.B. *Japan Surges Ahead* London: Weidenfeld & Nicolson, 1969.

Tett, Gillian *Fool's Gold*, London, Abacus, 2011.

Thurow, Lester C. *The Zero-Sum Society*, New York: Basic Books, 1980.

Tsoukalis, Loukas *The New European Economy*, Oxford: Oxford University Press, 1993.

US Council of Economic Advisers *Economic Report of the President*, Washington, DC: US Government Printing Office, 1999.

Warburton, Peter *Debt and Delusion*, London: Allen Lane The Penguin Press, 1999.

Wilkinson, Richard and Pickett, Kate *The Spirit Level* London: Allen Lane, 2009

Willetts, David *The Pinch* London: Atlantic Books, 2010.

Wilson, Edward O, *Consilience: The Unity of Knowledge*, London: Little Brown and Company, 1998.

Wray, L. Randall *Understanding Modern Money*, Northampton, Mass: Edward Elgar Publishing, Inc, 1998.

Index